Lecture Notes in Computer Science 8061

Commenced Publication in 1973
Founding and Former Series Editors:
Gerhard Goos, Juris Hartmanis, and Jan van Leeuwen

Andrea Kő   Christine Leitner
Herbert Leitold   Alexander Prosser (Eds.)

Technology-Enabled
Innovation
for Democracy, Government
and Governance

2nd Joint International Conference on Electronic Government
and the Information Systems Perspective,
and Electronic Democracy, EGOVIS/EDEM 2013
Prague, Czech Republic, August 26-28, 2013, Proceedings

 Springer

Volume Editors

Andrea Kő
Corvinus University of Budapest
Fővám tér 13-15, 1093 Budapest, Hungary
E-mail: ko@informatika.uni-corvinus.hu

Christine Leitner
Danube University Krems
Center for European Public Administration
Dr.-Karl-Dorrek-Strasse 30, 3500 Krems, Austria
E-mail: christine.leitner@donau-uni.ac.at

Herbert Leitold
A-SIT, Secure Information Technology Center - Austria
Inffeldgasse 16a, 8010 Graz, Austria
E-mail: herbert.leitold@a-sit.at

Alexander Prosser
University of Economics and Business Administration
Augasse 2-6, 1090 Wien, Austria
E-mail: prosser@wu.ac.at

ISSN 0302-9743   e-ISSN 1611-3349
ISBN 978-3-642-40159-6   e-ISBN 978-3-642-40160-2
DOI 10.1007/978-3-642-40160-2
Springer Heidelberg Dordrecht London New York

Library of Congress Control Number: 2013944641

CR Subject Classification (1998): K.5.2, K.4, H.4, H.5, K.6, J.1, K.3, I.2

LNCS Sublibrary: SL 3 – Information Systems and Application, incl. Internet/Web
and HCI

Typesetting: Camera-ready by author, data conversion by Scientific Publishing Services, Chennai, India

Printed on acid-free paper

Springer is part of Springer Science+Business Media (www.springer.com)

Preface

The public sector in Europe and elsewhere is under double pressure: On the one hand, the financial and debt crisis requires a massive re-alignment of state activities and state expenditures, which creates pressure to further increase the efficiency of public administration. On the other hand, citizens demand more say in public affairs and thanks to social media have ready access to powerful tools of self-organization. This second challenge is deepened by the demands of the Aarhus Convention, which grants citizens more information and participation rights including access to judicial remedies in environmental matters. These challenges are paralleled by a fundamental technology shift in the terminals people use to access Internet services: "Classic" PCs and laptop computers are increasingly complemented and even replaced by mobile devices ranging from smartphones via tablets to unconventional devices, such as computerized glasses.

The challenges to government ICT are indeed awe-inspiring: more flexible, more responsive, mobile – and all that at lower cost! The contributions to this conference are dedicated to showing ways to reconcile these requirements. The contributions focus on the currently most sensitive areas in the field, which are identity management as a core component in any eGovernment or participation system, open data, mobile government applications as well as intelligent and learning systems. Case studies and experiences from eGovernment and eParticipation present the best practice in the area.

Hence, this proceedings volume is dedicated to a better understanding of how to design and build successful government – citizen interaction and to implement it in ICT-enabled systems. As Program Committee Chairs, we wish to thank all reviewers and members of the Program Committee for ensuring a high-quality scientific selection process. We would also like to thank the organizers of DEXA for their great job in organizing the conference and providing a valuable infrastructure for the academic work. Above all, we would like to thank Gabriela Wagner from the DEXA Organizing Committee, who held it all together, provided help and suggestions and above all, made sure we kept to the time schedule.

We are assured the reader of this volume will find additional insight and valuable suggestions – whether practitioner or researcher in the field.

August 2013

Andrea Kő
Christine Leitner
Herbert Leitold
Alexander Prosser

Organization

Conference Program Chairs

Andrea Kő — Corvinus University of Budapest, Hungary
Christine Leitner — CEPA, Danube University Krems, Austria
Herbert Leitold — A-SIT Secure Information Technology Center, Graz, Austria
Alexander Prosser — University of Economics and Business Administration, Vienna, Austria

Honorary Chairs

Wichian Chutimaskul — King Mongkut's University of Technology, Thailand
Fernando Galindo — University of Zaragoza, Spain
Roland Traunmüller — University of Linz, Austria
Irina Zálišová — EPMA, Prague, Czech Republic

Program Committee

Georg Aichholzer — Austrian Academy of Sciences, Austria
Jan Aidemark — Växjö University, Sweden
Luis Álvarez Sabucedo — Universidade de Vigo, Spain
Majed Ayyad — NextLevel Technology Systems
Victor Bekkers — Erasmus University Rotterdam, The Netherlands
Trevor Bench-Capon — Liverpool University, UK
Jaro Berce — University of Ljubljana, Slovenia
Thomas Buchsbaum — Austrian Foreign Ministry, Austria
Marek Canecky — ITAPA, Slovakia
Alejandra Cechich — Universidad Nacional del Comahue, Argentina
Wojciech Cellary — Poznan University of Economics, Poland
Yannis Charalabidis — University of the Aegean, Greece
Eleni Christodoulou — University of Cyprus, Cyprus
Wichian Chutimaskul — King Mongkut's University of Technology, Thailand
Flavio Corradini — University of Camerino, Italy
Ignacio Criado — Universidad Autónoma de Madrid, Spain
Peter Cruickshank — Edinburgh Napier University, UK
Vytautas Cyras — Vilnius University, Lithuania
Annelie Ekelin — Blekinge Institute of Technology, Sweden

Julian Valero	Universidad de Murcia, Spain
Tom M. van Engers	University of Amsterdam, The Netherlands
Daniel van Lerberghe	European Center for Political Technologies
Lex van Velsen	University of Twente, The Netherlands
Costas Vassilakis	University of the Peloponnese, Greece
Mark Vermeulen	DNA, The Netherlands
Jorge Viera da Silva	Mobility Ticketing & Applications, Belgium
Gianluigi Viscusi	University of Milano Bicocca, Italy
Doug Vogel	City University Hong Kong, Hong Kong
Melanie Volkamer	Technische Universität Darmstadt, Germany
Roland Wagner	University of Linz, Austria
Silke Weiss	Austrian Federal Ministry of Finance, Austria
Andy Williamson	London School of Economics and Political Science, UK
Christopher C. Wills	Caris Research Ltd., UK
Frank Wilson	Interaction Design, UK
Robert Woitsch	BOC Asset Management, Austria
Chien-Chih Yu	National ChengChi University, China (Taiwan Province)

External Reviewers

Christian Broser	University of Regensburg, Germany
Francesco De Angelis	University of Camerino, Italy
Michael Diener	University of Regensburg, Germany
Prokopis Drogkaris	University of the Aegean, Greece
Evangelos Goggolidis	University of the Aegean (Mytilene), Greece
Patrik Hitzelberger	Centre de Recherche Public - Gabriel Lippmann, Luxembourg
Elisavet Konstantinou	University of the Aegean, Greece
Stephan Neumann	CASED/TU Darmstadt, Germany
Lise Schrøder	Aalborg University, Denmark
Thomas Tamisier	Centre de Recherche Public - Gabriel Lippmann, Luxembourg

Table of Contents

Mobile Government

Open Government Data

E-Participation

eParticipation on the European Union Level

Alexander Prosser

University of Economics and Business, Vienna
alexander.prosser@wu.ac.at

Abstract. This paper analyses the legal basis and technical possibilities for citizen participation by electronic means on the European Union level; in particular, the various forms of dialogue introduced by Art 11 TEU as well as Art 20 TFEU are analysed. [1a, 1b]

Keywords: eParticipation, European Union, citizens' initiative, petition.

1 Introduction

The European Union has developed into a geographically vast and cultural diverse area of 4,2m square kilometers and 502m inhabitants.[1] Even though an organization of sovereign member states, a large degree of decisions, particularly in the economic sphere, are today made on the EU level. This requires concrete interaction between law makers and the administration (Commission) on the European level on the one hand and the citizens on the other to avoid disenfranchisement and discontent. Art 10.1 TEU states that the Union is *"founded on representative democracy"* and gives political parties a central role (Art 10.4), however, every citizen is granted *"the right to participate in the democratic life of the Union"* (Art 10.3). The physical expanse of the EU, however, makes it imperative to utilize electronic means and the Internet for such communications.

This contribution tries to summarize the main instruments for citizen participation on the EU level and their implementation for real citizen interaction. It does not deal with the requirements of the Acquis for national legislation, eg, the Aarhus Convention.

2 The European Petition

Probably the most basic democratic right is the right to submit a petition as laid down in Art 20 TFEU [2]. The petition may be signed by one or several persons and there is no right vested in the petition beyond that to receive a reply in the same language (not even a time frame for the reply is given in the Treaty). The same applies to submissions to the European Ombudsman.

---

[1] http://bookshop.europa.eu/en/the-european-union-pbIK3111290/
?CatalogCategoryID= 5giep2IxSeYAAAEu.lwD0UdL (13/6/2013)

A. Kő et al. (Eds.): EGOVIS/EDEM 2013, LNCS 8061, pp. 1–7, 2013.

Petitions may be submitted online [2], however apart from the immediate confirmation of receipt, all further correspondence will be done by post as explicitly mentioned on the petitions form; possible attachments to the petition also have to be submitted by post and cannot be attached to the petition. Also, it is not possible to view and support existing petitions or to see, what came of petitions and how the legislators reacted to the petitions.

This procedure and functionality is definitely not state-of-the-art: Examples [3] and [4], for instance, offer registration of petitioners with no [3] or weak [4] – an email address is checked for validity – authentication. There is also a list of all submitted petitions, which can also be supported by registered users of the platform [3] or with a separate, again weak, authentication [4]. Both systems enable the user to follow-up on the further development around the petition including the parliamentary workflow and decisions made by the petitions committee. In both examples, the entire workflow is available electronically; it would hence be a value added to upgrade the EU Parliament's petitions functionality to at least these examples.

What is largely unsolved is the question of reliably identifying the citizens issuing a petition. Literally everybody can submit a petition and only by responding to the postal address indicated the European Parliament will recognize whether the petitioner's address is a valid one or not (however saying nothing about whether the petitioner is a European citizen). Processes, which are completely done in the electronic media, such as [3] and [4], necessarily rely completely on the data indicated by the petitioner. The petition may be a rather "uncritical" democratic right and may have lesser implications than an election; nevertheless, the deficit in identifying citizens in the electronic media is shown clearly. The topic will return with other instruments.

3   The Dialogues According to Art 11 TEU

3.1   General Remarks

Art 11 TEU defines four types of dialogue:

- The horizontal dialogue among citizens (paragraph 1);
- The vertical dialogue between the institutions and *representative associations and civil society*" (paragraph 2);
- The consultation process of the Commission (paragraph 3);
- The European Citizens' Initiative (paragraph 4).

The following sections discuss how far these dialogue types have been implemented in general and particularly in the electronic media.

3.2   The Horizontal Dialogue

"The institutions shall, by appropriate means, give citizens and representative associations the opportunity to make known and publicly exchange their views in all areas of Union action." Art 11.1

At first glance, this requirement seems to be somewhat strange in the age of social media and their massive use by citizens. One may argue that citizens did not wait for the European Union to start their brand of horizontal dialogue on an everyday basis, not exclusively on, but certainly also including, European topics. At second glance, however, there are some properties of such a dialogue, which can only be provided by government authorities:

- The legal provision seems to clearly describe a deliberative approach[2] ("*publicly exchange*"), which – if to be taken seriously – requires a certain degree of moderated dialogue to prevent the discussion from degenerating.
- The deliberation process needs reliable information as input, for instance if a new Directive is to be discussed, the partners to the Trilogue [7], in particular the Commissioner responsible, would have to provide dependable, authenticated and timely information on the state of the preparation of the Directive, even though the dialogue as such is a horizontal one. Otherwise, the dialogue among citizens may be based on inaccurate and possibly outdated information and hence be rendered useless – or even counter-productive. This requires a platform integrated in EU processes and administrative work.

To the knowledge of the author, there is no current activity to implement a structured process and electronic platform to support this kind of dialogue.

3.3 The Vertical Dialogue

"The institutions shall maintain an open, transparent and regular dialogue with representative associations and civil society." Art 11.2

There seems to be a degree of uncertainty how to interpret this provision [6, 8], in particular on the meaning of "*representative*" and whether this – depending on its construction by the institutions, potentially massive – qualification only refers to associations or also civil society. Nevertheless, it describes a deliberative process to be held between the (ie, all) institutions on the EU level and civil society. This is in many ways an enormous challenge, particularly in the electronic media:

- If the dialogue is to be taken seriously, it requires a certain degree of reliable identification and authentication of contributors to the deliberation process [5]. Such a register plus identification mode can only be provided by the authorities of the MS and on the basis of a reconciled EU voter register (for this issue cf. [9]); in this regard, technological advances may help overcome this issue (for an approach cf. [10]).

---

[2] Cf. Sigmund's elucidating remarks on the difficulties with the terminology of Art 11, also as compared to the Treaty of Nice [6]. For the definition of deliberation, see [5], [11].

- The dialogue has to be maintained in all official languages of the Union, which is not so much a technical, but a logistical issue; it also tends to fragment the discussion into separate tracks – or it may lead to a situation, where the English discussion track becomes the main, and possibly intellectually richest, track of all languages. In any case, this issue warrants some particular consideration.
- The organizer of each deliberation process seems unclear. The focus on "*institutions*" may lead to a situation, where several institutions in parallel may initiate deliberation on one and the same issue. Hence, some kind of co-ordination among institutions seems to be advisable.
- There is a clear link between vertical and horizontal dialogue and it appears not to be advisable to separate these two [11, 12]. Hence, one unified platform for both dialogue applications would seem indicated.[3]

The vertical dialogue currently seems to be largely implemented as Facebook pages. The Web page europa.eu/take-part/facebook offers links to the Facebook presence of various institutions and persons; similar pages exist for twitter accounts and other social media. However, the nature of mainstream social media does not allow for the above criteria, in particular for any kind of structured and dependable discussion process. Also, it seems doubtful to base any serious European deliberation process on social media which are subject to US jurisdiction.

3.4   Consultation

"The European Commission shall carry out broad consultations with parties concerned in order to ensure that the Union's actions are coherent and transparent." Art 11.3

The Web page ec.europa.eu/yourvoice offers a platform for managing the consultation process. Information gathering ranges from simple free text submission via email/attachment to structured questionnaires; also a differentiation between organizations (registered or not) and private individuals can be observed in some consultations. A follow-up after the consultation is closed is provided with the possibility to browse through the contributions and a summary document. [14]

Summarizing, this part is arguably the best-implemented part of the participation rights in Art 11 altogether.

3.5   European Citizens' Initiative, ECI

"Not less than one million citizens who are nationals of a significant number of Member States may take the initiative of inviting the European Commission, within the framework of its powers, to submit any appropriate proposal on matters where citizens consider that a legal act of the Union is required for the purpose of implementing the Treaties." Art 11.4

---

[3] In this regard, the engagement of the members of the civil society may then lead to addressing the institution; hence, one form of dialogue may seamlessly pass into the other. Cf. particularly the noteworthy remarks in [13] from the European Ombudsman's perspective.

This element arguably triggered the largest implementation effort in any of the dialogue elements in Art 11 TEU. The details were laid down in Regulation (EU) No 211/2011[4]. Due to software and other implementation issues [15], the first ECIs could start collecting support declarations in the second half of 2012. Currently, the ECI has a number of severe shortcomings, which are clearly rooted in the Regulation:

- The full personal liability for organisers in terms of criminal, civil and administrative charges (Art 13 of the Regulation); [16]
- This is aggravated by the fact that only natural persons can be organisers of an ECI (*"citizens' committee"*, Art 3 of the Regulation), which implies that organisers cannot protect themselves from the massive liabilities mentioned above. Derflinger [17] concludes that this is a *"very problematic dimension of this provision"* (p. 83) and suggest to take out liability insurance. It seems, however, doubtful, whether this risk is insurable and if so, whether the resulting insurance premiums would be affordable to grass-root initiatives.
- Annex III of the Regulation defines the assignment of support declarations to member states; it does so, however, in an inconsistent way, which results in a large number of EU citizens residing in the EU losing their right to support an ECI simply due to an inconsistent Annex of the Regulation [18].
- Random sampling is allowed to verify the support declarations at the member states' election authorities [19], which may considerably weaken the credibility of this democratic instrument.
- The lack of most of the necessary supporting infrastructure to support ECIs in technical, legal and also general terms [20].

Fortunately, Reg 211/2011 provides for a review period to modify the legal basis and the above-mentioned issues may be fixed. Most importantly, the reversial of the "privatisation" of the signature collection process appears to be instrumental in establishing the citizens' initiative as a main feature in the democratic dialogue forms created by Art 11 TEU.

4   The Way Forward

The individual potential for improvement for the instruments and their ICT implementation have already been mentioned in the respective sections. However, these instruments put together provide a powerful legal toolset for participatory democracy allowing for the fact that *"the dualism of representative and direct democracy is not sufficient any more for well-functioning democratic systems of the 21st century"*. [17, p. 85].

Furthermore, these instruments are inter-related: It was already shown that vertical and horizontal dialogue may seamlessly interact between one another; also the

---

[4] For downloads and details cf.
http://ec.europa.eu/citizens-initiative/public/welcome (19/6/2013).

citizens' initiative will definitely be accompanies by a horizontal, and possibly even a vertical dialogue and finally a consultation process may also involve both a horizontal and a vertical dialogue form. It would hence seem somewhat strange to consider these dialogues as distinctly different and – technically and organisationally – separate forms of citizen interaction. Therefore, a coherent strategy appears to be indicated not only to implement these dialogue forms completely and in a citizen-friendly way, but also to consider the integration scenario. Such integration of services would provide a number of advantages, such as unified handling of citizen identification or the "bundling" of different forms of dialogue grouped by topic and not by institution or type of dialogue.

There is hence a lot of future potential and promise in such integration of dialogues according to Art 11, but also still enough potential for improvement as far as the implementation of this primary law provision is concerned.

References

[1a]   Treaty on the European Union (TEU) (June 12, 2013),
       http://www.lisbon-treaty.org
[1b]   Treaty on the Functioning of the European Union (TFEU) (June 12, 2013),
       http://www.lisbon-treaty.org
[2]   European Parliament, Information on online petitions available at (June 12, 2013),
       http://www.europarl.europa.eu/aboutparliament/de/
       00533cec74/Petitions.html
[3]   Deutscher Bundestag, Information über Onlinepetitionen available at (June 12, 2013),
       https://epetitionen.bundestag.de/epet/peteinreichen.html
[4]   Österreichischer Nationalrat, Beteiligung der BürgerInnen available at (June 12, 2013),
       http://www.parlament.gv.at/PAKT/BB/index.shtml?jsMode=&xdoc
       umentUri=&NRBR=NR&BBET=PET&ZUSTIMM=ZU&SUCH=&listeId=104&LIS
       TE=Anzeigen&FBEZ=FP_004
[5]   Müller-Török, R.: Identification in Paper-based and Electronic Democracy Processes –
       A Comparison. In: Prosser, A. (ed.) Proceedings of EDEM 2011, pp. 121–128. OCG-
       Verlag, Vienna (2011)
[6]   Sigmund, A.-M.: Article 11 TEU in the perspective oft he EESC. In: Pichler, J.W., Bal-
       thasar, A. (eds.) Open Dialogue between EU Institutions and Citizens – Chances and
       Challenges, pp. 196–201. Neuer Wissenschaftlicher Verlag, Vienna (2013)
[7]   Tobler, C., Beglinger, J.: Essential EU Law in Charts, 2nd edn., Lisbon. HVG-ORAC,
       Leiden (2010)
[8]   Pichler, J., Balthasar, A.: Introduction. In: Pichler, J., Balthasar, A. (eds.) Open Dialo-
       gue between EU Institutions and Citizens – Chances and Challenges, pp. 17–26. Neuer
       Wissenschaftlicher Verlag, Vienna (2013)
[9]   Balthasar, A., Müller-Török, R.: Ein Vorschlag zur Effektuierung der Richtlinie
       93/109/EG. In: Schweighofer, E., Kummer, F. (eds.) Europäische Projektkultur als Bei-
       trag zur Rationalisierung des Rechts, Tagungsband der IRIS 2011, pp. 303–310. OCG
       Verlag, Vienna (2011)
[10]   Prosser, A.: Richtlinie 93/109/EG und In-Memory Computing. In: Schweighofer, E.,
       Kummer, F., Hötzendorfer, W. (eds.) Abstraktion und Applikation, Tagungsband IRIS
       2013, pp. 257–262. OCG Verlag, Vienna (2013)

[11]   Velikanov, C.: Responsibility of participants in e-deliberation. In: Leitner, C., Haase, M., Makolm, J., Traunmüller, R. (eds.) Eastern European e|Gov Days 2010, pp. 155–162. OCG Verlag, Vienna (2010)

[12]   Leitner, C., Müller-Török, R.: Evaluating E-Participation Projects in Austria – A Methodological Approach for a Decision on the Success of E-Participation. In: Prosser, A. (ed.) Proceedings of EDEM 2011, pp. 53–66. OCG-Verlag, Vienna (2011)

[13]   Harden, I.: Open dialogue between institutions and citizens – the Ombudsman's perspective – Opening Session – Workshop I. In: Pichler, J., Balthasar, A. (eds.) Open Dialogue between EU Institutions and Citizens – Chances and Challenges, pp. 124–128. Neuer Wissenschaftlicher Verlag, Vienna (2013)

[14]   Personal Web research by the author (June 18, 2013)

[15]   Häfner, G.: ECI – problems with online collection tool – concession of the Commission (June 19, 2013),
        `http://www.democracy-international.org/eci-software.html`

[16]   Müller-Török, R., Stein, R.: Die Rechtsakte zur Europäischen Bürgerinitiative – Offene Fragen und Risiken für Organisatoren. In: Schweighofer, E., Kummer, F., Hötzendorfer, W. (eds.) Transformation Juristischer Sprachen, Tagungsband der IRIS 2012, pp. 237–244. OCG Verlag, Vienna (2012)

[17]   Derflinger, W.: The democratic and integritive mission of the "European Citizens' Initiative" in the contect of "Civil Dialogue" and "Civil Society". In: Pichler, J., Balthasar, A. (eds.) Open Dialogue between EU Institutions and Citizens – Chances and Challenges, pp. 74–86. Neuer Wissenschaftlicher Verlag, Vienna (2013)

[18]   Müller-Török, R., Stein, R.: Die Europäische Bürgerinitiative aus Sicht nationaler Wahlbehörden. Verwaltung und Management 5, 255–262 (2010)

[19]   Balthasar, A., Prosser, A.: Die Europäische Bürgerinitiative – Gefährdung der Glaubwürdigkeit eines direktdemokratischen Instruments? Journal für Rechtspolitik 3, 122–132 (2010)

[20]   Sigmund, A.-M.: Towards a supportive infrastructure. In: Pichler, J., Kaufmann, B. (eds.) The Next Big Thing – Making Europe Ready for the Citizens' Initiative. Neuer Wissen-schaftlicher Verlag, Vienna (2011)

E-Government – New Challenges Ahead

Roland Traunmüller

Johannes Kepler Universität Linz
Altenbergerstraße 69
4040 Linz, Austria
traunm@ifs.uni-linz.ac.at

Abstract. The term "Electronic Government" became a common label Nineties turning a new century. So having been employed for more than a Decade it is the right moment to reflect. So the course of development is sketched recalling some key events and also connecting them with the Linz Institute. Subsequently, some prospects and future developments are considered. One advancement concerns smart and proactive Government with services using cross-border interoperability and identity management. Another field of progress is improving participation. A lot of progress will build on solid trends which add quite specific improvements and synergies to particular issues. In that way four clusters of issues are treated : a)The collaboration part which includes platforms, social media and mobile devices; b) The part of managing the knowledge domain; c)The drafting and modelling part concerning law and policy; d)The decision making part.

Keywords: Electronic Government, Digital Government, Electronic Governance.

1 The Year 2013 – An Occasion to Recollect Key Events

The year 2013 is an occasion to recollect some memorabilia. The first year to recollect is 1983. The Year 1983 brought a first joint event of the German and Austrian Computer societies GI (Bonn) and ADV and OCG (Wien). The 1983 conference was held in Linz with the title "Neue Informationstechnologien und Verwaltung" and one year later proceedings were published with Springer (Traunmüller at al., 1984).

Next year to recollect is 1998. It brought the IFIP World Conference in Vienna and Budapest, and this event was one of the first to use the notion E-Government. The sub-conference "Telecooperation" was divided in the parts E-Commerce und E-Government. Proceedings were published at the conference (Traunmüller and Cushaj, 1988).

Also to mention are some collective volumes on the state of the art. So on behalf of the GI (Bonn) and their respective steering committees two collective volumes were published:

a) In 1997 a general collective volume presenting a retrospective und describing the state of the art was published (title: Informatik in Recht und

A. Kő et al. (Eds.): EGOVIS/EDEM 2013, LNCS 8061, pp. 8–17, 2013.

Verwaltung). Editors were Klaus Lenk, Heinrich Reinermann and Roland Traunmüller.

b) In 1999 a collective volume describing e-Government was published (title: Öffentliche Verwaltung und Informationstechnik) with the editors Klaus Lenk und Roland Traunmüller.

2   The DEXA 2002 Conference– Proclaiming an E-Government Agenda

On the occasion of First EGOV Conference an E-Government Agenda was proclaimed. The EGOV Conference took place within DEXA 2002 in Aix-en-Provence in September 2002 and proceedings were published (Traunmüller and Lenk, 2002). The Memorandum proclaimed comprises the following seven points as requirements for E-Government:

1. A holistic view: Moving ahead means having an integral view. Clear strategies and perceptions are a prerequisite to facing the challenges and making the best of the opportunities created by technological progress and its intellectual mastery. E-Government is more than a new wave of administrative modernisation, e-Government means a permanent e-transformation that enables governance on a comprehensive scale.

2. Service provision as focus: Citizen Portals and service delivery to business, to individual citizens and to communities reflect the viewpoints of individual citizens or of companies, looking at government and administration from outside. So the portal part is of prime concern, yet is should be noted that communicating with agencies is only the tip of an iceberg: the entire scope of administrative action has to be involved.

3. Redefining governmental processes: Thus, a thorough rethinking of the machinery of Government is mandatory. It will reveal many more situations where IT as an enabling force can enhance effectiveness, quality and efficiency of public action as well as its legitimacy. In many respects the legal framework of these processes has to be changed, and new institutions will emerge which fit the new ways of producing and delivering public services.

4. Knowledge enhanced government: A shift of focus from structures and processes towards content reaches the very heart of administrative work: taking decisions. Management of legal/ administrative domain knowledge is a decisive driver in governance. In addition, understanding the connections between processes and knowledge will improve design. In the agency of the future human and software expertise become totally interwoven – knowledge enhancement at its best.

5. An engineering approach: A sound engineering approach is indispensable. At bottom level this means a suitable IT infrastructure - unhampered communication and cooperation, availability, security, data protection, etc. At the application level it means smooth cooperation, high usability and a design integrating important perspectives: citizen service, process reorganisation, knowledge enhancement.

6. Reference models and administrative standards: Reference models and pilot projects give an idea about the full extent of the possibilities available. Above all, issues of standards have to be tackled: establishing a common understanding of processes, building on widespread administrative concepts, ensuring interoperable platforms; providing definitions for data interchange.

7. Change Management: Success can only be achieved if a quantum leap in the innovative capacity of the public sector is achieved. Critical success factors include strategic thinking and a farsighted allocation of funds for creating infrastructures and avoiding reinventing the wheel in different places. Best practice and guidelines derived from landmark projects will have to replace the attitude of curious but indiscriminate trying out of different approaches. Competent change management will have to place people first, and an unprecedented qualification offensive is needed to communicate the necessary know-how.

3   The Como Conference 2003 – Opening the Forum of European Events

There was positive reaction to the Aix Memorandum and one of the consequences was an invitation by the EU: Lenk and Traunmüller were invited to become part of the team formulating an official EU State of the Art Report. The report was edited by Christine Leitner and was authored by Jean-Michel Eymeri, Roland Traunmüller, Klaus Lenk and Morten Nielsen. It was handed over on occasion of the 2003 Ministerial Conference in Como. The State of the Art Report aimed at helping decision makers which were confronted with the crucial process of implementing e-Government at all levels. Its purpose was to provide a broad and varied overview of both the reality and the vision of e-Government as well as to offer an account of the state of affairs in e-Government in Europe. The report clearly indicated that e-Government" it is not restricted to the use of all sorts of new information and communication technologies. More, e-Government aims at fundamentally transforming the production processes in which public services are generated. For more on the Report see (Leitner, 2003) and concerning E-Government in general see the Reader (Chen et al., 2007).

4   A Broad Picture on European E-Government

The Como conference and subsequent Ministerial conferences presented a vivid picture on the state of European E-Government. These events showed several factors differentiating government in different countries. Just to give examples: Governmental structures may vary concerning centralisation (UK vs. Germany) and e-Government strategies are based on different priorities. Other examples show the wide variety: Broadband (US), mobile (Finland), one huge database containing all files of all ministries (Austria), creating Public-Private-Partnerships (Eastern Europe).

Also interesting communalities between the different countries showed up. Countries with a strong service economy take the lead. Further size matters; many high advanced countries have a middle size like Ireland, Denmark, Austria and The Netherlands ("small is beautiful"). A reason therefore is that it is easier to have an overview about different initiatives, which happen in the field of e-Government. Then small countries are more flexible if changes are necessary. A further outcome was that a pronounced interest in technology favours progress. This point starts with trendsetters and is also given in a (common) awareness of government as prime catalyst for change.

5   Some Leading Contributions from Austria

Help.gv.at: Life Event Advice Systems is an important application. The project Help.gv.at was awarded the first prize at the EU-conference in Como 2003. It complies with a new way of thinking regarding the citizens as "customers" of the administration. Such Advice System contains information and help in order to facilitate orientation in public life. In principle it is a kind of administration lexicon, to answer common questions. The most important contents are proof and guide function as well as claim information about rights and/or administration services and about duties. Based on life-events, the citizen receives information about offices and institutions as well as up-to-date information on procedures, fees, deadlines, etc. In a similar manner, enterprises receive information on business situations.

RIS: This is the Legal Information System of the Republic of Austria operated as an electronic database managed by the Austrian Federal Chancellery. It serves the publication of legal texts which must be published in the Federal Law Gazette and information on the current law in the Republic of Austria.

SPOCS: This is a large-scale pilot project launched by the European Commission in order to overcome obstacles of interoperability. Basically, businesses seeking to expand into other countries often struggle to comply with all the regulations they need to follow. Applying for licenses permits and completing other administrative procedures in another country can be very complicated. One application is the EU Services Directive which requires a lot of compliances for establishing a business and providing services in another EU country. The SPOCS project is now taking things a step further by streamlining those procedures and offering seamless cross-border technology.

E-Europe Awards of e-Government: These competitions have been established to recognise innovative initiatives in the areas of e-Government. Most competitions for e-Europe Awards have been organised by CEPA at University Krems and have drawn on the support of the Information Society Technologies Programme of the European Commission. Accordingly model projects are selected for presentation on conference exhibitions and during international e-Government conference. Regarding the method; Basic provision is that an independent panel of experts identifies best cases.

At the e-Europe Awards the following criteria that were applied: innovation, effective management, real practical results, impact, relevance and transferability.

A general note on knowledge transfer should be added. Collecting model cases may provide a good start; but Best Practice needs complimentary transfer mechanism. The development has to be supported by intensive knowledge transfer. The range of means for knowledge transfer is broad: knowledge transfer conferences, vendor neutral transfer spaces, virtual communities of knowledge sharing, learning journeys, involving facilitators and mentors and organising twinning projects.

6   Smart/Proactive Government and Cross Border Services

Citizens want public-sector services to be comparable to the best in the private sector, with greater transparency and access. Consumerisation of E-Government is the answer as more citizens become more comfortable with all digital features. New expectations drive Government organizations for utilizing technology to make systems more comfortable. In that way information become available to the general public. Government increases its capability to cooperate across government entities to provide services and information for the public. So citizen articulate their problem and get answers dedicated to their needs. Agencies go for systems tailored for their needs and also building up service knowledge. In that way also proactive services become possible. Also public, private, and non- profit providers of public services will become more common replacing tasks that traditionally have been seen as the preserve of public policy.

Broad use of interoperability and identity management is a special point. Both are crucial for accomplishing the vision of a "joined up Government" and still are implemented fairly inadequately on the national level. Making the question even more complicated is that the issue has to be solved on a Pan-European level. The European Interoperability Framework has three main distinctions. Technical interoperability covers the technical issues of linking computer systems and services. Semantic interoperability ensures that the precise meaning of exchanged information is understandable by other applications. Organizational interoperability is concerned with business processes and cooperation of agencies also including governance issues such as covering political, legal and structural conditions. Identity management and security are another crucial part. Technically, signatures are data linked to other data for the purpose of proving authenticity of message and sender. There are several categories of signatures used. A qualified digital signature has a qualified certificate and a secure method of transmission; so it is EU minimum standard and is so legally recognized as substitute of manual signatures.

7   Supporting E-Participation

Government has to support the formation of a democratic culture. The initiative of the European Parliament defined three main challenges: the perceived democratic deficit requiring new relationships between state and citizens; reconnecting Europeans with politics and policy making; competing with the complexity of decision making and legislation.

Thus e-Participation develops and implements new forms of participation in decision and policy making processes for citizens. The communication will involve citizens, public authorities, elected representatives etc. Aims of e-Participation are to improve public responsiveness and to enhance public satisfaction. This reinforces democracy and helps fighting against corruption and fraud. So e-Participation is a major point in the European e-Government Action Plans.

The early foci of e-Participation were laid in e-Voting and transparency. There were several projects using the web for voting. But most projects ran without digital signature and were often directed to rather particular circumstances. This included voting on special issues or covering areas of less sensitivity such as professional bodies. New approaches centre more in e-Participation as core. Active participation is a further item – so supporting community development and the building up of democratic knowledge. Many such activities will involve the communication with quite a lot of persons and therefore ICT support is demanded. Basically, the provision of data and information is significant. Many tools are quite simple just as mailing lists, discussion forum, special portals or websites, and so on. Other tools for collaboration are a more advanced form. They were developed in the Nineties under the name of groupware and are discussed later on. In the following some examples are given.

Campaigning: It is an important field for citizens active in supporting their representatives at elections. The goal of e-Campaigning is raising awareness; then it engages with people and encourages people to engage with each other. So it channels the power of public opinion to advance a progressive drive. In e-Campaigning the tools used are quite diverse, so writing blogs, using twitter, forwarding campaign information, making fund raising web-sites, etc.

Monitoring: Citizens are also watching and observing public life in a critical mood. No wonder that diverse forms of monitoring have become a leading issue. The targets of monitoring are divers. They include: events such as elections, groups such as political parties, persons such as politicians, modes such as proper fund spending and spaces such as parks.

Consultation: Such systems may support actual decision making. There are many activities in several countries: opinion polls for getting input or portals which engage the citizens to learn making virtual budget decisions guided by budget modelling. This example can be considered as a modest start to the demanding concept of policy modelling.

Lawmaking: These are efforts involving politicians, administrations, citizens and experts. Connecting stakeholders makes law-making more effectively. There are big advantages in handling the flow with workflow management and using semi-structured text processing. Just to give an example, annually in Austria sixty tons of papers are spent less by electronic handling.

Policy modelling: Here the fan of issues is broad. They comprise policy modelling tools, opinion visualization, and large-scale societal simulations as well as managing the legal and administrative domain knowledge.

8   Managing the Collaboration Part: Platforms, Social Media and Mobility

Now we turn to a more general view. A lot of progress will build on solid trends which add quite specific improvements and synergies. Here we consider advancements in four clusters:

a) The collaboration part (platforms, portals, social media and mobile devices);
b) The part of managing the knowledge domain;
c) The part of modelling: law and policy;
d) The decision making part.

Platforms and portals offer a broad choice of methods and tools. Some tools are easy to use and low-cost, as in the case of discussion forums and mailing lists. Other more advanced solutions include brainstorming software and spatial technology for visualization. Such platforms and portals also support social media. Social media provide new ways for citizens to participate in decision-making and policy formation, thereby better tapping the expertise of citizens and providing political planning processes with more input. In such a way, decisions can be improved and are more likely to be supported. Creation of collaborative content is mainly done by blogs and wikis: Blogs are online notebooks open to comment for other users while a wiki is built by collaborative edition of content. In addition, a form of information co-sharing is organized by references such as bookmarks, and URLs. Characteristic features comprise activities of different type in an intertwined mode. Thus, collaborative work blends different modes: informal collaborative modes alternating with strictly structured cooperation sustained by workflow or phases in searching for information and distributing of information.

Social media and mobile business reinforce each other in a co-evolutionary manner. Furthermore, the fact that such a large proportion of citizens use mobile devices such as smartphones and tablets to access the Internet has serious consequences. For example, the widespread usage of such devices has necessitated changes in modes of access and communication. Furthermore, the level and the intensity of service usage have increased. It follows that businesses and governments must adapt their business procedures and communication methods accordingly.

9   Managing the Domain Knowledge Part

Government has to keep up with the knowledge society. For administrations knowledge is top: agencies have respectable and extensive riches of knowledge; decision-making is the public official's daily occupation; all in all knowledge work is omnipresent. So a better management of knowledge will lead to forms of "smart government". Innovation is a key link relating Government and Knowledge Society - so it is worth to regard their mutual relationship. According to OECD a cycle of innovation has to be established: So discovery and development have to meet delivery and diffusion. Further favourable conditions have to be built. They include: collaboration, networks, value chains, and openness. Thus e-Government is perceived as a support as well as a field of innovation. Legal and Administrative Domain Knowledge is also the basis for internal improvements.

The field of Knowledge grows. A further field of knowledge is unlocked with Open Government Data. The idea dates back as the Freedom of Press was proclaimed in the American (1776) and French (1789) Revolution. General goals are improving transparency and making public value from Government data. Thus commercial use in joint ventures is promoted. A number of institutions provide open data creating an e-Government demand pull. Public value is linked to individual and societal interests. There is an intrinsic value in Government as well as in openness and transparency. In addition a broad consensus consists that more openness will promote good govern-ance. Several marks of good governance are influenced: participation, consensus reaching, accountability and responsiveness. E-Transparency has several aspects such as documents and data, benchmarks, processes, meetings.

Knowledge Management in the public sector has become an important issue, yet obstacles persist. Knowledge is omnipresent, but the task of managing legal and ad-ministrative domain knowledge is not easy. One reason is that Governments are not mentally prepared to KM. The administrators do not conceive themselves as knowledge workers. Second, several hindrances are rooted in the pronounced distinct-iveness of the legal domain. Legal information is collected in special forms and is organised following types of legal sources (norms, decisions, legal facts etc.). It is this conventional form of legal documentation that makes retrieval an onerous task.

In sketching the realm of Public Administration we present three different knowl-edge perspectives, which also show the immense cosmos of knowledge types and repositories: i) A first coarse distinction, which is based on the task of the public sec-tor, makes out three big clusters: registers, legal databases and management informa-tion. ii) A second perspective discerns the layers of government: The top government institutions as strategic-political layer, administrative bodies as tactical layer, and agencies as executive layer have different requirements on knowledge. iii) A third perspective takes a closer view on administrative action. Manifold types of knowl-edge on diverse subjects such as: on legal regulations, on standards on the policy field to be influenced, on the internals of the administrative system in general, on the re-spective environment, on means and modalities of action, on the effectiveness of measures etc.

10   Improving the Modelling Part: Law and Policy

There exists a long history of legal modelling. Here listing some spotlights may suf-fice. After some precursors legal modelling started in the Eighties with legal expert systems. It covered various subjects ranging from practical applications such as deci-sions support systems and configuration of legal documents to methodical issues. Our decade has brought continuous development as well as a new application – legal modelling for data exchange. Legal Information Retrieval has changed little in the past several decades, also poses problems. The key problem is that such systems are still keyword-oriented even thought finding a correct answer typically requires understanding the question, not just knowing the keywords. Case- based reasoning tools offer a possible solution. Prototypes using logical reasoning, including deontic logic, probabilistic methods and neuronal nets exist. However, such systems are experimental. Thus, they belong to the scientific realm and have not achieved large-scale use.

Recently in Public Governance working on policy formulation a novel topic emerged: ICT for governance and Policy modelling. The fan of questions is broad: policy modelling tools, opinion visualisation, mass collaborative platforms, and large-scale societal simulations. For example on-line collaborations have the potential to trigger and shape significant changes. Governance and participation toolboxes may comprise advanced tools from gaming and virtual reality technologies. This would include opinion visualisation and simulation solutions based on modelling, simulation, visualisation, mixed reality technologies, data mining etc. Further employing systems dynamics methodology helps analyse and model complex systems.

11   Improving the Decision Making Part

Supporting Individual Decision Making: A broad range of methods and tools, such as analytical systems, information retrieval, simulation and knowledge-based systems are available to support decision-making.

Supporting Group Decision Making: Collaborative decision-making adds a new dimension to conventional decision support systems. Groupware systems include many different types of systems such as brainstorming, argumentation, video-conferencing, and meeting support. Classical examples of situations in which collaborative decision support systems can be useful are negotiation and mediation procedures as well as policy formulation. Key characteristics of such domains include complex procedural regulations, activities of different types intertwined and conflicting interests of stakeholders. Generally, any cooperative work relationship is characterised by the fact that multiple actors transform or control an ensemble of mutually interacting objects and processes.

Giving Meeting Support: Such systems attempt to support the meeting process itself and perform various sub tasks. The different subtasks comprise the scheduling of the overall negotiation procedure, clarifying procedural questions and the planning of meetings and implied sub-activities. Further, one has to support the agenda setting and the documenting of processes and results. A lot of work is necessary for sustaining meetings in various ways: drawing on supplementary information, commenting on that information, spotting experts, structuring issues, summing up results etc. It follows that such working environments must blend collaborative methods with phases of strictly structured cooperation such as distributing information by workflow and searching for information. Transitions between these methods and auxiliary functions are needed too.

Adding Knowledge-based Components: Administrative applications can often be improved through the addition of knowledge-based components, which increase the capacity to understand the meaning of queries. It is highly desirable to incorporate knowledge into software. Improving the ability of citizen advice systems to comprehend requests and provide explanations is an important goal. Including knowledge can help bridge the divide between user language and the legal-administrative jargon that is often used by public agencies. The ultimate goal is to develop intelligent multilingual and multi-cultural personal assistants that are integrated in electronic public services.

Building on Semantic Technologies: In particular, semantic-based technologies show great promise. Semantic technologies are also applied to improve help-systems providing advice for life events and business situations. Furthermore, semantic technologies can be used to build repositories of administrative process knowledge. Such repositories gather experience from different cases and their usage can assist new-hires in their work. A quite universal and comprehensive solution for adding meaning is the Semantic Web. The Semantic Web means collective intelligence on the internet. So a world-wide sharing of unstructured information and informal knowledge becomes possible. This is allowed by architecture of layering and standardisation.

References

1. Chen, H., Brandt, L., Gregg, V., Traunmüller, R., Dawes, S., Hovy, E., Macintosh, A., Larson, C. (eds.): Digital Government: E-government Research, Case Studies, and Implementation. Springer-Verlag, New York Inc. (2007) ISBN 978-0387716107
2. Leitner, C. (ed.): e-Government in Europe: The State of Affairs, presented at the Ministerial e-Government Conference in Como, EIPA, Maastricht (2003)
3. Lenk, K., Traunmüller, R. (Hrsg.): Öffentliche Verwaltung und Informationstechnik: Perspektiven einer radikalen Neugestaltung der öffentlichen Verwaltung mit Informationstechnik. Schriftenreihe Verwaltungsinformatik Bd. 20, im R. v. Decker's Verlag, Heidelberg (1999)
4. Lenk, K., Reinermann, H., Traunmüller, R. (Hrsg.): Informatik in Recht und Verwaltung, Entwicklung, Stand, Perspektiven, Schriftenreihe Verwaltungsinformatik. R. v. Decker's Verlag, Heidelberg (1997)
5. Traunmüller, R., Lenk, K. (eds.): EGOV 2002. LNCS, vol. 2456. Springer, Heidelberg (2002)
6. Traunmüller, R., Fiedler, H., Grimmer, K., Reinermann, H. (Hrsg.): Neue Informationstechnologien und Verwaltung, Informatik-Fachberichte 80. Springer, Heidelberg (1984)
7. Traunmüller, R., Csuhaj, E. (eds.): Telecooperation. Proceedings of the XV. IFIP World Computer Congress, Vienna and Budapest, August 31-September 4. OCG Schriftenreihe, Wien (1998)

Digital Identity into Practice:
The Case of UniCam

Damiano Falcioni, Fabrizio Ippoliti, Fausto Marcantoni, and Barbara Re

Computer Science Division
School of Science and Technologies
University of Camerino
62032 – Camerino (MC), Italy
{damiano.falcioni,fausto.marcantoni,barbara.re}@unicam.it,
fabrizio.ippoliti@studenti.unicam.it

Abstract. Identity management is a set of technologies and processes supporting identity information. Its adoption in Public Administration, in particular in the domain of university, maintains organization autonomy giving at the same time students and staff support to access the services that are delivered. In this paper we present a project lead by University of Camerino with the Italian Banking Group UBI and the Namirial Certification Authority. The project consists in the issue of Enjoy my UniCam card allowing users to have, on a single physical card, several functionalities about facilitated banking account, university services and digital signature certificate. First results about the testing phase are presented as well as the next steps of the project.

1 Introduction

Over the time, managing personal identity on-line has become a serious issue. It has become increasingly important in terms of personal security, partly because organisations are now highly networked when it comes to information. Digital Identity (ID) is spread among different organisations. Small amounts of information cannot reveal enough about people to impact on us in a negative way but, when using the internet extensively, we can find several more information than expected [1]. So, depending on the context, person may be represented by different "partial identities". For example, a person may use one or more partial identities for work and others in spare time, e.g., with the family, doing sports, or dealing with companies like a bank, an Internet service provider, or a supermarket [2].

The project is based on a prepaid card named "Enjoy", that made possible the creation of a project leaded by University of Camerino (UniCam)[1] in collaboration with the Italian Banking Group UBI and the Namirial Certification Authority. This initiative has also made possible the creation of a digital scenario "Enjoy Ecosystem", resulting from a collaboration of five Italian universities and

---

[1] http://www.unicam.it

A. Kő et al. (Eds.): EGOVIS/EDEM 2013, LNCS 8061, pp. 18–28, 2013.
© Springer-Verlag Berlin Heidelberg 2013

many UBI local branches. Aim of the paper is to present the UniCam experience in digital identity management (IdM). The goal is to create a card for students, faculty and administrative staff that allow you to have, on a single physical card, several functionalities such as bank services, academic services and digital signature, letting the owners to save time and increase their satisfaction toward the university. The "all-in-one" solution has been chosen to guarantee safety, privacy and trust.

In order to complete the project, several issues have been addressed and solved. From the political point of view, the project is a valuable means of bringing innovation in UniCam. About the legal point of view, it also allowed the adoption of the Italian Digital Administration Code. For what concerns the organisational issues, an agreement was signed among UniCam, Italian Banking Group UBI and Namirial Certification Authority, it regulates terms and conditions in order to achieve the whole project objective. Finally, about the technical aspects, a new system was implemented. It is integrated with all the other existing infrastructures in the university, supporting different technologies. For instance, to set data flows among stakeholders, some web services have been implemented and SFTP (Secure Shell File Transfer Protocol) server has been integrated. Finally, from the administrative point of view, the use of Enjoy My UniCam card allows a remarkable simplification of the paperwork.

Section 2 presents a brief state of art about eID solutions in Europe and in Italy. Section 3 discusses the whole Enjoy my UniCam card project, with a deep description of actors, system architecture and processes. Section 4 introduces all the features of the card. Section 5 describes the services available with Enjoy my UniCam card. Finally, Section 6 concludes the paper.

2   Background: Digital Identity from Europe to UniCam

Over the years smart cards are being increasingly applied in the Public Administrations (PA). They provide great value to the use of services and they provide users identification and authentication.

For what concerns the eID solutions, limiting our analysis to government initiative, the European situation shows as the most adopted ones are implemented with smart card technology [3]. The majority of the European eID smart cards are national ID cards (in 13 countries) or tax cards. 6 other countries have already planned similar initiatives. The second most popular choice is password-based system (9 countries). Less adopted solutions are based on One Time Passwords (OTP) or Mobile Subscriber Identity Module (SIM) cards. Furthermore, in some cases, PA is assisted by private companies or the initiative is only private. The most common services offered by the European eID solutions are about tax declarations, pension and healthcare. In most cases, it also offers to the user the possibility to digitally sign documents.

The European Commission, through the Community Research and Development Information Service, founded several projects about Digital Identity and related subjects. They are financed in the 6th and the 7th Framework Programme funded by European Research and Technological Development respectively from 2002 until 2006 and from 2007 to 2013. In the 6th one, **FIDIS** (Future of Identity in the Information System, *http://www.fidis.net/*) was funded between April 2004 and June 2009. It aimed to integrate European research regarding technologies in order to support identity and identification; interoperability of identity and identification concepts; ID-theft, privacy and security; profiling and forensic implications. The achieved results regard integrated approaches to research; legal, socio-economic, usability and application requirements; public architecture and specifications. Further projects have been funded in the 7th Framework Programme such as: PrimeLife (Privacy and Identity Management in Europe for Life), GINI-SA (Global Identity Networking of Individuals - Support Action), DigIDeas and FutureID. Each of them has been funded by the ICT programme except DigIDeas which was funded under the programme IDEAS. **PrimeLife** (*http://primelife.ercim.eu/*) was funded from March 2008 to June 2011. It is the successor of the project PRIME (PRivacy and Identity Management for Europe, *https://www.prime-project.eu/*). PrimeLife mainly focused on: addressing the problem of digital footprints in the emerging Internet, in communities, and Web2.0 and through user-centric and configurable technology; making results of the projects PRIME and PrimeLife widely usable and deployed through standards, open source and education; advancing the state of the art about privacy and identity management. **GINI-SA** (*http://www.gini-sa.eu/*) was funded between June 2010 to May 2012. It aimed to investigate and establish the foundations for the architectural, legal, regulatory requirements, as well as the provisioning and privacy enhancing aspects, of a framework of user-centric identity management services. GINI-SA was based on the assumption that individuals, i.e. citizens, consumers, users of any related services, should be able to manage their own identity data and provide it in an open and flexible manner. The **DigIDeas** project (*http://www.digideas.nl/*), funded between October 2008 and September 2013, examines the social and ethical aspects of digital identities in the context of an increasingly digital world. The overall aims of DigIDeas are to increase understanding of the social and ethical aspects of digital identity management, to further theorize the concept of identity, and to contribute to the quality and social/ethical acceptability of technological developments. **FutureID** (*http://www.futureid.eu/*) is the most recent research project and it will finish in November 2015. The FutureID project builds a comprehensive, flexible, privacy-aware and ubiquitously usable identity management infrastructure for Europe, which integrates existing eID technology and trust infrastructures, emerging federated identity management services and modern credential technologies to provide a user-centric system for the trustworthy and accountable management of identity claims. Every stakeholder involved in the eID value chain, will benefit from the availability of a ubiquitously usable open source eID client that is capable of running on arbitrary desktop PCs, tablets and modern smartphones.

For what concerns more application oriented project we can refer the Information and Communication Technologies Policy Support Programme (ICT-PSP) as part of the Competitiveness and Innovation framework Programme (CIP). They are SSEDIC (Scoping the Single European Digital Identity Community), STORK (Secure idenTity acrOss boRders linKed) and STORK 2.0 (Secure idenTity acrOss boRders linKed 2.0). **SSEDIC** (*http://www.eid-ssedic.eu/*), funded from December 2010 to December 2013, it is a network with the goal to provide a platform for all the stakeholders of eID, to work together and collaborate to prepare the agenda for a proposed Single European Digital Identity Community. The network will identify the actions and the timetable for the Digital Agenda and the successful launch of the European Large Scale Action, as well as to provide a multi stakeholder planning resource to assist its implementation. **STORK** project (*https://www.eid-stork.eu/*) was funded from June 2008 to June 2011. It implemented an EU wide interoperable system for recognition of eID and authentication that should enable businesses, citizens and government employees to use their national electronic identities in any sember state. Project goals were: develop common rules and specifications to assist mutual recognition of eIDs across national borders; test, in real life environments, secure and easy-to-use eID solutions for citizens and businesses and interact with other EU initiatives to maximize the usefulness of eID services. **STORK 2.0** (*https://www.eid-stork2.eu/*), funded from April 2012 to April 2015, is going to contribute to the realization of a single European electronic identification and authentication area. It is based on the results of STORK, establishing interoperability of different approaches at national and EU level, eID for persons, eID for legal entities and the facility to mandate.

For what concerns the Italian scenario, we refer to the Italian Digital Administration Code. The National Card of Services ("Carta Nazionale dei Servizi" - CNS) and the Electronic Card of Identity ("Carta di Identità elettronica" - CIE) are the standards. In the last years, CNS model has been adopted by several Italian regions in order to realize Regional Card of Services ("Carta Regionale dei Servizi" - CRS) that are standard CNS. In most cases CRS are integrated with the Regional Health Card ("Tessera Sanitaria Regionale" - TS-CNS). At the end of 2012, regions have already been distributed to citizens over 20 million cards for access to services. The most massive distribution was of the Lombardy Region, which has completed distributing the card to all the population. The card are used to access health and government services such as enabling digital signatures. For what concerns identity enabling infrastructures, we cite ICAR (Interoperability and Applicative Cooperation between Regions) and IDEM (IDEntity Management for federated access). **ICAR** project (*http://www.progettoicar.it/*) supports implementation of an interregional federated authentication system aimed to define and implement a federated authentication system at interregional level. **IDEM** (*https://www.idem.garr.it/*) is the first Italian Federation of Authentication and Authorization Infrastructure (AAI) involving Institutions of the scientific and academic community and service and content providers on the web. The main purpose of the IDEM Federation is to make easier and more secure user identification and authorization to access to the services in the university country. Thanks to the federated approach, successfully developed in the

ICAR and IDEM projects, users can more easily access to networked resources provided by different organizations [5][6].

3   Enjoy My UniCam Project

3.1   Overview

Even if the paper focuses on the role of Enjoy My UniCam card, it's important to have a wider point of view considering the whole Enjoy My UniCam card project in Fig. 1. Every UniCam user can be identified and authenticated by the Enjoy My UniCam card. In this way, it's possible to benefit of the various services making available directly by UniCam. The basic idea allows to establish a trust federation, respecting the SAML 2.0 standard[2], between UniCam Identity Provider (IdP) and Idp of other organisations. The infrastructure is based on Shibboleth[3]: an open-source project that provides Single Sign-On capabilities and allows sites to make informed authorization decisions for individual access of protected on-line resources in a privacy-preserving manner. The Shibboleth software implements widely used federated identity standards, principally OASIS' Security Assertion Markup Language, to provide a federated single sign-on and attribute exchange framework. By doing so, users of an organization can use the services offered by the new federated organization and vice versa. All data are managed in full compliance with current privacy policies. Some personal information are exchanged between different actors.

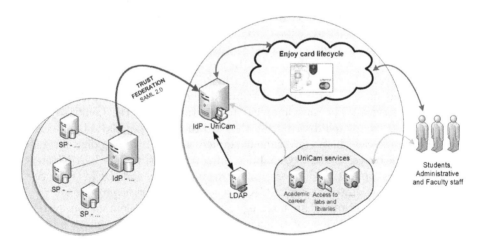

Fig. 1. The whole Enjoy My UniCam card project

---

[2] http://saml.xml.org/saml-specifications
[3] http://shibboleth.net/

3.2   Stakeholders

Following we sum up the main stakeholders involved in the project.

- University of Camerino is the services and cards provider, it manages control and data flow.
- UBI is a banking group which has a wide coverage, with about 1,800 branches, on the whole national territory. It assigns an International Bank Account Number (IBAN) to each person requesting Enjoy My UniCam card, offering its banking services. The group is also responsible for the emission of the card. About control and data flow management, UBI performs some operations in order to obtain and exchange data flows with UniCam and Oberthur.
- Oberthur is a company and it deals with the creation and issuance of personalized cards, according to the explicit applicant request and after obtaining the confirmation that the applicant has the right to get the card.
- Namirial Certification Authority is a computer company and web engineering that has found its own specific place in the field of IT and it's one of Certification Authority recognized by Italian Public Administration. In the project, Namirial is responsible for the issuance, management and termination of the digital signature certificates.

The stakeholders exchange information between their systems, according to the architecture represented in Fig. 2, where it is possible to see also the components diagram of the system.

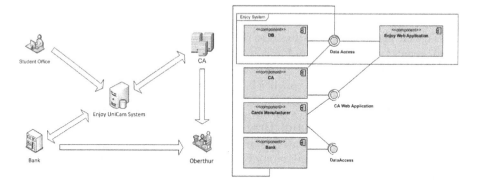

Fig. 2. Enjoy My UniCam system architecture and component diagram

3.3   Implemented Process

Following the main business process supported by Enjoy My UniCam, in Fig. 3 we provide the use cases diagram of every processes about the process to obtain the card.

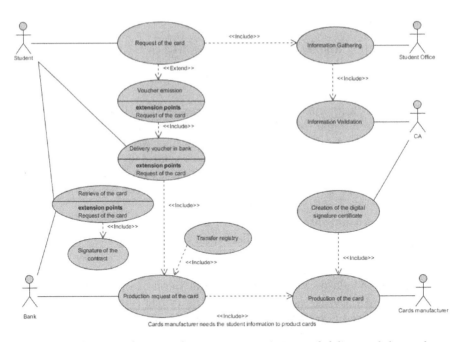

Fig. 3. Use cases diagram about request, emission and delivery of the card

Request of the Card - Student Office. For the students interested in the Enjoy My UniCam initiative, Student Office collects the students data and their pictures to be used for the card production. During the registration phase, UniCam uses the Namirial web portal to insert the student data, which performs the necessary checks of formal correctness. Based on these data, Namirial produces digital signature certificates and makes them available to Oberthur. Finally, the Student Office issues a voucher to present to the bank, which proves to be eligible for the card request. The voucher is recognized by UniCam and UBI like an official document.

Request of the Card - Bank Branch. The student goes to a branch authorized to issue cards, presenting the voucher given to him/her by UniCam during request phase. The bank employee collects the voucher and performs the following tasks:

- Identification of the users and insertion his/her data in the system;
- Request of the card in the system;
- Ask the student to subscribe the necessary contracts;
- Notifies the student when approximately the card will be ready and also that he/she will receive an envelope containing the Personal Identification Number (PIN) and the invitation to come to the branch to get the card.

Every day, via the SFTP server, UBI provides UniCam a file with a list of requests for cards issuance. UniCam acquires via SFTP the file, completes with the additional information and for each record includes a photograph to be printed on the card. According to UBI needs, UniCam adds in the photograph file properties the information about the fiscal code and the IBAN assigned to the holder.

Production of the Card. UBI transmits the requests, the personal data necessary for the production of cards and photographs of the owners to Oberthur, which performs the following activities:

- Customization with UniCam logo, Namirial logo and photo of the owner;
- Insertion of digital signature certificates in the cards, that are available on the Namirial web portal.

When the card is produced, on behalf of the UBI shipping office, Oberthur sends:

- The cards to the bank branches from which the request was made;
- The envelopes containing the PIN and the notification that the card is available in the bank, to the students' home address.

Activation of the Digital Signature Certificate. The issuance process of digital signature certificates involves the following steps:

- Namirial concludes a LRA agreement (Local Registration Authority)[4] with UniCam for the issuance of signature devices;
- Namirial provides UniCam of its web portal, with which a UniCam application refers to validate the data of the applicant;
- After the UniCam registration is complete and, data has been validated from Namirial web application, digital signature certificates are made available for Oberthur, without UBI participation;
- Oberthur loads the digital signature certificates on the cards, realizing the customization and sends them to the UBI branches.

Delivery of the Card. When the card and PIN have been produced, the student receives at his/her home address the PIN and the invitation to go to the bank branch to receive the card. When the student is at the office, he/she was handed the envelope containing the card and the delivery device signature module. The student signs the module and UBI sends it via mail to Namirial. Every day Namirial will call a procedure to communicate to UniCam the information acquired. At this point Namirial sends directly to the students' home address PIN and Personal Unblocking Key (PUK) of the digital signature certificate.

Reissue of the Card. In case of theft or loss of card, the student must:

- Request the freezing of money services in the way specified in the contract documents: that is calling the customer service or going directly to the bank branch;

---

[4] An LRA (Local Registration Authority) is an agent of the Certifying Authority who collects the application forms for digital signature certificates and related documents, does the verification and approves or rejects the application based on the results of the verification process.

- Request the freezing of digital signature certificate, as specified by Namirial in the documentation attached to the envelope containing PIN and PUK;
- Go to the Student office to request the release of a new voucher with which to present the replacement request of the card at the bank branch, in order to maintain the same IBAN;
- Go to the bank branch where the student originally requested the issuance of the first card, showing the new voucher. In this way the replacement request is processed as a standard procedure for a new Enjoy My UniCam card.

The process then follows the normal process of issuing a card. The voucher is a prerequisite, without which the student can't request the card. It's the only document obtained from the Student Office, certifying the students have the right to become cardholders.

Early Extinction of the Card. If a student loses the right to ownership of the card (e.g. in the case of drop-out), the Student office must inform the student that, before closing the relationship with the University, he must go to the bank branch to return the Enjoy My UniCam card, according to the usual banking regulations about the extinction of the cards.

4   Device

Starting from the basic information that can be found on any prepaid card, Enjoy My UniCam card has some customizations. On the front, the card is personalized with the UniCam Logo, Namirial logo and the holder photograph. On the back, instead, the card has only one customization: an indication of the code needed to handle the blocking activity of digital signature certificates.

The card used for the project is a card produced and commercialized by Oberthur Technologies^{TM}, named *ID-One Cosmo V7*. All interfaces of communication are available: it can be used in the following ways: Dual, Contact (Interface ISO 7816 T=0/T=1), Full-Contactless (ISO 14443 Type A and Type B).

Implementing Java Card^{TM} and GlobalPlatform Industry standards and featuring on-board applications, it has been specifically designed for identity and government market needs. It implements the most recent cryptographic mechanisms implemented, such as 3DES, AES, RSA and Elliptic curves. It also has 128 KB of free memory to load applications, as the UniCam services.

Anyone can understand how many risks need to be addressed in a project of this size, but the first and the most important one is about security. In particular, digital signature certificates, having legal value, must not be altered. This is the reason why the ID-One Cosmo card has been used, it's the only one to satisfy very high security standards.

- **Common Criteria EAL5+**: The *Evaluation Assurance Level* (EAL1 through EAL7) of an IT product or system is a numerical grade assigned following the completion of a Common Criteria security evaluation, an international standard in effect since 1999. The EAL5+ grade means the ID-One

Cosmo has been certified as "Semiformally Designed and Tested". As a result, we obtain that, even if an untrusted application were loaded and run, safety won't be compromised as the digital signature certificate remain valid.

- **FIPS 140-2 level 3**: The *Federal Information Processing Standard* is a U.S. government computer security standard used to accredit cryptographic modules. The standard provides four increasing, qualitative levels of security intended to cover a wide range of potential applications and environments. The security requirements cover areas related to the secure design and implementation of a cryptographic module. These areas include cryptographic module specification; cryptographic module ports and interfaces; roles, services, and authentication; finite state model; physical security; operational environment; cryptographic key management; electromagnetic interference/electromagnetic compatibility (EMI/EMC); self-tests; design assurance; and mitigation of other attacks [4].

Compliance with these two international standards is a prerequisite for the legal value of the digital signature certificate. This is supported by Enjoy my UniCam card.

5   Supported Services

The card allows the students to have, in a single physical device, several functionalities, in different areas: bank and university services.

- **Bank services**. The card is technically a prepaid card with an associated IBAN. It is valid for 5 years and it has not fixed fee. It allows you to make the usual banking operations, with special facilitations, such as paying anywhere displaying the MasterCard^{TM} symbol in Italy and abroad, making free withdrawals at every Bancomat cash machines in Italy, making and/or receiving transfers using home banking, paying bills and making RID payments and so on.
- **UniCam services**. The card allows the student to be recognized in UniCam facilities giving the possibility to access to laboratory and library, pay the meal at the canteen, register for exams, display and summary of the academic career, require internships and thesis, enrollment to university sports center.
- As already mentioned, the card contains a **digital signature certificate**, with legal value, with which you can digitally sign documents. In order to use the UniCam services about the request of particular documents or, for example, to require thesis, it's possible to fill the document directly from your laptop and then, finally, sign it with digital signature certificate. In this way the document will have official and legal value.

UniCam also partecipates in the IDEM Federation. So organizations in IDEM become Identity Provider: identities of own users can be exchanged, providing appropriate safeguards and always respecting the privacy of users [7][8][9]. With Enjoy my UniCam card it will be possible, in every university or organization participating to IDEM, to access to any service available such as libraries, logging in in computer labs, connecting to universities WiFi networks, which are often present in squares and public areas of faculties, and so on.

6 Conclusion and Future Works

In this paper we present the experience of the University of Camerino about the multi-services card. The adopted solution presents several advantages. On one hand, it avoids the possibility to have many and many cards to benefit different services. On the other, in term of identity federation it is part of community making advantages of related benefits.

Enjoy My UniCam card obtained good results during the testing phase, delivering over 330 cards in the first 9 months. The waiting time between the request and the final delivery has been about 15 days, that is a nice result considering the processing. In the next future, UniCam is going to activate several more services such as paying photocopies, coffees or snacks at the vending machines and about public transport service aiming to build up a smart campus.

References

1. Hansen, M.: Me, Myself and I! Manage your IDs safely (2007)
2. Clauß, S., Köhntopp, M.: Identity management and its support of multilateral security. Computer Networks (2001)
3. Bour, I.: Electronic Identities in Europe - Overview of eID solutions connecting Citizens to Public Authorities. Technical report, Transaction Security (2013)
4. NIST: Security requirements for cryptographic modules. Technical report, National Institute of Standards and Technology (2001)
5. Eve Maler, D.R.: The Venn of Identity: Options and Issues in Federated Identity Management. Technical report, European Commission (2010)
6. Gaedke, M., Meinecke, J., Nussbaumer, M.: A modeling approach to federated identity and access management. In: WWW 2005 Special Interest Tracks and Posters of the 14th International Conference on World Wide Web (2005)
7. Carota, S., Corradini, F., Falcioni, D., Maggiulli, M.L., Marcantoni, F., Piangerelli, R., Polzonetti, A., Re, B., Sergiacomi, A.: FedCohesion: Federated Identity Management in the Marche Region. In: Kő, A., Leitner, C., Leitold, H., Prosser, A. (eds.) EDEM 2012 and EGOVIS 2012. LNCS, vol. 7452, pp. 112–124. Springer, Heidelberg (2012)
8. Morgan, R., Cantor, S., Carmody, S., Hoehn, W., Klingenstein, K.: Federated Security: The Shibboleth Approach. Technical report, EDUCAUSE Quarterly (2004)
9. Baldoni, R.: Federated Identity Management Systems in e-Government: the Case of Italy (2012)

Trust-Service Status List Based Signature Verification

Opportunities, Implementation and Survey

Klaus Stranacher, Thomas Lenz, and Konrad Lanz

Institute for Applied Information Processing and Communications (IAIK),
Graz University of Technology, Graz, Austria
{klaus.stranacher,thomas.lenz,konrad.lanz}@iaik.tugraz.at

Abstract. Interoperability and cross-border services are on the top of the agenda of the Digital Agenda for Europe and the e-Government action plan. Here, electronic signatures and their verification play a major role. Especially electronic signatures relying on qualified certificates and produced by secure signature creation devices are of special interest – as they are legally equivalent to handwritten signatures. To facilitate the recognition of such qualified signatures, trust-service status lists have been established. Current signature verification applications lack on a sufficient support of trust-service status lists. To solve this problem, we propose an efficient, adaptable and easy to use trust-service status list enabled signature verification application. Our solution bases on the Austrian signature verification component MOA-SP. It extends the existing architecture to support trust-service status list functionalities. Finally, our implementation is evaluated in real life scenarios and we give a survey about the implementation status of trust-service status lists in Europe.

Keywords: Trust-service Status List, Signature Verification, Qualified Certificate, Secure Signature Creation Device, Cross-Border Services.

1 Introduction

Digital services have gained importance in the last years, especially in the area of e-Government and e-Administration. The increasing mobility of citizens and companies raises new challenges regarding cross-border services and interoperability. These issues have been taken up by the European Commission. Several activities, such as the Digital Agenda for Europe [9], the e-Government action plan [10] and the Services Directive [1] exist, which aim to remove the obstacles for creating a European digital market.

Within e-Government services, authenticity and integrity of the electronic data plays a major role. Usually, authenticity and integrity is achieved by using electronic signatures. The legal basis is formed by the EU Signature Directive [7]. Nevertheless there exist interoperability issues, especially for the verification of the validity of signatures. As there exist a variety of signature formats, the European Commission Decision 2011/130/EU [2] define standard signature formats which must be able to be processed by all concerned competent authorities.

A. Kő et al. (Eds.): EGOVIS/EDEM 2013, LNCS 8061, pp. 29–42, 2013.
© Springer-Verlag Berlin Heidelberg 2013

For many e-Government processes it is essential to know if an electronic signature is legally equivalent to a handwritten signature. To facilitate this verification the EU Member States are obliged to publish a trusted list of certification service providers issuing qualified certificates. These trusted lists rely on the ETSI standard on Trust-service Status List (TSL) [8].

Existing signature verification applications do not support trust-service status lists (trusted certification service providers can only be configured manually) or they do not support them sufficient. In the present paper we show an efficient, adaptable and easy to use TSL enabled signature-verification application, which bases on the Austrian component MOA-SP for signature verification.

The remainder of this paper is organized as follows. In Section 2, we describe the legal and technical framework our solution bases on. Section 3 elaborates on the Austrian component MOA-SP and other existing signature-verification applications. The subsequent Section 4 gives details about our develop library for processing and handling trust-service status lists. In section 5 we show the integration of this library into MOA-SP including a requirement analysis, the extended architecture and extended process flows. Section 6 gives an evaluation of our solution and presents a survey of the implementation status of the different EU Member State trust-service status lists. Finally, we draw conclusions and discuss future work.

2   Legal and Technical Framework

2.1   Legal Background

In 1999 the European Commission published the Directive on a Community framework for electronic signatures, better known as the Signature Directive [7]. The Directive includes a definition of different levels of electronic signatures and their legal effects. In particular it defines that an electronic signature is legally equivalent to a handwritten signature (Article 5), if the electronic satisfies following requirements:

— The signature must be an advanced electronic signature
— The signature must base on qualified certificate (QC)
— The signature must be created using a secure signature creation device (SSCD)

In many e-Government processes such a 'qualified signature'[1] is a precondition for further processing. Especially in cross-border services[2] the verification on qualified certificate and secure signature-creation device becomes difficult, as qualified certificate can only be issued by certification service providers, which are accredited or under supervision. To facilitate the verification of the status of certification service provides (and so the QC and SSCD property of an electronic signature), EU Member

---

[1] The Signature Directive does not explicitly define the term qualified signatures. Nevertheless this term is often used in literature.

[2] For instance, it is of special interest for the cross-border identification and authentication of persons. See EU large scale pilots STORK (https://www.eid-stork.eu/) and STORK 2.0 (https://www.eid-stork2.eu/).

States are obliged to maintain a trusted list of certification service providers issuing qualified certificates.

These trusted lists are implemented by the ETSI standard on Trust-service Status List (TSL). Additionally, to provide a single point of contact, the European Commission maintains and published a central trusted list (EU-TSL), which holds references to the different Member State trusted lists (MS-TSL).

2.2   Trust-Service Status Lists

Trust-service status lists (TSL) have been specified by ETSI [8]. The main objective is to publish information about the status of a trust-service provider in such a way *"that interested parties may determine whether a trust service is or was operating under the approval of any recognized scheme at either the time the service was provided, or the time at which a transaction reliant on that service took place."* [8].

The trust-service provider status includes information about the provider including whether the provider is or was acting under the scheme[3] of a certain scheme operator[4]. In relation to electronic signatures, the EU-TSL holds status information about certification service providers, which are issuing qualified certificates under the scheme of a certain accredited or supervised body.

The logical structure of a TSL consists of following four components:

— Information about the TSL and the scheme itself facilitating its identification
— Information about the trust service providers and whose services are within the scope of the scheme
— For each trust service provider: information about current status of each service operated by the provider (including the certificate which represents the particular service)
— For each service: information about historical status information

For authentication purposes the whole TSL is signed. Additionally a TSL must be published in a human readable and machine processable form.

3   Signature Verification Services

Signature verification is often required in many processes and procedures. Therefore various tools and applications exist. In our survey on existing signature verification services, we are focusing on services, which have a strong cross-border context. Following services exist on a European level:

---

[3] The TSL specification defines scheme as *"any organized process of supervision, monitoring, approval or such practices that are intended to apply oversight with the objective of ensuring adherence to specific criteria in order to maintain confidence in the services under the scope of the scheme"* [8].

[4] I.e. it contains the current status and historical status information. Historical status information is important to verify if a certification service provider was accredited or supervised at the issuing time of a certain qualified certificate.

— SD-DSS[5]: The SD-DSS tool is commissioned by the European Commission. It supports the verification of electronic signatures formats according to the Commission Decision on establishing minimum requirements for the cross-border processing of documents [2]. Its focus lies on applications in the area of the EU Services Directive.

— PEPPOL signature verification: The EU large scale pilot PEPPOL developed a signature verification service[6] with focus on public procurement processes in a cross-border context.

— SPOCS eDocuments verification: The EU large scale pilot SPOCS implemented a signature verification services as part of the validation and verification of electronic documents. This service has been developed for use cases concerning the EU Services Directive, but is not limited to them.

— MOA-SP: The signature-verification service MOA-SP is part of the Austrian software bundle MOA-ID/SP/SS[7]. The functionality is divided into three different modules, whereas MOA-SP enables the verification of XML, XAdES and CMS signatures[8]. MOA-SP is widely used in Austria, but also in other countries[9] and in applications of the European Commission Authentication Service (ECAS)[10].

All of these verification services are licensed under the European Public License EUPL [3] and therefore freely available on the platform Joinup.

4   TSL Implementation

In this section we describe the TSL library which is used to download, parse and handle the particular trust-service status lists. We give an overview about the architecture of the TSL library. In addition, we present detailed information about the main parts of our TSL library and finally we describe measures for TSL schema error-handling.

4.1   TSL Library Architecture

Figure 1 illustrates the architecture of the TSL library. The key component is the TSL Engine. It coordinates the TSL import and the certificate-extension verifications. These operations are implemented in sub-modules to achieve a modular architecture of the TSL library.

---

[5] http://joinup.ec.europa.eu/software/sd-dss/home
[6] http://www.peppol.eu/peppol_components/esignature/esignature
[7] http://joinup.ec.europa.eu/software/moa-idspss/home
[8] The other components enable the creation of XML and XAdES signature on the server side (MOA-SS) and provide a unique identification and authentication of Austrian and foreign citizens as well as citizens using electronic mandates (MOA-ID). See [5] for details on these identification and authentication processes.
[9] As essential part of the STORK pilot applications:
https://www.eid-stork.eu/pilots/index.htm
[10] https://webgate.ec.europa.eu/cas/

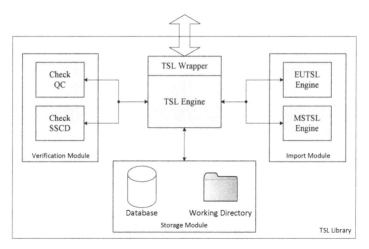

Fig. 1. TSL library architecture

The entire functionality which is required to import and verify the particular TSL information's are implemented in the Import Module. The verified TSL information is stored in a structured format in a Database. Additionally, certificates (extracted from the TSL information) are stored in a local file system based Working Directory. All store and read functionality is encapsulated in the Storage Module. The Verification Module implements functionalities to verify certificate extensions depending on the information which is stored in the Storage Module. The benefit of this architecture is fast processing, due to the internal database and the separate certificate extension verifications (as they must be performed for each certificate validation during a signature verification process).

4.2   TSL Library Sub-modules

In this sub-section, we present detailed information about the Import Module and den Verification Module.

Import Module
A TSL import operation consists of several steps and therefore we split this operation into two modules. The two modules are the EUTSL Engine, which is used to download, verify and import the EU TSL information and the MSTSL Engine which process the Member States TSLs. Figure 2 illustrates the process flow of a TSL import operation. The following steps are performed after a Download TSLs request has been received:

1. The TSL Engine initializes the database connection and setup the URL to EU trust-service status list.
2. Processing of the EU TSL:
   (a) The EU-TSL is downloaded and stored in the local working directory.

(b) Afterwards, the TSL gets validated (XML schema validation and verification of the applied TSL signature).

(c) Finally, the pointers to the Member State TSLs are stored in the database and the signer certificates of the particular TSL are stored in the working directory.

3. Processing of the Member State TSLs. This step is repeated for each Member State TSL[11].

(a) The MS-TSL is downloaded and stored in the local working directory.

(b) Afterwards, the MS-TSL gets validated (XML schema validation and verification of the applied TSL signature).

(c) Finally, the TSL information and all extracted certificates are stored.

4. In the last step, the import and validation errors are stored into the database and the database connection is closed.

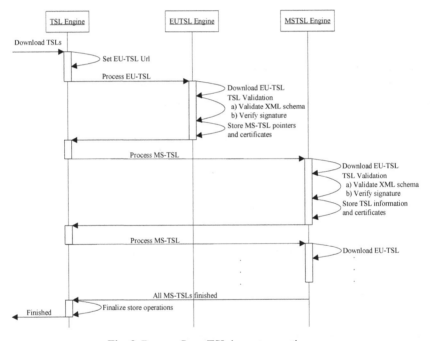

Fig. 2. Process flow: TSL import operation

Verification Module

The Verification Module is used to verify the QC or SSCD property of an electronic signature. This property check requires several steps and uses information from the local Database. Figure 3 shows the process flow of a verification of these properties.

---

[11] Two modes of operation exit to import the Member State TSLs. Default mode of operation is sequential processing of the MS-TSLs. As an alternative, a parallel mode of operation is supported, which uses multi-threading to process all MS-TSLs simultaneously.

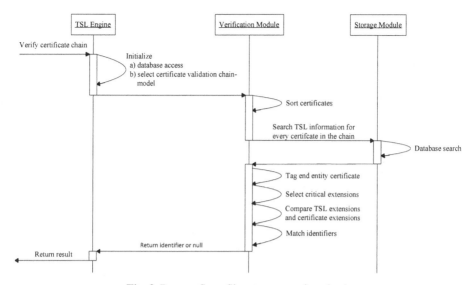

Fig. 3. Process flow: Signature extension check

The following steps are performed after a CheckQC or CheckSSCD request has been received.

1. Initialization of the Database access and selection of the certificate validation-model.
2. The certificate chain is sorted beginning with the end-entity certificate.
3. Search for information in the TSL Database for every certificate in the chain.
4. Select the critical extensions in the end-user certificate and the TSL information.
5. Compare these extensions according the TSL criteria-list element.
6. For every match extension, check if a QC or SSCD property exists
7. Return the result.

4.3   TSL Library Error Handling

Actually only a few TSLs are strictly conform to the corresponding XML schema and therefore, a schema-validation error-handling becomes necessary (see also Section 6). During the TSL import operation, all validation error get logged and stored in the Database to obtain an overview of the current situation. The error handling can also be used to correct a subset of errors on the fly during the XML schema-validation process. If such a special defined error is found, a specific error-correction method is started to solve the fault and afterwards the strict XML schema validation is restarted. If a second error is found on the same place, then the TSL is rejected. The advantage of this solution is a combination of a strict XML schema validation which can be loosen for a specific subset of XML schema error.

5   TSL Integration

In this section we elaborate on the integration of the TSL library into the Austrian open source software module MOA-SP. In the following sub-sections we give a brief overview about the existing functionality of MOA-SP focusing on the certificate validation. Next we give requirements which have to be taken into consideration for the TSL integration. The last two sub-sections elaborate on the extended architecture and modified process flows in detail.

5.1 Existing Functionality

Figure 4 shows the architecture of MOA-SP. According to the general signature verification process, MOA-SP performs the core signature-verification and the following certificate validation. During the core signature-verification MOA-SP verifies the cryptographic validity of the signature (Core Signature Verification Unit) based upon the supported signature formats. The certificate validation-process (Certificate Validation Unit) verifies if the signer certificate is valid and performs following validations:

— Validation of the signer certificate itself. That means to verify if the certificate is timely valid (e.g. has not expired) or is not revoked (e.g. due to a key compromise).
— Built a certificate chain from the signer certificate up to a root CA[12] certificate according to the PKI specification [6] and verify the validity of all certificates in this chain.
— Validation if a certificate of the chain matches a certificate in a defined trustprofile. Such trustprofiles are configured in the MOA-SP configuration and define a set of trusted certificates (=truststore). This last validation is very important to define which signer certificates are trusted.

Only if all validation steps have a positive result, the whole certificate validation is positive. Actually this trustprofile mechanism only bases on manually added trusted certificates. In the following this mechanism is extended to support TSL.

5.2 Requirements

Basis for our requirement analysis have been the application operators and users of MOA-SP. Their needs and preconditions have been the leading factors for our analysis. Here it was essential to find a trade-off between the widespread functionality of the TSL library and a still easy configurable and useable MOA-SP module. Our analysis led to following main requirements:

— Backward compatibility: MOA-SP is widely used. Therefore it is of high importance to retain the existing functionalities, especially for all application operators and users which do not need TSL support. This means in particular that current configurations and user interfaces must be still usable after the TSL integration.
— Minimal effort: The installation and configuration effort of the TSL functionality should be reduced to a minimum. At the same moment, really needed configuration options should be easily modifiable.
— Integration: The TSL support should fit well into the existing architecture of MOA-SP and should allow an easy integration into existing applications.

---

[12] CA is a certification authority, which issues certificates.

Based upon these requirements following section elaborates on the developed extended architecture.

5.3   Extended Architecture

Figure 4 illustrates the extended architecture and the extended trustprofile mechanism. The extended mechanism allows adding TSL support for trustprofiles (TSL-enabled trustprofiles). This means that TSLs can be used as an additional[13] trust anchor during the certificate validation.

Due to the wide range of functions of the TSL library, a TSL Wrapper has been developed following the KISS principle. This wrapper encapsulates the functionalities of the TSL library and provides specific methods, which are needed by MOA-SP. In addition, this wrapper provides an easy applicable interface for other verification services, which intends to use the TSL library functionalities. These interface methods are:

— Initialization: This method initializes the TSL library (creation and initialization of the TSL database, define a TSL working directory, etc.)
— Download: In this method the national TSLs are downloaded, parsed and the information in the TSL library is updated.
— Export: This method exports a set of CA certificates, whose CA issues qualified certificates and its certification service provider is under supervision or accredited.
— QC and SSCD Check: These last methods verify if the signer certificate is qualified and if the signer signature has been created by the use of a secure signature-creation device.

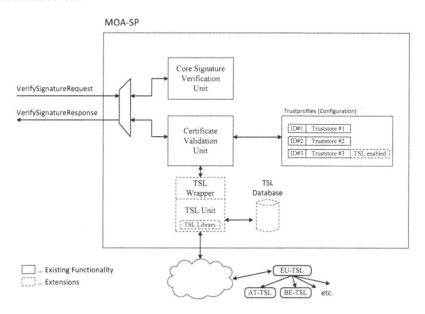

Fig. 4. MOA-SP architecture (basic functionality and extensions)

---

[13] I.e. in addition to optional, manually, added certificates.

5.4   Extended Process Flows

Based upon the extended architecture, the process flows have been changed in case of a configured TSL support. In the following the modified process flows during the server startup and the certificate validation process are explained.

Startup and TSL Unit Initialization

During the server start MOA-SP performs different initializations based upon the MOA-SP configuration. The corresponding process flow (in case of TSL-enabled trustprofiles are configured) is illustrated in Figure 5 and consists of following process steps:

1. After the server startup MOA-SP performs the non-TSL specific initializations based upon the configuration.
2. Initialization of the TSL Unit, e.g. definition of database location.
3. Update of the TSL-enabled trustprofiles:

   (a) Download of the actual national TSLs via the EU-TSL.
   (b) Parsing the TSLs and update of the information in the database.
   (c) For each TSL-enabled trustprofile:

       (i) Export all CA certificates matching the properties defined in the MOA-SP configuration (i.e. CA certificate from all or only selected countries)
       (ii) Update of the truststore, i.e. storing the exported certificates in the truststore.

In addition, the update of the TSL-enabled trustprofiles is executed on a regular basis. The update interval is adjustable via the configuration.

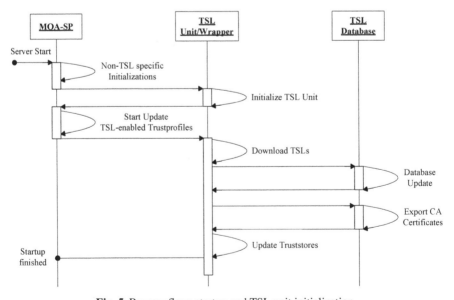

Fig. 5. Process flow: startup and TSL unit initialization

Signature Verification and TSL Based Certificate Validation

Figure 6 shows the process flow for verifying a signature based upon a TSL-based trustprofile. After receiving a VerifySignatureRequest following process steps are performed:

1. MOA-SP performs the cryptographic signature verification.
2. The Certificate Validation Unit builds the certificate chain and verifies the validity of all certificates.
3. Via the TSL Unit it is verified if the signer certificate is qualified and if the signature has been created using a secure signature creation device.
4. Finally MOA-SP consolidates all verification and validation results and returns a VerifySignatureResponse.

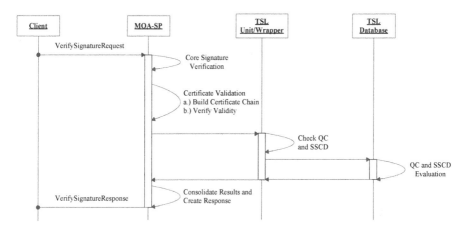

Fig. 6. Process flow: Signature verification and TSL based certificate validation

6   Evaluation and Survey

In this section we evaluate our implementation in a real life environment. Afterwards, we discuss issues arising from the use of trust-service status lists and finally we illustrate some actual TSL issues.

6.1   Evaluation

In Austria, a Web based signature-verification tool [11] has been developed which is in common use and enables the verification of different document and signature formats. This tool uses MOA-SP in the backend for the core signature-verification. Thus we decided to evaluate our solution within this application. For the evaluation the automatic test-framework, which is a part of the Web based signature-verification tool, is used to verify the electronic signatures of a wide range of signed documents. For our tests, we use a set of 99 documents which are signed with certificates from 15 European countries. As basic principle for this evaluation, we use the same MOA-SP configuration which is also in use in the productive application. Figure 7 illustrates the certificate validation result, if no TSL information is used. Actually more the 60 per cent of the documents failed the verification process, because no valid certificate chain[14] can be determined.

If we use the MOA-SP module with TSL support, then the certificate validation-result shows a clearly better result (see Figure 8). By using information from the TSLs, the verification results are much better, because valid certificate chains can be determined by using the adding information for the TSL. Thus, from a functional view TSLs are beneficial for certificate validation. Nevertheless, correct verification results strongly depend on valid trust-service status lists, which are issued by the respective Member States. However, there are still problems with valid Member States TSLs because actually more than three quarters of them have structural flaws.

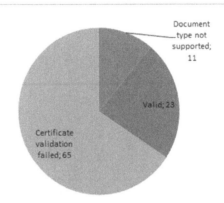

Fig. 7. Certificate validation without using TSL information (as at 04.06.2013)

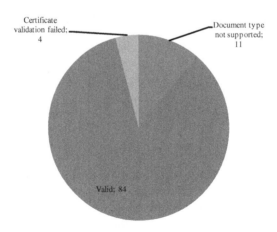

Fig. 8. Certificate validation with TSL information (as at 04.06.2013)

---

[14] Not valid in terms of no trust anchor has been found.

6.2   TSL Usage Issues

Actual, only seven of 27 currently available Member State TSLs have no structural flows[15]. To overcome these problems we use the error handling and correction functionality, which is described in section 4.3. Figure 9 illustrates the distribution of TSLs, which we actually can handle with the TSL library depending on the errors which we found. Actually, we reject six Member State TSLs[16], because they have serious schema issues, such as missing XML elements, or the XMLDsig signature of the TSL cannot be verified.

Actually, we accept 14 Member State TSLs after an error correction is performed. The following enumeration illustrates the structural flaws which must be corrected.

- The XMLDsig signature can be verified but uses an XML transformation which is not allowed, according to the TSL standard [8]. This error can be corrected for ten Member State TSLs[17].
- Deletion of some characters, like hyphens, which are included in front of or after XML elements. This error can be corrected in three Member State TSLs[18].
- Solve problems with an incorrectly used XML xsd:ID type. This error can be corrected in three Member State TSLs[19].

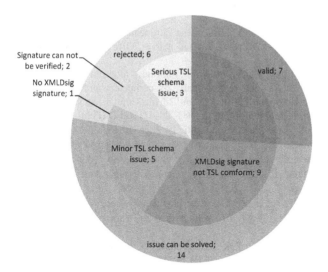

Fig. 9. Distribution of TSLs used in our implementation according to their validation flaws (as at 04.06.2013)

---

[15] AT, BE, CZ, FI, HU, LI, LU.
[16] BG, DE, DK, EE, MT, RO.
[17] CY, ES, FR, LT, LV, NL, PL, PT, SE, SI.
[18] GR, IT, PL.
[19] CY, LV, NL.

7 Conclusions

Signature verification is essential for many e-Government processes. Especially the recognition of electronic signatures based on a qualified certificate and a secure signature creation device is of high importance. In this paper we have presented a trust-service status list based signature verification enabling the recognition of 'qualified signatures'. We have demonstrated the practical applicability, flexibility and efficiency of our presented solution. Our application is able contribute to a higher volume of interoperable cross-border service.

Our developments will be incorporated into the new release of the component MOA-SP. The publication of this release is planned for the third quarter of this year.

Nevertheless, our survey on the status of the different national trusted lists has shown that in some cases the trusted list of certain Member States is inconsistent or contains shortcomings. The quality of the trusted list of the affected Member States should be improved to guarantee a higher interoperability for cross-border services. This has been recognized by the European Commission, which currently elaborates on an amendment of the European Commission Decision 2009/767/EC. Most likely this amendment includes a common template for the "Trusted List of supervised/accredited Certification Service Providers".

References

1. European Union, Directive 2006/123/EC of the European Parliament and of the Council of 12 December 2006 on services in the internal market, Official Journal L 376, pp. 36–68 (December 27, 2006)
2. European Commission Decision, Establishing minimum requirements for the cross-border processing of documents signed electronically by competent authorities under Directive 2006/123/EC of the European Parliament and of the Council on services in the internal market, notified under document C(2011) 1081, 2011/130/EU (February 25, 2011)
3. European Community, European Union Public Licence (EUPL v.1.1) (2007), http://joinup.ec.europa.eu/software/page/eupl/licence-eupl
4. Posch, R., Orthacker, C., et al.: Open Source Bausteine als Kooperationsgrundlage. In: Eixelsberger, W., Stember, J. (eds.) E-Government - Zwischen Partizipation und Kooperation
5. Stranacher, K., Tauber, A., et al.: The Austrian Identity Ecosystem – An e-Government Experience. In: Martínez, A.R. (ed.) Architectures and Protocols for Secure Information Technology (Note: in press)
6. Cooper, D., Santesson, S., et al.: RFC 5280, Internet X.509 Public Key Infrastructure Certificate and Certificate Revocation List (CRL) Profile (May 2008)
7. European Union, Directive 1999/93/EC of the European Parliament and of the Council of 13 December 1999 on a Community framework for electronic signatures, Official Journal L 13, pp. 12–20 (January 19, 2000)
8. ETSI, Technical Specification 102 231, Electronic Signatures and Infrastructures (ESI); Provision of harmonized Trust-service status information, V2.1.1 (2006)
9. European Commission, Communication from the Commission to the European Parliament, the Council, the European Economic and Social Committee and the Committee of the Regions A Digital Agenda for Europe, COM/2010/0245 (May 19, 2010)
10. European Commission, The European eGovernment Action Plan 2011-2015 Harnessing ICT to promote smart, sustainable & innovative Government, COM/2010/743 (December 15, 2010)

Towards a Federated Identity as a Service Model

Bernd Zwattendorfer, Klaus Stranacher, and Arne Tauber

E-Government Innovation Center (EGIZ), Graz University of Technology, Graz, Austria
{bernd.zwattendorfer,klaus.stranacher,arne.tauber}@egiz.gv.at

Abstract. Identity management plays a key role in e-Government. Giving the increasing number of cloud applications, also in the field of e-Government, identity management is also vital in the area of cloud computing. Several cloud identity models have already emerged, whereas the so-called "Identity as a Service"-model seems to be the most promising one. Cloud service providers currently implement this model by relying on a central identity broker, acting as a hub between different service and identity providers. While the identity broker model has a couple of advantages, still some disadvantages can be identified. One major drawback of the central identity broker model is that both the user and the service provider must rely on one and the same identity broker for identification and authentication. This heavily decreases flexibility and hinders freedom of choice for selecting other identity broker implementations. We bypass this issue by proposing a federated identity as a service model, where identity brokers are interconnected. This federated identity as a service model retains the benefits but eliminates the drawbacks of the central cloud identity broker model.

Keywords: Cloud Computing, Identity as a Service, Federated Identity as a Service, Identity Broker, Identity Management.

1 Introduction

Electronic identity management [1] is the key enabler for reliable identification of users, which is essential in e-Government applications. The main tasks of identity management comprise secure management of identities, management of attributes corresponding to identities in a specific context, and identification and authentication processes [2]. Identification of users is a main requirement for many applications, especially for those which are processing confidential or sensitive data.

Numerous identity management initiatives and systems exist since many years. In the enterprise sector, directory services such as LDAP (Lightweight Directory Access Protocol) [3] or Kerberos [4] are still present. Within the Web, systems or standards such as the Security Assertion Markup Language (SAML) [5], the Liberty Alliance Project[1] (that evolved to the Kantara initiative[2]) or Shibboleth[3] gained

---

[1] http://www.projectliberty.org
[2] http://kantarainitiative.org
[3] http://shibboleth.net

A. Kő et al. (Eds.): EGOVIS/EDEM 2013, LNCS 8061, pp. 43–57, 2013.

increased popularity, to just name a few. Also a couple of research projects covered the topic on identity management, e.g. FIDIS[4], PRIME[5] and PrimeLife[6], or PICOS[7].

Secure identity management also plays an important role for governments. Many European countries have already national eID solutions to be used in public or private sector applications in place since years [6]. Additionally, within Europe the project STORK[8] successfully piloted secure identification and authentication across borders using various national eIDs. Those results are further taken up by its successor project STORK 2.0[9], which started in 2012. In relation to that, the USA introduced its "National Strategy for Trusted Identities in Cyberspace"[10] (NSTIC), which aims on the creation of a secure and trusted identity ecosystem in the US.

In most electronic identity management systems, identity providers are the means of choice for identification of users and authentication at the service provider. Identity providers are usually an essential entity within an identity model. We briefly introduce traditional identity models for central, user-centric, or federated approaches in Section 2.

Given the increasing number of cloud applications, also in the field of e-Government, identification of users gains also more and more importance in the field of cloud computing. Hence, different cloud identity models have already been defined to cover new requirements particularly relating to cloud computing. The main distinctive criterion between these cloud identity models is the entity, which operates the identity provider in relation to the cloud application. We overview these cloud identity models in Section 3. Thereby, the so-called "Identity as a Service"-model [7] specifies the very cloud identity model, which takes best advantage of the cloud computing paradigm. In this model, the identity provider is fully operated in the cloud. This allows for a separation between cloud service providers, which host and operate the application, and cloud service providers, which host and operate the identity provider. Therefore, this model is currently the most promising identity model for cloud-based identity management.

Based on the "Identity as a Service"-model, a couple of so-called cloud identity brokers have already emerged. The identity broker model consists of a central identity broker in the cloud, which acts as a hub between various service and identity providers. The benefit of this approach is decoupling the service provider from multiple identity providers, which in fact facilitates identity management.

Nevertheless, the cloud identity broker model has one major drawback, which has not been solved yet. Users and service providers must rely on the same central identity broker for identification and authentication, if this model is applied. Obviously, this causes strong dependencies on the availability and functionalities of the identity broker. To overcome this issue, we present a new identity model for the cloud relying on

---

[4] http://www.fidis.net
[5] https://www.prime-project.eu
[6] http://primelife.ercim.eu
[7] http://www.picos-project.eu/
[8] https://www.eid-stork.eu/
[9] http://www.eid-stork2.eu/
[10] http://www.nist.gov/nstic

a federated approach between multiple identity brokers. This federated identity as a service model retains the benefits, but eliminates the drawbacks of the cloud identity broker model.

The remainder of this paper is structured as follows. In Section 2, we describe traditional identity models and their basic approaches. Section 3 elaborates on existing cloud identity models and classifies them. The subsequent Section 4 introduces the centralized cloud identity broker model based on the "Identity as a Service" approach of Section 3. In Section 5, we present our idea of a federated identity as a service model. Finally, we draw conclusions including future work.

2   Traditional Identity Models

Identification and authentication are by far no new issues, thus several different identity management systems have evolved [8]. In most identity management systems, user identification and authentication at a service provider is carried out via a so-called identity provider. Such an identity provider is responsible for user authentication and transferring user's identity and authentication data to the requesting service provider. Not all systems follow the same methodological approach. For instance, some systems store identity data centrally, whereas other systems follow a federated approach. In this section we briefly describe three types of traditional identity models (central, user-centric, and federated approach) based on the work of Palfrey and Gasser [9]. Distinction criteria are the storage location of identity data (i.e. central database, user domain, or distributed storage). Each of these three models has its specific characteristics. One may have advantages on privacy and user control, another one on scalability. This classification of identity models can also be found in [10]. However, also other classification approaches such as by Alpár, Hoepman, and Siljee [11] exist.

2.1   Central Approach

In the central identity model identity data are stored in a central database at the service provider or the identity provider. Before being allowed to use a service, users usually have to register. This registration has to be done at an affiliated identity provider. Once registered, the identity data are managed and stored in central repositories in the identity provider's domain. When accessing a certain service or application at a service provider, the user must have been successfully authenticated at the identity provider before. After that, the identity provider forwards the identity data to the service provider. In this approach, the user has no control anymore on which data are stored or actually transmitted to the identity information requesting service provider.

2.2   User-Centric Approach

In the user-centric model, the user herself always remains the owner of her identity data. Identity data are managed and stored within the user's domain (e.g. on a smart card) and are transferred to a service provider only if the user explicitly gives her consent. Using this approach, a direct communication channel between the user and the service provider can be achieved and end-to-end security without involving third parties can be guaranteed.

2.3 Federated Approach

In this model, user or identity data are distributed across various identity providers, which have a trust relationship amongst each other. Such trust relationships are usually established on organizational level, whereas enforcement is carried out on technical level. Commonly, the data repositories of the individual identity providers are linked and data can be easily exchanged. In most cases, data exchange takes place based on an agreement of a common identifier for a certain user.

3   Cloud Identity Models

Identification and authentication are not less important in the area of cloud computing. Many e-Government applications are being migrated into the cloud [12] because of cost benefits and higher scalability. Hence, also new cloud identity models, which are tailored to the needs of cloud computing, have emerged. For example, Gopalakrishnan [13] or Cox [14] classify such cloud identity models in their publications. Classification criteria are mainly how and where identities are managed.

Gopalakrishnan concludes that three different identity management patterns in the cloud can be distinguished. Within the first identity management pattern (Trusted IDM Pattern), the identity management system is running within the trusted domain of the cloud provider, which is also hosting the application to be secured by the identity management system. According to her remarks, this pattern is intended for smaller and less scalable cloud models, such as private clouds. In contrast to that, the second identity management pattern (External IDM Pattern) is intended for public clouds, which have high scalability. In this pattern, the identity management system is external to the cloud provider's domain. Identity data and attributes are provisioned through a well-defined protocol, such as SAML [5]. The last and most flexible proposed identity management pattern is the so-called Interoperable IDM pattern. In this pattern, a central identity management system is capable of various authentication technologies and is serving multiple identity consuming service providers.

Cox focuses on public clouds in his identity model classification. In his opinion, identity management in private clouds is obvious, as the identities are managed by the private cloud's organization on their own and no trust relationship to external providers is required. He actually defines four different models and particularly pays attention for provisioning and de-provisioning of users or identities, respectively. In the first model, the cloud service provider generates and manages the identities for the enterprise. There is no external connection to e.g. an enterprise data source. The second model of Cox deals with synchronization. Thereby, the identity management system of an enterprise is synchronized with the user management of the cloud service provider. In the third model, identities are federated. This means that identities are still managed by the enterprise but are consumed by the cloud service provider. Similar to the Interoperable IDM pattern of Gopalakrishnan, Cox proposes a unified model implementing features of the three other described models as a fourth identity model for the cloud.

Also Goulding [15] classifies such cloud identity models in his whitepaper. The models are based on three use cases. The first model serves the use case of extending the enterprise identity management system up to the cloud. The second model deals with the use case of securing cloud services with an enterprise identity management system. In the third model, identity services are delivered to various applications down from the cloud.

In addition to those classifications, also the Cloud Security Alliance (CSA) [16] discusses three identity architectures for the cloud. In the so-called "hub-and-spoke"-model identities are managed by a central broker or proxy, which serves multiple identity and service providers. In the "free-form"-model, the service provider itself is responsible for managing several and disparate identity providers. The third model described by the CSA constitutes a hybrid model, which synthesizes advantages of the hub-and-spoke model and the free-form model.

In the following, we take the different identity models described before as a basis and classify three cloud identity models, which have already been deployed in several cloud computing environments. In addition, we list advantages and disadvantages of the individual model.

3.1   Identity in the Cloud

The "Identity in the Cloud"-model constitutes the simplest cloud identity model. In this model, the cloud service provider, which hosts the cloud application, also acts as identity provider. This means that the cloud service provider has its own user management, which is used for identification and authentication at its cloud applications. Hence, identity data are stored *in the cloud*. Fig. 1. illustrates the "Identity in the Cloud"- model.

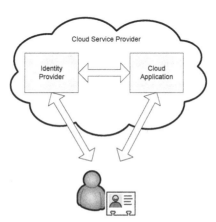

Fig. 1. Identity in the Cloud

This model can be seen as a special case of the traditional central identity model described in section 2.1, where the identity provider and service provider define the same entity for this cloud case. This model has been also discussed by Gopalakrishnan [13] or Cox [14]. Typical practical and already deployed examples of this model are the cloud service providers Google or Salesforce.com. Both cloud service providers host, maintain, and offer their own user management for their Software as a Service (SaaS)[11] applications.

The advantage of this cloud identity model is that organizations can just rely on the existing user management of the cloud service provider. This saves costs and maintenance efforts as no separate user management is required and accounts are created and maintained directly at the cloud service provider, which also hosts the organization's applications. However, this transfer of responsibility to the cloud service provider means also less control for the organization on identity and user data. Additionally, transfer of identity data to the cloud service provider or synchronization (e.g. as discussed by Cox [14]) cannot be easily achieved, because the cloud service provider might rely on different data models in its storage systems.

3.2   Identity to the Cloud

The "Identity to the Cloud"-model actually puts the traditional central identity model of section 2.1 into the cloud domain. In the traditional case, the user management is outsourced by the service provider to an external identity provider. The only difference in the cloud identity model is that the service provider is cloud-based and not only simply web-based. In addition, we assume that the identity provider is not cloud-based equally as in the traditional model. We will consider the scenario of a fully cloud-based identity provider in the next Section 3.3. However, Fig. 2 illustrates the "Identity to the Cloud"-model.

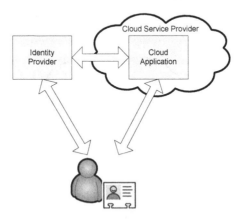

Fig. 2. Identity to the Cloud

---

[11] Software as a Service (SaaS) constitutes a cloud computing service model, where software is provided as a service by a cloud service provider to customers.

The identity provider is responsible for the complete user management, such as provisioning or de-provisioning of identities, user authentication, etc. The cloud service provider is responsible for the cloud application only and just consumes identity data or information respectively from the identity provider. In other words, identity data is transferred *to the cloud*. Transfer of identity data between the identity and the cloud service provider is usually carried out based on well-defined interfaces and standardized protocols. Such protocols dealing with the secure exchange of identity and authentication data are e.g. SAML [5], OpenID[12], or OAuth[13].

Many existing cloud service providers, in particular public cloud providers such as Google or Salesforce.com, rely on such interfaces or protocols for external identity provisioning. For instance, both mentioned cloud service providers rely on SAML and OpenID for their identity provisioning or so-called Single Sign-On (SSO) interfaces. In contrast to Salesforce.com, Google additionally allows external authentications via OAuth. The use of such interfaces does not only allow the implementation of the traditional central identity model, but moreover enables the application of the federated identity model described in section 2.3.

When applying this model, advantageous is the possibility to re-use existing identity management systems (e.g. an internal identity management system of an organization or enterprise) for external identification and authentication at cloud providers and cloud services. In contrast to the previous model (Identity in the Cloud), no new user management at the cloud service provider or any migration to the cloud service provider is required. While the application or service is operated in the cloud, the user management stays under full control of the individual organization. In contrast to that, an issue might be interoperability (e.g. technical or semantic interoperability). Many cloud service providers, which offer SSO interfaces for external identification or identity federation, rely on standardized protocols. Although standardized protocols should actually guarantee technical interoperability, the implementations of such protocols may have a different behavior, as shown in [17]. In addition, the respective cloud service provider might not support the desired identity protocol for external authentication, which could cause additional implementation efforts and costs at the organization's or enterprise's site. Semantic interoperability constitutes another issue, as user attributes of the external identity provider might not be understood by the cloud service provider. Hence, a thorough attribute mapping between the identity provider and the cloud service provider is required.

3.3   Identity from the Cloud

Within the third introduced cloud identity model identities are provided from an identity provider, which fully resides in the cloud. In fact, identities are provided as a service *from the cloud*. Therefore, the proposed model can also be seen as an "Identity as a Service"-model [7]. Fig. 3 illustrates the so-called "Identity from the Cloud"-model.

---

[12] http://openid.net
[13] http://oauth.net

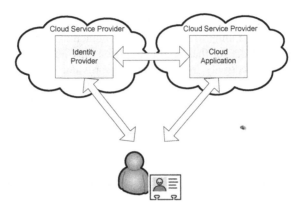

Fig. 3. Identity from the Cloud

In this model, both the identity provider and the application are operated in the cloud. Contrary to the "Identity in the Cloud"-model of Section 3.1, the identity provider need not necessarily be operated by the same cloud service provider that also hosts the application. Needless to say that still just one cloud service provider can operate both, the identity provider and the application. However, the precondition is that the user management of the identity provider is separated from the application's cloud service provider.

Basically, this cloud identity model is independent of the underlying cloud deployment or operational model. In fact, this "Identity as a Service"-model can be operated in a public, private, or community cloud. Due to the interconnection of different cloud deployment models (the cloud model used for operating the identity provider might be different than the cloud model for hosting the application), this cloud identity model can also be seen as hybrid cloud model. However, although within the illustrating Fig. 3 only cloud applications are shown acting as identity consuming services, this "Identity as a Service"-model can also be applied to traditional web-based applications of service providers.

Besides cost advantages and less maintenance efforts due to the outsourcing of identity management tasks into the cloud, the main advantage of this model is the separation of the cloud service providers. I.e., the cloud service provider for the application is usually different to the cloud service provider acting as identity provider. This allows organizations or enterprises an individual selection, which service provider they are going to trust to host and maintain their user management. A requirement for selecting a particular cloud service provider to act as identity provider might be, for instance, specific data protection regulations, such as enforcement that sensitive data is only allowed to be stored in selected or specific countries. Disadvantages of this model are, however, the need to move identity data into the cloud and thus trust a third party (the cloud service provider) for the user management. Furthermore, although complexity is decreased due to the take up of management tasks through the cloud service provider, organizations or enterprises need to think about how identity data can be easily transferred to this cloud service provider.

4   The Cloud Identity Broker Model

The "Identity as a Service"-model seems to be a promising concept for identity management in the cloud. In the previous section, we provided a more general view on this model, just illustrating the basic idea that identities are provided from the cloud. However, according to the Cloud Security Alliance [16] or Huang et al. [18] this "Identity as a Service"-model can be more seen as an identity broker model. This means that the identity provider in the cloud, which provides identities as a service, acts as central identity broker between various other identity providers and several service providers. In other words, the cloud identity provider plays some kind of hub between multiple service and identity providers [16]. Fig. 4 gives a more detailed view on the "Identity as a Service" model with central identity broker functionality.

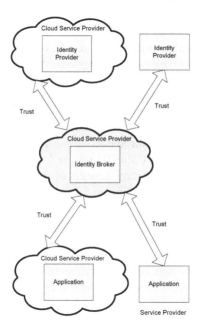

Fig. 4. Identity as a Service using a central Identity Broker

The main idea of this model is to decouple the service provider from multiple identity providers. Hence, instead of having multiple dependencies to various identity providers, only one strong dependency to the identity broker is given. This has further advantages, both on technical and organizational level. On technical level, the service provider only needs to implement the communication protocol to the identity broker and thus can ignore specific protocols of the individual identity providers. To lower the implementation efforts for service providers, the identity broker can offer standardized and well-established interfaces and protocols for secure data exchange (e.g. SAML, OpenID, etc.), where service providers can easily connect to. On organizational level, the strength of this model is aggregating multiple different trust relationships between service and identity providers to just one, namely between the service provider and the identity broker. The identity broker now takes over these various trust relationships with the individual identity providers. In other words, the trust relationship between the service provider and the identity provider is brokered through the cloud identity broker. Having just one trust relationship simplifies the contractual model for the service provider. Needless to say that this centralized model has one general drawback. If the identity broker breaks down, users are cut off service provisioning. Nevertheless, this risk is not specific to this model and can be found in several other identity models, where identification and authentication are outsourced to an external entity.

The identity broker model is not new and has already been implemented and deployed by several organizations. For instance, the Cloud SSO[14] product of Intel constitutes a ready implementation. Intel Cloud SSO offers strong user authentication and connectivity to different identity stores and more than 100 external Software as a Service (SaaS) applications. For achieving that, Intel Cloud SSO relies on existing federation interfaces provided by the different SaaS vendors. Another implementation of the identity broker model constitutes the results of the SkIDentity project[15]. SkIDentity especially focuses on eIDs, providing secure access to cloud services by supporting various types of eIDs. Hence, the SkIDentity implementation might also be interesting for e-Government adoption. In contrast to Intel Cloud SSO, for identity provisioning SkIDentity requires a special connector module to be installed at the cloud service provider. Other products implementing the identity broker model are e.g. RadiantOne's Cloud Federation Service[16], McAfee's Cloud Identity Manager[17], VMWare's Horizon[18], or Fugen's Cloud ID Broker[19].

Although we have identified several benefits of this model, still some drawbacks can be found. One major drawback is that users and service providers must rely on the same central service, the identity broker. This means that both the service provider and the user must have a trust relationship with the same authenticating authority. In terms of trust, this model is similar to the traditional central identity model (see Section 2.1), which uses a pairwise trust model as described in [19]. Brokered trust only comes into play between the service providers and the different identity providers.

In addition, another disadvantage is that both the service provider and the user are more or less dependent on the functionality and features of the identity broker. For instance, on the one hand service providers are dependent on the interfaces the identity broker supports. If the identity broker suddenly quits the support of a particular interface, the service provider is cut off of any identity service and requires much effort for implementing another supported interface. On the other hand, users are dependent on the type and number of identity providers the identity broker supports. If a user wants to authenticate at a specific identity provider, which has no affiliation

---

[14] http://www.intelcloudsso.com

[15] http://www.skidentity.com

[16] http://www.radiantlogic.com/products/radiantone-cfs

[17] http://www.mcafee.com/uk/products/cloud-identity-manager.aspx

[18] http://www.vmware.com/products/desktop_virtualization/
horizon-application-manager/overview.html

[19] http://fugensolutions.com/cloud-id-broker.html

with the identity broker, or if a user wants to use a particular authentication mechanism, which is not supported by the identity broker, accessing the service provider becomes impossible. In other words, the user has actually no real free choice which identity provider to use and is dependent on the support of the identity broker.

To bypass these disadvantages, we propose a new identity model for the cloud. This new model relies on a federated approach between multiple identity brokers. We will discuss this federated identity broker model or federated identity as a service model in more detail in the next section.

5   Federated Identity as a Service Model

A federated identity as a service (or federated identity broker model) solves the issue on being dependent on just one and the same identity broker for both, the service provider and the user. In this federated model, users and service providers do not need to rely on the same identity broker as authenticating authority. Both can actually contract their individual identity broker of choice, which offers greater flexibility. In addition, the individual identity broker can easier respond on individual requirements, either from the user or the service provider. Such requirements might be some local or domestic regulations specific to a country. This means for example, a user can rely on her desired identity broker, which acts compliant to such local or national regulations. Although there is no direct trust relationship between the user and the affiliated identity broker of the service provider, due to identity broker federation the user is still able to authenticate at the service provider. Fig. 5 illustrates this federated identity as a service model.

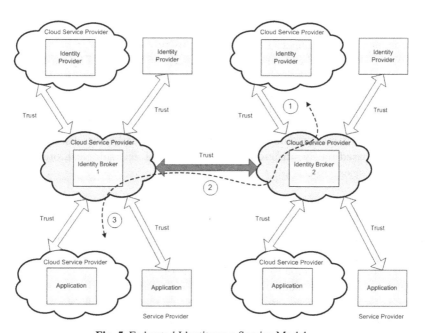

Fig. 5. Federated Identity as a Service Model

In this federated model it is possible that the service provider has a contractual relationship with identity broker 1, whereas the user has a contractual relationship with identity broker 2. In addition, both identity brokers have some kind of trust and contractual relationship amongst each other. Hence, this model fully features the brokered trust model according to [19] across multiple identity brokers.

Having a closer look at the information and process flow, in a first step the user contacts a service provider by stating that she wants to consume a protected resource. For accessing this protected resource, proper identification and authentication is required. The service provider has a contractual and trust relationship with identity broker 1. However, the user only has a contractual and trust relationship with identity broker 2, which supports – in contrast to identity broker 1 - the identity provider the user actually wants to use for authentication. To use this intended identity provider, in a next step the user is forwarded to her affiliated identity broker 2. After that, identity broker 2 initiates the identification and authentication process with the desired identity provider. The user provides appropriate credentials for successful authentication at the desired identity provider. If authentication was successful, identification and authentication data will be transmitted to identity broker 2. Subsequently, identity broker 2 forwards the user's identity and authentication data to identity broker 1, which in turn transmits these data to the service provider. Based on the received data, the service provider either grants or denies access to the protected resource.

In this model, there are three communication channels (cf. Fig. 5) where identity data are transferred, namely between

1. Identity Provider and Identity Broker 2
2. Identity Broker 2 and Identity Broker 1
3. Identity Broker 1 and Service Provider

The communication channels 1 (between identity provider and identity broker 2) and 3 (between identity broker 1 and service provider) can be covered by existing identity protocols, such as SAML, OAuth, etc. However, for communication channel 2 (between identity broker 2 and identity broker 1) it must be investigated whether existing protocols might be sufficient or whether new protocols need to be developed.

In the following, we list some requirements that must be fulfilled to set up and build such a federated identity as a service model. Thereby, we distinguish the requirements based on five different aspects (functional, technological, organizational, legal, and business aspects).

5.1   Functional Requirements

For such a system, the support of basic identity management functionality such as registration, collection and proofing of attributes, credential management, or claims issuance and transformation by the different identity brokers are required. In addition, the vision is to not only support natural persons, but also legal persons such as companies or governments as users. This support might also enable person to person transactions (e.g. two natural persons are exchanging identity data via this network), without involving a service provider in between.

In particular, the framework should be designed user-centric (information control remains with the individual) and should be claims-based. User-centricity means that in every transaction the user always has maximum control over her personal data. The use of claims instead of attributes particularly preserves privacy. By using claims, only the minimum set of personal data required may be disclosed. In addition, single sign-on (SSO) should be supported to allow seamless authentication between various service providers without re-authentication or any further interactions. Finally, the network should be simple to use and especially transparent and auditable to allow for compliance with legal regulations.

5.2   Technological Requirements

As a main technological requirement, the proposed framework should be secure and should automatically preserve users' privacy. In addition, the brokered trust pattern should be modeled accordingly at technological level. This implies the implementation of a proper trust protocol.

Furthermore, the technological framework should build upon existing infrastructures and rely on open standards wherever possible. Application programing interfaces (APIs) should be provided to adopt further applications and business models. Finally, the technical implementation of such a framework should be location independent and agnostic of the user's client used for accessing the network.

5.3   Organizational Requirements

The use of open standards constitutes also an important organizational requirement because it facilitates interoperability between network entities. Moreover, if possible, existing standards should be relied on instead of developing new ones.

A reliable trust framework and meta model needs to be taken up or defined to ensure interoperability between different entities, such as identity brokers. Especially, on semantic level, regulations or guidelines should be defined. This particularly includes a common understanding on identity attributes or claims, which are transferred. Additionally, a common understanding on used authentication mechanisms, e.g. authentication assurance levels as defined in STORK [20], is required. Furthermore, data verification processes need to be defined.

5.4   Legal Requirements

Especially for national identity management systems, compliance with data protection laws or regulations defines an essential requirement. For instance, when supporting national eID solutions, the identity brokers must act compliant to any specific national law or regulation. This requirement might involve not only one but several laws and regulations. However, data protection will be one of the most important legal requirements to suffice. In addition, legal requirements might also include the support of special contracts, certifications, or terms of use according to national laws.

5.5   Business Requirements

Entering and the use of this identity management network in the cloud will probably be not free of charge. Therefore, appropriate accounting and pricing models need to be developed. Moreover, incentives must be generated to involve businesses to participate in such a network and to cooperate. During business model generation, focus should also lie on the re-use of existing infrastructure and API provisioning for further business generation.

6   Conclusions

Identity management and the processes of identification and authentication are essential when protected applications or resources need to be accessed. Identity management is of particular importance in e-Government. While identity management does not define a new topic, identity management in the cloud brings up new challenges. Traditional identity models have already been transferred to the cloud, hence different cloud identity models have emerged. Depending on the cloud identity model, identity data are either provided in the cloud, to the cloud, or from the cloud. The most promising cloud identity model is the "Identity from the Cloud"-model, which can also be called "Identity as a Service"-model. As the name already indicates, identities are provided from a cloud service provider as a service. Current implementations of this model rely on the so-called identity broker model, where a central identity broker acts as a hub between several identity and service providers. While this model has a couple of advantages, also one major drawback can be identified. Both the user and the service provider must rely on the same identity broker during an identification and authentication process, which causes strong dependency on the central identity broker. To bypass this issue, we proposed a federated identity broker model (federated identity as a service model), which guarantees freedom of choice on the desired identity broker for the user and the service provider. Furthermore, we listed requirements (functional, technological, organizational, legal, and business requirements) that must be taken into account when setting up and implementing such a federated identity broker approach.

Future work will include further research on how these requirements can be fulfilled for setting up such a federated identity broker model. In more detail, this will include research on the required trust framework and the transport protocol required for secure message and data exchange between identity brokers.

References

1. Bertino, E., Takahashi, K.: Identity Management: Concepts, Technologies, and Systems. Artech House Inc. (2010)
2. ISO/IEC JTC 1/SC 27/WG 5: A framework for IdM
3. Sermersheim, J.: Lightweight Directory Access Protocol (LDAP): The Protocol. RFC 4511. Internet Engineering Task Force (IETF) (2006)

4. Neuman, C., Yu, T., Hartman, S., Raeburn, K.: The Kerberos Network Authentication Service (V5). RFC 4120. Internet Engineering Task Force (IETF) (2005)
5. Lockhart, H., Campbell, B.: Security Assertion Markup Language (SAML) V2.0 Technical Overview. OASIS Committee Draft 02 (2008)
6. Siddhartha, A.: National e-ID card schemes: A European overview. Inf. Secur. Tech. Rep. 13(2), 46–53 (2008)
7. Emig, C., Brandt, F., Kreuzer, S., Abeck, S.: Identity as a Service – Towards a Service-Oriented Identity Management Architecture. In: Pras, A., van Sinderen, M. (eds.) EUNICE 2007. LNCS, vol. 4606, pp. 1–8. Springer, Heidelberg (2007)
8. Bauer, M., Meints, M., Hansen, M.: D3.1: Structured Overview on Prototypes and Concepts of Identity Management System, FIDIS (2005)
9. Palfrey, J., Gasser, U.: Digital Identity Interoperability and eInnovation, Case Study. Berkman Publication Series (2007)
10. Jøsang, A., Pope, S.: User centric identity management. In: AusCERT Asia Pacific Information Technology, pp. 1–13 (2005)
11. Alpár, G., Hoepman, J.-H., Siljee, J.: The Identity Crisis - Security, Privacy and Usability Issues in Identity Management. CoRR (2011)
12. Kurdi, R., Taleb-Bendiab, A., Randles, M., Taylor, M.: E-Government Information Systems and Cloud Computing (Readiness and Analysis). In: Developments in E-systems Engineering, DeSE 2011, pp. 404–409 (2011)
13. Gopalakrishnan, A.: Cloud Computing Identity Management. SETLabs Briefings 7(7), 45–55 (2009)
14. Cox, P.: How to Manage Identity in the Public Cloud. InformationWeek reports (March 2012)
15. Goulding, J.: Identity and Access Management for the Cloud: CA's strategy and vision. Whitepaper, CA Cloud Business Unit (Mai 2010)
16. Cloud Security Alliance: Security Guidance for Critical Areas of Focus in Cloud Computing V3.0 (2011)
17. Zwattendorfer, B., Tauber, A.: Secure Cloud Authentication using eIDs. In: Proceedings of IEEE CCIS 2012, pp. 515–519 (2012)
18. Huang, H.Y., Wang, B., Liu, X.X., Xu, J.M.: Identity Federation Broker for Service Cloud. In: 2010 International Conference on Service Sciences, pp. 115–120 (2010)
19. Boyen, S., Ellison, G., Karhuluoma, G., MacGregor, W., Madsen, P., Sengodan, S., Shinkar, S., Thompson, P.: Trust Models Guidelines. Draft. OASIS (2004)
20. Hulsebosch, B., Lenzini, G., Eertink, H.: D2.3 - Quality authenticator scheme. STORK Deliverable (2009)

Ontology-Based Compliance Checking on Higher Education Processes

Katalin Ternai, Ildikó Szabó, and Krisztián Varga

Department of Information Systems, Corvinus University of Budapest
1093 Budapest, Fővám tér 13-15., Hungary
katalin.ternai@uni-corvinus.hu,
{iszabo,kvarga}@informatika.uni-corvinus.hu

Abstract. This paper introduces a method using ontology matching for compliance checking on higher education processes. The main goal of our approach is to transform business processes into process ontologies in order to apply ontology matching procedure to restructure the business processes. The „conceptual models - ontology models" converter maps the Business Process Modeling elements to the appropriate Ontology elements in meta-level. We have created an evaluating algorithm of the structured report resulted by the ontology matching process. Having processed the report, we can gain such information, which facilitate to plan action to restructure our current process.

Keywords: semantic business process management, ontology matching, higher education, compliance check.

1   Introduction

One assumption of sustaining competitive edge of an economy is to transfer and use of relevant knowledge to the right place and in the right time. It means to overcome the barriers to mobility and to create a competitive education area. The financial crisis emphasized the importance of higher education in qualifying students in the light of the needs of labor market and „creating and maintaining a broad, advanced knowledge base and stimulating research and innovation" [1].

The Hungarian government has recognized that there is a mismatch between the learning outcomes of higher education qualifications and the competences required by companies. So the Hungarian higher education reform taking place in nowadays wants to rationalize qualification obtained in the higher education in the light of requirements of the world of labor. [2]

The actual economic status of the Hungarian higher-education institutions implies a compliance checking on their institutional processes. This paper introduces a method using ontology matching for compliance checking on higher education processes. In our approach the business process modelling and some part of the ontology-based methodology is mixed to ground a solution for this kind of compliance checking (see in Section 2). The applicability of our solution is presented through the

A. Kő et al. (Eds.): EGOVIS/EDEM 2013, LNCS 8061, pp. 58–71, 2013.

student application handling use case because it is a resource-intensive and time-consumed process. Our solution starts with building the actual business process model and the ideal business process model (see in Section 3.1). The ontology approach gives unified view about these processes, so these models are transformed into ontology in Section 3.2. The discrepancies between the structures of these processes reveal problem areas for decision makers, so an ontology matching procedure is executed on these ontologies in Section 3.3. The last section contains conclusions and outlook.

2   Theoretical Background

2.1   BPM, SBPM

Business processes ought to perform well within dynamically changing organizational environments. The main challenge in Business Process Management (BPM) is the continuous translation between business requirements view on the process area and the actual process area. It can be expected that Business Process Management will only come closer to its promises if it allows for a better automation of the two-way translation. Semantic Business Process Management (SBPM) is a new approach of increasing the level of automation in the translation between these two levels, and is currently driven by major players from BPM, and Semantic Web Services domain. The core paradigm of SPBM is to represent the two spheres using ontology languages and to employ machine reasoning for automated or semi-automated translation.

A competitive enterprise has to adapt core value-added processes with unprecedented speed, to act appropriately regardless of the situation. The focus of process designers is to make more sophisticated use of process architectures and continuous improvement of processes. Modern BPM suites are evolving to automate the modeling, monitoring and redesign of complex, collaborative processes to achieve these goals.

Conceptual model captures the semantics of an application through the use of a formal notation, but the descriptions resulting from conceptual model are intended to be used by humans and not machines. The semantics contained in these models are in a large extent implicit and cannot be processed. With the web-based semantic schema such as Web Ontology Language (OWL), the creation and the use of the conceptual models can be improved, furthermore the implicit semantics being contained in the models can be partly articulated and used for processing.

The basic idea of Semantic Business Process Management is to combine Semantic Web Services frameworks, ontology representation, and Business Process Management methodologies and tools, and to develop a consolidated technology. The use of web-based ontologies and their contribution to business innovation has received a lot of attention in the last years. [3]

The consortium of SUPER project elaborated a semantic framework for compliance management. They presented five perspectives on compliance checking: design-time/run-time;   forward/backward;   active/passive;   task   checking/process checking or engine-based/query-based perspective. [4] We would like to give a feedback about the structure of our current *student application handling* process, in the light of the expected process, in order to plan actions to restructure it. So our compliance checking approach is executed on the engineering desk, so it doesn't require data from running of the process. So our approach is suitable for design-time, forward, passive; process checking and engine-based perspective.

2.2   Ontology Approach

Ontologies facilitate to create a process model by providing a unified view about the elements, their attributes and their relationships of this model. The process ontology is capable of representing a real business process. We can build them by reusing or extending an existing ontology (like PSL Ontology [5]), using a framework (like the framework of SUPER project [4]) or transforming the output of a BPM tool (like ARIS or ADONIS) into an ontology format [6].

The importance of process ontologies in SBPM is to help to exchange process information between applications in the most correct and complete manner [5], or to restructure business processes by providing a tool for examining the matching of process ontologies [7]. Semantic or structural discrepancies between process ontologies may be derived from different viewpoint or background knowledge used by the experts in the process of building ontology, or the different structure of real business processes. An ontology matching procedure applied in the domain of process ontologies helps to reveal these discrepancies in order to prepare the decision making about the business process reengineering.

Alasoud et al. [8] define ontology matching problem as follows: "given ontologies O1 and O2, each describing a collection of discrete entities such as classes, properties, individuals, etc., we want to identify semantic correspondences between the components of these entities."

The goals of combining ontologies are to merge, transform, integrate, translate, align or map etc. them into a new or an existing ontology. The goal of this paper is to present a solution for executing a compliance check between an actual and an expected higher education process. So ontology mapping, matching or alignment can be counted in our solution.

The general ontology mapping tools enumerated by Noy [9] or Choi et al. [10], or developed by Protégé community use different kind of method to identify the semantic correspondences between two ontologies. So we can take into the consideration methods searching axiomatic correspondences (e.g. OWLDIFF [11], Compare Ontologies function in Protégé 4.X) or calculating similarity values etc.. The latters take probability distributions (e.g. Glue [12], OMEN [13]) or text similarity functions (e.g. LOM [14]) as a basis.

Process specific methods can be considered by us. Jung [8] used logical assertations and similarity measures to facilitate the interoperability among processes.

Koschmider and Oberweis [15] used Petri nets „to obey an operational semantics that facilitates composition, simulation, and validation of business processes".

But we may mix these approaches too.

In our case, we focus on process ontologies, the relationships have most important role in. They put the tasks into a sequential or parallel order. So the examination of the components is focus on their relationships instead of their semantic meaning, hence the tools providing axiomatic comparison, like the tools developed on Protégé 4.X, seem to be the most appropriate tool to achieve our goals.

2.3 Compliance Checking

Compliance checking is an important area in semantic business process management. Combining the semantics with the business process management made it possible to not only model processes but define intelligent queries on them, and check their compliance with regulations, laws, best practices or other standard processes [16].

Ly et al. [17] presents a framework for semantic process verification to ensure system correctness after arbitrary process changes by defining semantic constraints over processes. El Kharbili et al. [18] presents eight requirements for a compliance management framework and discuss different ways of conducting compliance checking with a proposed policy-based framework for business process compliance management. They emphasize the use of business process ontologies as well.

3 The 'Student Application Handling' Use Case

Our aim is to check process compliance with the normative processes. The main goal of our approach is to transform business processes into process ontologies in order to apply ontology matching procedure to restructure the business processes. We use the 'Student application handling' process as a use case to demonstrate our approach.

3.1 The Characteristics of the Hungarian Higher-Education

The Hungarian government has recognized that there is a mismatch between the learning outcomes of higher education qualifications and the competences required by companies. So the Hungarian higher education reform taking place in nowadays wants to rationalize qualification obtained in the higher education in the light of requirements of the world of labor. [2]

Although, there is a huge budget cutback in the Hungarian higher education, too. In exchange, the universities focus on cost reductions and downsizing, instead of following the needs of labor market. The rector of Corvinus University of Budapest has started a reorganization project to find cost-savings possibility. The reorganization of institutional processes can facilitate to reach this goal.

In 2004 a comprehensive, high level process model of an ideal higher education institution was developed, financed by the formal Ministry of Education. In 2005 - 2006 two consortia of higher education institutions have started to develop further this model [19]. The aim of this *HEFOP-3.3.1-P-2004.09.0134/1.0 (Structural and Organizational Development of Higher Education[1])* project was to create a normative set of models from the processes, organizational and informational architecture of the higher education. Based on those, closed and consistent governance of the operational processes can be achieved, which leads to transparency and accountability. The models can be the base of supporting IT systems' specifications, too. All of these can lead to high-quality operations and education.

In the project the two consortia had conducted a complex process-measurement survey, made the process models and made business process reengineering, than laid down the definitive set of ideal models. 12 universities and colleges developed a sophisticated process model. The program and its projects intended to remove the deficiencies in the administrative aspects of the whole higher education system [19].

In the conservative academic world the organizational structure is very hierarchical and the knowledge transfer is fragmented. The real world requirements are just the opposite; there is a vast demand for students and professionals having the ability of integration, cooperation, knowledge absorption. During the last years, European countries went through an intensive development and changing phase in which the experiences of transition and coping with the information society requirements mixed up. The newest business methods and technology, which are in line with enterprises demands, are needed.   The processes in the higher education are significantly differing from a manufacturing or commercial enterprise, and even from a service enterprise, not mentioning the differences between the organizational cultures. Therefore many cases, development issues should be handled in a unique way.

The actual economic status of the Hungarian higher-education institutions implies a compliance checking on their institutional processes. We can use the processes developed in the HEFOP project as normative processes, so they are the base of the compliance check.

3.2   Business Process Modeling

Business Process Modeling is the first phase of the Business Process Management lifecycle. In the use case discussed in this paper, the business process models were implemented by using BOC ADONIS modeling platform. [20] We selected this modeling platform because of its popularity in modeling practice. However, our approach is principally transferable to other semi-formal modeling languages.

ADONIS is a graph-structured Business Process Management language. The integral model element is the activity. The ADONIS modeling platform is a business meta-modeling tool with components such as modeling, analysis, simulation, evaluation, process costing, documentation, staff management, and import-export. Its main feature is its method independence. A part of our 'Student application handling' business process model can be seen in Figure 1.

---

[1] http://informatika.bke.hu/hefop

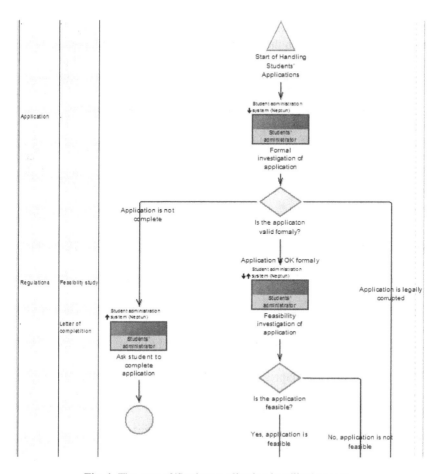

Fig. 1. The start of 'Student application handling' process

There are several parameters that can be set or defined when modeling a business process in this tool, and in others as well. The shell of a business process can be easily formed with activities, decision points, parallelism or merging objects, logical gateways and events, but this is just the beginning.

The vertical level in details of a business process model gives the focus point of the model: whether we specify operational areas only, or process areas, process models, sub processes, activities, or even deeper; the algorithms.

The horizontal level in details of a business process model gives the level of extra information modeled within the business process: organizational information can be specified in an organogram (working environment model) then the roles can be referred in the RACI matrix of the process model, the inputs needed and the outputs and products generated can be added to the business process model with the IT system elements as well. More detailed, key performance indicators and risk with controls can be specified for the process models, if needed.

The decision about which levels to use from the mentioned ones, and how detailed to be that, is always depend on the usage of the models. A business process model is complete, when it is detailed enough for proper usage. That is why all projects with business process modeling start with the specification of the usage and the needs, leading to the composing of the conventions of modeling. The book of conventions has to be known and accepted by everybody who is concerned. Based on this, everybody can model business processes in the same way, with the same level in details, and the models will mean the same for everybody.

In our paper, the business process models are used for their compliance checking by matching them with ideal, normative process models. To achieve this goal, during the modeling of business processes the following parameters have to be set:

- the logical shell of the business process model with the core objects (e.g. task, parallelity, merge, etc.);
- the organizational structure needed for the business process model, in one or more working environment model;
- the inputs and outputs needed for the business process model, in one or more document model;
- the IT elements needed for the business process model, in one or more IT system model;
- name of activities in the business process models;
- description of activities in the business process models;
- the Responsible role for all the activities in the business process models;
- input, output, IT system information for all the activities in the business process models, where available.

These parameters are required because the level in details of the ideal processes. To match the ideal and the current processes, their level in detail need to be the same, otherwise the results will be misleading.

3.3   Process Ontology

In this section, the focus is given to the mapping conceptual models to ontology models by using meta-modeling approach. Meta-models offer intuitive way of specifying modeling languages and are suitable for discussion with non-technical users. Meta-models are particularly convenient for the definition of conceptual models.

In our proposed approach, we discuss how to establish the links between model elements and ontology concepts. Ontologies basically provide semantics and they can describe both semantics of the modeling language constructs as well as semantics of model instances. [21] There were several projects creating business process ontologies such as the SUPER[2] project, but in our solution we used a process ontology we have created in our own way.

For the extension and mapping the conceptual models to ontology models, the models are exported in the structure of ADONIS XML format. All objects from the business process model will be an 'instance' in the XML structure, the attributes have

---

[2] http://ip-super.org

the tag 'attribute', while the connected objects (such as the performer, or the input/output data, which are stored in another model in the Adonis tool) have the tag 'interref'. A part of an XML export can be seen in Figure 2.

```
<INSTANCE id="obj.13793" class="Activity" name="Making the decision">
<ATTRIBUTE name="Description" type="STRING"></ATTRIBUTE>
<INTERREF name="Responsible role">
<IREF type="objectreference" tmodeltype="Working environment model" tmodelname="Roles"
tmodelver="" tclassname="Role" tobjname="Dean"></IREF>
</INTERREF>
<INTERREF name="Input">
<IREF type="objectreference" tmodeltype="Document model" tmodelname="Input / Output"
tmodelver="" tclassname="Document" tobjname="Application"></IREF>
</INTERREF>
<INTERREF name="Output">
<IREF type="objectreference" tmodeltype="Document model" tmodelname="Input / Output"
tmodelver="" tclassname="Document" tobjname="Decision"></IREF>
</INTERREF>
<INTERREF name="Referenced IT system elements"></INTERREF>
```

Fig. 2. XML export of the business process model (fraction)

The „conceptual models - ontology models" converter maps the Adonis Business Process Modeling elements to the appropriate Ontology elements in meta-level. The model transformation aims at preserving the semantics of the business model. The general rule we follow is to express each ADONIS model element as a class in the ontology and its corresponding attributes as attributes of the class. This transformation is done by the means of XSLT script that performs the conversion. The converted OWL ontology in the structure of   Protege/OWL XML format is imported into the editor of Protege 4.2. A sample part of the transforming XSLT code (mapping the 'Responsible role to an ontology element) can be seen in Figure 3.

```
<xsl:if test="INTERREF[@name='Responsible role']/IREF">
<ObjectAllValuesFrom>
    <ObjectProperty IRI="#performed_by"/>
    <xsl:for-each select="INTERREF[@name='Responsible role']/IREF">
        <Class >
            <xsl:attribute name="IRI">#<xsl:value-of select=
            "functx:words-to-camel-case(@tobjname)" /></xsl:attribute>
        </Class>
    </xsl:for-each>
</ObjectAllValuesFrom>
</xsl:if>
```

Fig. 3. Fraction of XSLT code transforming 'Responsible role' attribute to an ontology element

To specify the semantics of ADONIS model elements through relations to ontology concepts, the ADONIS business model first must be represented within the ontology. In regard to the representation of the business model in the ontology, one can differentiate between a representation of ADONIS model language constructs and a representation of ADONIS model elements. ADONIS model language constructs such as "activity", as well as the control flow are created in the ontology as classes and properties. Subsequently, the ADONIS model elements can be represented through the instantiation of these classes and properties in the ontology. The linkage of the ontology and the ADONIS model element instances is accomplished by the usage of properties. These properties specify the semantics of an ADONIS model element through a relation to an ontology instance with formal semantics defined by the ontology. The final ontology can be seen in the Protégé editor in Figure 4.

Fig. 4. The process ontology in Protege 4.2

By means of a concrete process we show the applicability of the method.

3.4   Ontology Matching

As we opted for ontology matching tools built-in Protégé 4.2 (see 2.2 section), their methods and outputs were studied by us.

OWL DIFF [11] is a Java-based Protégé plugin, which is capable of merging and comparing ontologies. It focuses on executing the matching process mostly structurally. It investigates axiomatic correspondences between two ontologies. It can use logical comparisons and set functions in the procedure. It shows the differences graphically in two trees, one for each ontology.

Compare Ontologies is a built-in function in Protégé 4.X. It is capable of comparing ontologies with different name space, which OWL DIFF isn't. It searches axiomatic correspondences too, but it presents the report in table format. It distinguishes three actions: created, deleted, or modified elements. It groups the results based on this classification.

We investigated the usage of these system based on such questions that the decision makers might conceive through the compliance checking process:

- Do the activities follow the same order in both processes?
- Which activities are missing (appeared just in the expected business process) or useless (appeared just in the current business process)?
- How can we characterize the new expected activities (considering their relationships with other activities, I/O documents, supporting IT systems, or its responsible persons)?
- Are the actors responsible for the same activities?
- Does the expected business process give any new information about the I/O documents, the supporting IT systems or the actors related to the common activities?

Based on these questions, we can state that a structured report using sections related to the new, deleted or modified building blocks of the process model is very useful for decision makers. So Compare Ontologies function was chosen to execute the compliance checking.

The Results of the Ontology Matching

The main goal of Compare Ontologies function is to compare two versions of the same ontology, so it requires an original and an updated version of the ontology. In our case, the ontology model related to the Handling Student Application process used in nowadays was considered as the original model. We would like to update it, so the updated version was the ontology model related to the process expected by the HEFOP Consortium.

Having executed the ontology matching process, we set an evaluating algorithm of the report. First of all, we identified new expected process steps by using SubClass of Process_step text marker. So we gained AskStudentToCompleteApplication and OfferingPossibilityToReview as new process steps. These activities were characterized by the steps followed by them, their actors, I/O documents etc. (see in Table 1.).

Table 1. The new process steps expected by HEFOP project in the ontology matching report

Block		Created: AskStudentToCompleteApplication
Action	Original version	Updated version
Added		Class: AskStudentToCompleteApplication
Added		AskStudentToCompleteApplication SubClassOf Process_step
Added		AskStudentToCompleteApplication SubClassOf followed_by only End-13424
Added		AskStudentToCompleteApplication SubClassOf performed_by only Students'Administrator

Table 1. (*Continued*)

Added		AskStudentToCompleteApplication SubClassOf produces_output only LetterOfCompletition
Added		AskStudentToCompleteApplication SubClassOf uses_system only StudentAdministrationSystem(Neptun)
Block		Created: OfferingPossibilityToReview
Action	Original version	Updated version
Added		Class: OfferingPossibilityToReview
Added		OfferingPossibilityToReview SubClassOf Process_step
Added		OfferingPossibilityToReview SubClassOf followed_by only End-13447
Added		OfferingPossibilityToReview SubClassOf performed_by only Rector'sOffice

Their previous process steps could be discovered by using followed_by AskStudentToCompleteApplication and followed_by OfferingPossibilityToReview searching term. The IsTheApplicatonValidFormaly? and SendingRejectionNotification process steps were found. Because there were in Modified block, so there are existing process steps in nowadays. As we see in the next table, SendingRejectionNotification should receive an input and its next step should be replaced by OfferingPossibilityToReview step.

Table 2. The modified process steps

Block:	Modified: IsTheApplicatonValidFormaly?	
Action	Original version	Updated version
Added		IsTheApplicatonValidFormaly? SubClassOf followed_by only AskStudentToCompleteApplication
Block:	Modified: SendingRejectionNotification	
Action	Original version	Updated version
Added		SendingRejectionNotification SubClassOf followed_by only OfferingPossibilityToReview
Added		SendingRejectionNotification SubClassOf uses_input only Decision
Deleted	SendingRejectionNotification SubClassOf followed_by only End-13447	

If a current process step or other building block is missing in the updated version, it appears in Deleted block.

But we can collect information about actors, IT systems, I/O documents, actors or decision points too in this way.

Table 3. Modified actors

Block:	Modified: MakingTheDecision	
Action	Original version	Updated version
Superclass changed	MakingTheDecision SubClassOf performed_by only Dean	MakingTheDecision SubClassOf performed_by only Committee

Summarized, this process based compliance checking was executed by using ontology relationships as searching term in the ontology matching report.

The SubClassOf <<class>> relationship found in Created block means to insert new expected building element (e.g. process step, actor etc.) into our current process. The Modified or Deleted blocks suggest to change or delete the building blocks of the current process model

The classes appeared in Created or Modified block must be tracked by using their relationships as searching terms. These terms give us new information about what we should create, delete or change e.g. joint points (by tracking followed_by relationship), actors (by performed_by relationship) or any other building blocks.

According to the ontology matching report, we can state that the expected HandlingStudentsApplication process is more student friendly than the current one. Because it enables to complete the application after checking its validity and it offers an automation by highlighting Neptun as supporting IT system. Moreover it enables a new submission of the application after sending the rejection, but it puts the decision into the responsibility of the Rector's office, which is a new expected actor in the process. And it requires a role change in the decision making (from the dean to the committee).

4   Conclusion and Outlook

The Hungarian higher education reform taking place in nowadays. There is a huge budget cutback in the institutions but it is very important to rationalize qualification obtained in the higher education in the light of requirements of the world of labor. Our paper introduced a method using ontology matching for compliance checking on higher education processes. In our approach the business process modeling and some part of the ontology-based methodology is mixed to ground a solution for this kind of compliance checking. The applicability of our solution is presented through the student application handling use case because it is a resource-intensive and time-consumed process. Our solution starts with building the actual business process model and the expected processes provided by HEFOP Consortium. The ontology approach gives unified view about these processes, so these models are transformed into ontology. The discrepancies between the structures of these processes reveal problem areas for decision makers, so an ontology matching procedure is executed on these ontologies. Having executed the ontology matching process, we set an evaluating algorithm of the report so we can gained such information, which facilitate to plan action to restructure the actual process.

Having investigated general ontology matching tools, we chose a built-in function in Protégé 4.2 called Compare Ontologies, because ontology axioms represents relationships in process models well and this tool focuses on searching axiomatic correspondences between ontologies. It gives a report, which can be processed by using the above-mentioned algorithm written in a given programming language. Having processed the report, we can gain such information, which facilitate to plan action to restructure our current process.

The disadvantage of this tool is that, it doesn't compare the name of ontology elements semantically and its report may be less transparent in the case of complex process ontologies. But it is open source software, so in the future we can improve its algorithm by using similarity measures or extending by a new report processing program.

The transforming script can be improved by adding support of transforming the triggers of a business process model, and supporting complex process sets. Business processes may have subprocesses, incoming and outgoing cross-reference processes as well, ant those need to be supported for a full-scale compliance check.

References

1. BolognaProc: The Bologna Process 2020 - The European Higher Education Area in the new decade (2009), http://www.ond.vlaanderen.be/hogeronderwijs/bologna/conference/documents/leuven_louvain-la-neuve_communiqu%C3%A9_april_2009.pdf
2. SZKTerv: A következő lépés Széll Kálmán terv 2.0 (2012), http://www.kormany.hu/download/3/e8/80000/1-A_k%C3%B6vetkez%C5%91_l%C3%A9p%C3%A9s%20%28SzKT%2020%29.pdf
3. Hepp, M., Cardoso, J., Lytras, M.D.: The Semantic Web: Real-World Applications from Industry. Springer (2007) ISBN: 0387485309
4. El Kharbili, M., et al.: Towards a framework for semantic business process compliance management. In: Proceedings of the Workshop on Governance, Risk and Compliance for Information Systems, pp. 1–15 (2008)
5. Staab, S., Studer, R.: Handbook on ontologies. Springer (2009)
6. Kő, A., Ternai, K.: A Development Method for Ontology Based Business Processes. In: eChallenges e-2011 Conference Proceedings. IIMC International Information Management Corporation Ltd., Florence (2011)
7. Jung, J.J.: Semantic business process integration based on ontology alignment. Expert Systems with Applications 36(8), 11013–11020 (2009)
8. Alasoud, A., Haarslev, V., Shiri, N.: An Effective Ontology Matching Technique. In: An, A., Matwin, S., Raś, Z.W., Ślęzak, D. (eds.) ISMIS 2008. LNCS (LNAI), vol. 4994, pp. 585–590. Springer, Heidelberg (2008)

9. Noy, N.F.: Semantic integration: a survey of ontology-based approaches. SIGMOD Rec. 33, 65–70 (2004)
10. Choi, N., et al.: A survey on ontology mapping. SIGMOD Rec. 35, 34–41 (2006)
11. OWLDiff: OWL Diff Documentation (2008),
    http://krizik.felk.cvut.cz/km/owldiff/documentation.html
12. Doan, A.H., et al.: Ontology matching: A machine learning approach. In: Staab, S., Studer, R. (eds.) Handbook on Ontologies, pp. 385–516 (2004)
13. Mitra, P., Noy, N., Jaiswal, A.R.: OMEN: A Probabilistic Ontology Mapping Tool. In: Gil, Y., Motta, E., Benjamins, V.R., Musen, M.A. (eds.) ISWC 2005. LNCS, vol. 3729, pp. 537–547. Springer, Heidelberg (2005)
14. Li, J.: LOM: a lexicon-based ontology mapping tool. In: Information Interpretation and Integration Conference (I3CON) (2004)
15. Koschmider, A., Oberweis, A.: Ontology based business process description. In: Proceedings of the CAiSE, pp. 321–333 (2005)
16. Hepp, M., Roman, D.: An Ontology Framework for Semantic Business Process Management. In: Proceedings of Wirtschaftsinformatik 2007, Karlsruhe, February 28-March 2 (2007) (forthcoming)
17. Ly, L.T., Rinderle-Ma, S., Dadam, P.: Integration and verification of semantic constraints in adaptive process management systems. Data & Knowledge Engineering 64, 3–23 (2007)
18. El Kharbili, M., Stein, S., Markovic, I., Pulvermüller, E.: Towards a Framework for Semantic Business Process Compliance Management. In: Sadiq, S., Indulska, M., zur Muehlen, M. (eds.) Proceedings of the Workshop on Governance, Risk and Compliance for Information Systems (GRCIS 2008), Montepellier, France. CEUR Workshop Proceedings, vol. 339, pp. 1–15 (June 2008)
19. Gábor, A., Szabó, Z.: Knowledge based institutional capacity building in the Hungarian Higher Education. In: Berdai, A., Sekhari, A. (eds.) The Proceeding of the International Conference on Software, Knowledge, and Information Management and Applications (SKIMA 2009), Fez, Morocco, October 21-23, pp. 78–85 (2009) ISBN: 9781851432516
20. BOC Group: Business Process Management with Adonis (2013),
    http://www.boc-group.com/products/adonis/
21. Kramler, G., Murzek, M.: Business Process Model Transformation Issues (2006)

Managing Emergent Processes
with Information-Based Agents

John Debenham

QCIS, University of Technology, Sydney, Australia
john.debenham@uts.edu.au

Abstract. Emergent processes are business processes whose execution
is determined by the prior information of the agents involved and by
the information that emerges during a process instance. The path that
they follow is determined on-the-fly by the decision-makers involved.
Multiagent systems are an established platform for managing complex
business processes. What is needed for emergent process management is
agents that support decision-making and do not attempt to manage the
process in pursuit of some fixed process goal. This paper describes how
the information-based agent architecture is highly suited to emergent
process support.

1 Introduction

Emergent processes are business processes that are not predefined; their execution is determined by the prior information of the agents involved and by the
information that emerges during a process instance [1]. They are opportunistic in
nature whereas production workflows are routine. Production workflows may be
managed by event-condition-action rules for example [2]. The amount of process
knowledge that is relevant to an emergent process can be enormous and may
include common sense knowledge [3]. The term "business process management"
is generally used to refer to the simpler class of workflow processes [4].

If a process' knowledge can not be represented then that process can not be
managed. This does *not* mean that process management has nothing to offer
emergent process [5]. Emergent processes are principally concerned with human
agents making decisions [6]. Decision making relies on good advice from individuals and individuals working in groups [7,8]. Estimating the veracity of advice
and identifying effective groupings are examples of tasks that software agents
can perform impartially on the basis of observed history.

Process management is an established application area for multi-agent systems
[9] although emergent processes are typically handled either manually or by
CSCW systems [10] rather than by process management systems. The use of
these two technologies is not elegant and presents a barrier to a unified view of
of the full process management spectrum.

Former work on emergent process management was based on conventional,
BDI agents [5]. More recent work on agent architectures describes information-
based agents [11] for which the atomic act is passing information the effect of

A. Kő et al. (Eds.): EGOVIS/EDEM 2013, LNCS 8061, pp. 72–86, 2013.

which is to reduce the listener's uncertainty about the world. Working relationships [12] are founded on the exchange of information and information based agents are a natural choice to model them [13]. Advice is of little use unless the listener trusts its veracity [14]. This paper examines the information-based agent model as a foundation for emergent process management.

Information-based agents attempt to fuse interaction with the information that is generated both by and because of it. To achieve this, they draw on ideas from information theory rather than game theory. This provides the decision-making apparatus with two powerful, and sometimes contradictory, bases for decision-making: making choices with greatest expected utility and making choices with greatest expected information gain so reducing uncertainty.

In supporting emergent process, information-based agents estimate the veracity of advice given by a human agent and index it using an ontology. This enables the reputation of human agents to develop within their area of expertise. Information-based agents model all uncertainties using probabilities and assume that unknown probabilities can be inferred using *maximum entropy inference* which is based on random worlds [15]. This impartial stance is appropriate for emergent process in which each agent represents the interests of it human owner.

In the context of emergent process management all interaction is referred to as *advice*. So advice includes `inform` illocutions, e.g. "The Managing Director of XYZ Inc is Ms B", `opinion` illocutions, e.g. "In my opinion you have lost your mind", as well as suggested `action` illocutions, e.g. "I advise you to sell your shares in XYZ Inc.". This simplification is made possible by the architecture of information-based agents.

In emergent process advice flows from individuals and from groups; for example, a manager may call a meeting to form considered opinion on something. When agents interact their growing history of illocutionary dialogues is their *relationship*. An agent understands its relationships using various measures that summarise its dialogue history.

Two components of the information-based model are particularly relevant:

- The computation trust mechanism that is used to forecast the veracity of advice based on past performance. This does not burden the human agents — all that the system needs to know is the identities of the speaker and the listener, the ontological context of the advice, and in good time the listener's valuation of the advice.
- The relationship model that is used to model the strength of working relationships between individuals. This requires that all communication between humans is known to the system — as this may not be feasible in some applications it is discussed separately in Section 4.

Section 2 describes the information-based model of emergent process and is divided into subsections 2.1 that introduces the core apparatus, 2.2 estimates the veracity of advice and so leads to estimates of trust in the advice-giver, and Section 3 then considers directly the business of supporting emergent process. Section 4 models the working relationships between human agents. Section 5 concludes.

2   Information-Based Model for Emergent Process

2.1   Modelling Advice

The multiagent system $\{\alpha, \beta_1, \ldots, \beta_o, \xi, \theta_1, \ldots, \theta_t\}$, is described from the point of view of agent α that interacts with agents, $\mathcal{X} = \{\beta_i\}$, information providing agents, $\mathcal{I} = \{\theta_j\}$, and a *system agent*, ξ, that represents the overall interests of the system. The *information providing agents* are a formalisation of net-based information sources — the veracity of their advice is measured along with that provided by humans. The *system agent* ξ may form opinions on the agents and may publish reputation estimates.

The agents are information-based, they are endowed with machinery for valuing the information that they have, and that they receive. Everything in their world, including their information, is uncertain; their only means of reducing uncertainty is acquiring fresh information. To model this uncertainty, their world model, $\mathcal{M}^t$, consists of random variables each representing a point of interest in the world. Distributions are then derived for these variables on the basis of information received. Over time agents acquire large amounts of information that are distilled into convenient measures.

The agent's trust machinery forecasts the veracity of advice. Agent α's trust of agent β is derived from β's past actions that are aggregated to form an expectation of β's future actions. We show how α forms these expectations, how α compares those expectations with observations, and how α then determines whether β's actions as performed are better or worse than α's expectation.

α forms expectations of the veracity of β's advice on the basis of all that it has: its full interaction history $H_\alpha \in \mathcal{H}_\alpha$ where $\mathcal{H}_\alpha$ is the set of all possible interaction histories that is expressed in terms of α's ontology — that is not made explicit to avoid overburdening the notation. H_α is a record of all interactions with each agent in $\mathcal{X}$ and with each information providing agent in $\mathcal{I}$. Let $\mathcal{B} = (b_1, b_2, \ldots)$ denote that space of all outcomes. α's expectations of β's behaviour will be represented as probability distributions over $\mathcal{B}$.

Suppose α requests some advice b from β at time t, and that β deliver the advice b' at time t'. At some later time t'' α compares b' with α's expectations of β's actions, β having promised at time t to deliver b at time t'. That is:

$$\text{compare}_\alpha^{t''}(\mathbb{E}_\alpha^t(\text{Enact}_\beta^{t'}(b)|\text{request}_{\alpha,\beta}^t(b), H_\alpha^t), b')$$

where $\text{request}_{\alpha,\beta}^t(b)$ is a predicate meaning that α requested that β provide b at time t, and $\text{Enact}_\beta^{t'}(b)$ is a random variable over $\mathcal{B}$ representing α's expectations over β's enactment action at time t', $\mathbb{E}_\alpha^t(\cdot)$ is α's expectation, and $\text{compare}(\cdot, \cdot)$ somehow describes the result of the comparison.

Expectations over β's enactment actions:

$$\mathbb{E}_\alpha^t(\text{Enact}_\beta^{t'}(b)|\text{request}_{\alpha,\beta}^t(b), H_\alpha^t)$$

could form the basis for trust in the veracity of advice in the case that there is a history of requests with a high degree of similarly to b. Given such an expectation an agent may be prepared to use the structure of the ontology to propagate these expectations. For example, if α has a history of observing β's 'trusted' executions of requests for advice about Australia then it may be prepared to partially propagate this expectation to advice about New Zealand — perhaps on the basis that Australia and New Zealand are semantically close concepts in the ontology.

The discussion above is based on expectations of *what action* β will do. It makes more practical sense to develop a sense of expectation over *the evaluation of* β's actions. Let $\mathcal{V} = (v_1, v_2, \ldots, v_V)$ be the valuation space. Then α's expectation of the evaluation of a particular action that β may make is represented as a probability distribution over $\mathcal{V}$: $(f_1, f_2, \ldots, f_V)$. For example, a very simple valuation space could be $(good, ok, bad)$. The sequence $\mathcal{V}$ will generally be smaller than the sequence $\mathcal{B}$, and so developing a sense of expectation for the value of β's actions should be easier than for the actions themselves. That is, it is simpler to form the expectation:

$$\mathbb{E}^t_\alpha(\text{Value}^{t''}_\beta(b)|\text{request}^t_{\alpha,\beta}(b), H^t_\alpha)$$

where $\text{Value}^{t''}(b)$ is a random variable over $\mathcal{V}$ representing α's expectations of the value of β's delivered advice given that b was requested and given H^t_α. At time t'' it remains to compare expectation, $\mathbb{E}^t_\alpha(\text{Value}^{t''}_\beta(b)|\text{request}^t_{\alpha,\beta}(b), H^t_\alpha)$, with observation, $\text{val}_\alpha(b')$, where $\text{val}(\cdot)$ represents α's valuation of β's advice.

We are now in a position to define 'trust'. *Trust*, $\tau_{\alpha\beta}(b)$, is a computable[1] estimate of the distribution: $\mathbb{E}^t_\alpha(\text{Value}^{t''}_\beta(b)|\text{request}^t_{\alpha,\beta}(b), H^t_\alpha)$. τ is a summarising function that distils the trust-related aspects of the (probably very large) set H_α into a probability distribution that may be computed. $\tau_{\alpha\beta}(b)$ summarises the large set H_α. The structure of the ontology is used to aggregate estimates into suitable classes, denoted by $\hat{b}$, such as John's trustworthiness in advising on pacific rim countries.

In real world situations the interaction history may not reliably predict future action, in which case the notion of trust is fragile. No matter how trust is defined trusted relationships are expected to develop slowly over time. On the other hand they can be destroyed quickly by an agent whose actions unexpectedly fall below expectation. This highlights the importance of being able to foreshadow the possibility of untrustworthy behaviour.

2.2   Trust Model

The informal meaning of the statement "agent α trusts agent β" is that α expects β to deliver advice that α values [13]. Human agents seldom trust another for *any* action that they may take — it is more usual to develop a trusted expectation with respect to a particular set of actions. For example, "I trust John's advice on mining" whilst the quality of John's advice on agriculture may be terrible.

---

[1] *Computable* in the sense that it is finitely computable, and hopefully not computationally complex.

Ontology. We model ontologies following an algebraic approach as: an *ontology* is a tuple $\mathcal{O} = (C, R, \leq, \sigma)$ where:

1. C is a finite set of *concept symbols* (including basic data types);
2. R is a finite set of *relation symbols*;
3. $\leq$ is a reflexive, transitive and anti-symmetric relation on C (a partial order)
4. $\sigma : R \to C^+$ is the function assigning to each relation symbol its arity

where $\leq$ is a traditional *is-a* hierarchy, and R contains relations between the concepts in the hierarchy.

The semantic distance between concepts plays a fundamental role in the estimation of trust. The concepts within an ontology are closer, semantically speaking, depending on how far away they are in the structure defined by the $\leq$ relation. Semantic distance plays a fundamental role in strategies for information-based agency. How requested advice, Request($\cdot$) in a particular semantic region, and their enactment Observe($\cdot$), *affect* our decision making process about requesting advice on nearby semantic regions is crucial to modelling the common sense that human beings apply in managing working relationships.

A measure bases the *semantic similarity* between two concepts on the path length induced by $\leq$ (more distance in the $\leq$ graph means less semantic similarity), and the *depth* of the subsumer concept (common ancestor) in the shortest path between the two concepts (the deeper in the hierarchy, the closer the meaning of the concepts). Semantic similarity is:

$$\text{Sim}(c, c') = e^{-\kappa_1 l} \cdot \frac{e^{\kappa_2 h} - e^{-\kappa_2 h}}{e^{\kappa_2 h} + e^{-\kappa_2 h}} \tag{1}$$

where e is Euler's number (≈ 2.71828), l is the length (i.e. number of hops) of the shortest path between the concepts, h is the depth of the deepest concept subsuming both concepts, and κ_1 and κ_2 are parameters scaling the contribution of shortest path length and depth respectively. If $l = h = 0$ then $\text{Sim}(c, c') = 1$; in general $\text{Sim}(c, c') \in [0, 1]$.

The Core Trust Mechanism. This subsection describes the core trust estimation mechanism. The general idea is that whenever α evaluates $\text{val}_\alpha^{t''}(b')$ for the enactment b' of some previously requested advice b the trust estimates are updated. The advice space is typically very large and so estimates are not maintained for individual chunks of advice; instead they are maintained for selected abstractions based on the ontology. Abstractions are denoted by the 'hat' symbol: e.g. $\hat{b}$. For example, "large engineering firms" or "pacific rim countries'. Whenever an evaluation $\text{val}_\alpha^{t''}(b')$ is performed the trust estimates, $\tau_{\alpha\beta}(\hat{b})$, for the appropriate abstraction, $\hat{b}$, are updated.

In the absence of incoming information the integrity of an information-based agent's beliefs decays in time. In the case of the agent's beliefs concerning trust, incoming information is in the form of valuation observations $\text{val}_\alpha^{t''}(b')$ for each enacted request. If there are no such observations in an area of the ontology then the integrity of the estimate for that area should decay.

In the absence of valuation observations in the region of $\hat{b}$, $\tau_{\alpha\beta}(\hat{b})$ decays to a *decay limit distribution* $\overline{\tau_{\alpha\beta}(\hat{b})}$ (denoted throughout by 'overline'). The decay limit distribution is the zero-data distribution, but not the zero-information distribution because it takes account of reputation estimates and the opinions of other agents. We assume that the decay limit distribution is known for each abstraction $\hat{b}$. At time s, given a distribution for random variable $\tau_{\alpha\beta}(\hat{b})^s$, and a decay limit distribution, $\overline{\tau_{\alpha\beta}(\hat{b})^s}$, $\tau_{\alpha\beta}(\hat{b})$ decays by:

$$\tau_{\alpha\beta}(\hat{b})^{s+1} = \Delta(\overline{\tau_{\alpha\beta}(\hat{b})^s}, \tau_{\alpha\beta}(\hat{b})^s) \tag{2}$$

where s is time and Δ is the *decay function* for the X satisfying the property that $\lim_{s\to\infty} \tau_{\alpha\beta}(\hat{b})^s = \overline{\tau_{\alpha\beta}(\hat{b})}$. For example, Δ could be linear:

$$\tau_{\alpha\beta}(\hat{b})^{s+1} = (1-\mu) \times \overline{\tau_{\alpha\beta}(\hat{b})^s} + \mu \times \tau_{\alpha\beta}(\hat{b})^s$$

where $0 < \mu < 1$ is the decay rate.

We now consider what happens when valuation observations are made. Suppose that at time s, α evaluates β's enactment b' of commitment b, $\text{val}_\alpha^s(b') = v_k \in \mathcal{V}$. The update procedure updates the probability distributions for $\tau_{\alpha\beta}(\hat{b})^s$ for each $\hat{b}$ that is "moderately close to" b. Given such a $\hat{b}$, let $\mathbb{P}^s(\tau_{\alpha\beta}(\hat{b}) = v_k)$ denote the prior probability that v_k would be observed. The update procedure is in two steps. First, estimate the posterior probability that v_k would be observed, $\mathbb{P}^{s+1}(\tau_{\alpha\beta}(\hat{b}) = v_k)$ for the particular value v_k. Second, update the entire posterior distribution for $\tau_{\alpha\beta}(\hat{b})$ to accommodate this revised value.

Given a $\hat{b}$, to revise the probability that v_k would be observed three things are used: the observation: $\text{val}_\alpha^s(b')$, the prior: $\mathbb{P}^s(\tau_{\alpha\beta}(\hat{b}) = v_k)$, and the decay limit value: $\mathbb{P}^s(\overline{\tau_{\alpha\beta}(\hat{b})} = v_k)$. The observation $\text{val}_\alpha^s(b')$ may be represented as a probability distribution with a '1' in the k'th place and zero elsewhere, $\boldsymbol{u}_k$. To combine it with the prior its significance is discounted for two reasons:

- b may not be semantically close to $\hat{b}$, and
- $\text{val}_\alpha^s(b') = v_k$ is a single observation whereas the prior distribution represents the accumulated history of previous observations.

to discount the significance of the observation $\text{val}_\alpha^s(b') = v_k$ a value is determined in the range between '1' and the zero-data, decay limit value $\mathbb{P}^s(\overline{\tau_{\alpha\beta}(\hat{b})} = v_k)$ by:

$$\delta = \text{Sim}(b, \hat{b}) \times \kappa + (1 - \text{Sim}(b, \hat{b}) \times \kappa) \times \mathbb{P}^s(\overline{\tau_{\alpha\beta}(\hat{b})} = v_k)$$

where $0 < \kappa < 1$ is the learning rate, and $\text{Sim}(\cdot,\cdot)$ is a semantic similarity function such as that shown in Equation 1. Then the posterior estimate $\mathbb{P}^{s+1}(\tau_{\alpha\beta}(\hat{b}) = v_k)$ is given by:

$$\mathbb{P}^{s+1}(\tau_{\alpha\beta}(\hat{b}) = v_k) = \frac{\rho\delta(1-\omega)}{\rho\delta(1-\omega) + (1-\rho)(1-\delta)\omega} = \hat{b} \tag{3}$$

where $\rho = \mathbb{P}^s(\tau_{\alpha\beta}(\hat{b}) = v_k)$ is the prior value, and $\omega = \mathbb{P}^s(\overline{\tau_{\alpha\beta}(\hat{b})} = v_k)$ is the decay limit value.

It remains to update the entire posterior distribution for $\tau_{\alpha\beta}(\hat{b})$ to accommodate the constraint $\mathbb{P}^{s+1}(\tau_{\alpha\beta}(\hat{b}) = v_k) = \hat{b}$. Information-based agents [11] employ a standard procedure for updating distributions, $\mathbb{P}^t(X = x)$ subject to a set of linear constraints on X, $c(X)$, using:

$$\mathbb{P}^{t+1}(X = x|c(X)) = \text{MRE}(\mathbb{P}^t(X = x), c(X))$$

where the function MRE is defined by: $\text{MRE}(\boldsymbol{q}, \boldsymbol{g}) = \arg\min_{\boldsymbol{r}} \sum_j r_j \log \frac{r_j}{q_j}$ such that $\boldsymbol{r}$ satisfies $\boldsymbol{g}$, $\boldsymbol{q}$ is a probability distribution, and $\boldsymbol{g}$ is a set of n linear constraints $\boldsymbol{g} = \{g_j(\boldsymbol{p}) = \boldsymbol{a}_j \cdot \boldsymbol{p} - c_j = 0\}, j = 1, \ldots, n$ (including the constraint $\sum_i p_i - 1 = 0$). The resulting $\boldsymbol{r}$ is the *minimum relative entropy distribution*[2]. Applying this procedure to $\tau_{\alpha\beta}(\hat{b})$:

$$\mathbb{P}^{s+1}(\tau_{\alpha\beta}(\hat{b}) = v) = \text{MRE}(\mathbb{P}^s(\tau_{\alpha\beta}(\hat{b}) = v), \mathbb{P}^{s+1}(\tau_{\alpha\beta}(\hat{b}) = v_k) = \hat{b}) \qquad (4)$$

where $\hat{b}$ is the value given by Equation 3.

Whenever α evaluates an enactment $\text{val}^s_\alpha(b')$ of some commitment b, the above procedure is applied to update the distributions for $\mathbb{P}(\tau_{\alpha\beta}(\hat{b}) = v)$. It makes sense to limit the use of this procedure to those distributions for which $\text{Sim}(b, \hat{b}) > y$ for some threshold value y.

Prior Knowledge. The decay-limit distribution plays a key role in the estimation of trust. It is not directly based on any observations and in that sense it is a "zero data" trust estimate. It is however not "zero information" as it takes account of opinions and reputations communicated by other agents. The starting point for constructing the decay-limit distribution is the maximum entropy (zero-data, zero-information) distribution. This gives a two layer structure to the estimation of trust: opinions and reputations shape the decay-limit distribution that in turn plays a role in forming the trust estimate that takes account of observed data. Communications from other agents may not be reliable. α needs a means of estimating the reliability of other agents before they can be incorporated into the decay-limit distribution — reliability is discussed at the end of this section.

Reputation is the opinion (more technically, a social evaluation) of a group about something. So a group's reputation about a thing will be related in some way to the opinions that the individual group members hold towards that thing. An *opinion* is an assessment, judgement or evaluation of something. Opinions are represented as probability distributions on a suitable ontology that for convenience is identified with the *evaluation space* $\mathcal{V}$. That is, opinions communicated by β concerning another agent's trustworthiness are assumed to be expressed as

---

[2] This may be calculated by introducing Lagrange multipliers $\boldsymbol{\lambda}$: $L(\boldsymbol{p}, \boldsymbol{\lambda}) = \sum_j p_j \log \frac{p_j}{q_j} + \boldsymbol{\lambda} \cdot \boldsymbol{g}$. Minimising L, $\{\frac{\partial L}{\partial \lambda_j} = g_j(\boldsymbol{p}) = 0\}, j = 1, \ldots, n$ is the set of given constraints $\boldsymbol{g}$, and a solution to $\frac{\partial L}{\partial p_i} = 0, i = 1, \ldots, I$ leads eventually to $\boldsymbol{p}$.

predicates using the same valuation space as $\mathcal{V}$ over which α represents its trust estimates.

An opinion is an evaluation of an *aspect* of a thing. An aspect is the "point of view" that an agent has when forming his opinion. An opinion is evaluated in context. The *context* is everything that the thing is being, explicitly or implicitly, evaluated with or against. The set of valuations of all things in the context calibrates the valuation space; for example, "this is the best paper in the conference". The context can be vague: "of all the presents you could have given me, this is the best". If agents are to discuss opinions then they must have some understanding of each other's context.

Summarising the above, an *opinion* is an agent's evaluation of a particular aspect of a thing in context. A representation of an opinion will contain: the thing, its aspect, its context, and a distribution on $\mathcal{V}$ representing the evaluation of the thing. α acquires opinions and reputations through communication with other agents. α estimates the reliability of those communicating agents before incorporating that information into the decay-limit distributions. The basic process is the same for opinions and reputations; the following describes the incorporation of opinions only.

Suppose agent β' informs agent α of his opinion of the trustworthiness of another agent β using an utterance of the form: $u = \texttt{inform}(\beta', \alpha, \tau_{\beta'\beta}(b))$, where conveniently b is in α's ontology. This information may not be useful to α for at least two reasons: β' may not be telling the truth, or β' may have a utility function that differs from α's. We will shortly estimate β''s "reliability", $R_\alpha^t(\beta')$ that measures the extent to which β' is telling the truth and that α and β' "are on the same page" or "think alike"[3]. Precisely, $0 < R_\alpha^t(\beta') < 1$; its value is used to moderate the effect of the utterance on α's decay-limit distributions. The estimation of $R_\alpha^t(\beta')$ is described below.

Suppose that α maintains the decay limit distribution $\overline{\tau_{\alpha\beta}(\hat{b})^s}$ for a chosen $\hat{b}$. In the absence of utterances informing opinions of trustworthiness, $\overline{\tau_{\alpha\beta}(\hat{b})^s}$ decays to the distribution with maximum entropy. As previously this decay could be linear:

$$\overline{\tau_{\alpha\beta}(\hat{b})^{s+1}} = (1 - \mu) \times \text{MAX} + \mu \times \overline{\tau_{\alpha\beta}(\hat{b})^s}$$

where $\mu < 1$ is the decay rate, and MAX is the maximum entropy, uniform distribution.

When α receives an utterance of the form u above, the decay limit distribution is updated by:

$$\overline{\tau_{\alpha\beta}(\hat{b})^{s+1}} \mid \texttt{inform}(\beta', \alpha, \tau_{\beta'\beta}(b)) =$$
$$\left(1 - \kappa \times \text{Sim}(\hat{b}, b) \times R_\alpha^s(\beta')\right) \times \overline{\tau_{\alpha\beta}(\hat{b})^s}$$
$$+ \kappa \times \text{Sim}(\hat{b}, b) \times R_\alpha^s(\beta') \times \tau_{\beta'\beta}(b)$$

---

[3] The reliability estimate should perhaps also be a function of the commitment, $R_\alpha^t(\beta', b)$, but that complication is ignored.

where $0 < \kappa < 1$ is the learning rate and $R_\alpha^s(\beta')$ is α estimate of β''s *reliability*. It remains to estimate $R_\alpha^s(\beta')$.

Estimating $R_\alpha^s(\beta')$ is complicated by its time dependency. First, in the absence of input of the form described following, $R_\alpha^s(\beta')$ decays to zero by: $R_\alpha^{s+1}(\beta') = \mu \times R_\alpha^s(\beta')$. Second, describe how $R_\alpha^s(\beta')$ is increased by comparing the efficacy of $\tau_{\alpha\beta}(\hat{b})^s$ and $\tau_{\beta'\beta}(b)^s$ in the following interaction scenario. Suppose at a time s, α is considering requesing advice b with β. α requests β''s opinion of β with respect to b, to which β may respond $\mathtt{inform}(\beta', \alpha, \tau_{\beta'\beta}(b))$. α now has two estimates of β's trustworthiness: $\tau_{\alpha\beta}(\hat{b})^s$ and $\tau_{\beta'\beta}(b)^s$; $\tau_{\alpha\beta}(\hat{b})^s$ and $\tau_{\beta'\beta}(b)^s$ are both probability distributions that each provide an estimate of $\mathbb{P}^s(\mathrm{Value}_\beta(b) = v_i)$ for each valuation v_i. α increases its reliability estimate of β if the trust estimate in β's $\mathtt{inform}$ is 'better' than α's current decay limit value. Suppose that α requests the advice b at time t, and at some later time t'' evaluates β's enactment $\mathrm{val}_\alpha^{t''}(b') = v_k$, say. Then:

$$\mathbb{P}(\tau_{\beta'\beta}(b)^s = v_k) > \mathbb{P}(\overline{\tau_{\alpha\beta}(\hat{b})^s} = v_k)$$

and β''s trust estimate is better than α's; α increases $R_\alpha^s(\beta')$ using:

$$R_\alpha^{s+1}(\beta') = \kappa + (1 - \kappa) \times R_\alpha^s(\beta')$$

where $0 < \kappa < 1$ is the learning rate.

3   Emergent Process Management

Following [4] a *business process* is "a set of one or more linked procedures or activities which collectively realise a business objective or policy goal, normally within the context of an organisational structure defining functional roles and relationships". Implicit in this definition is the idea that a process may be repeatedly decomposed into linked sub-processes until those sub-processes are *activities* which are atomic pieces of work. Following [4] "An activity is a description of a piece of work that forms one logical step within a process.".

This definition of a business process incorporates the notion of emergent process [16] where the atomic activities are the illocutionary act of giving advice [17]. As we have remarked previously, advice may flow from individuals or from groups. In this model, the deliberative process by which the advice was formed is not considered — what matters is the advice, from whom it came, its ontological context, and whether it proved to be sound. This abstraction focusses on the valuation of advice givers; for example, "The advice given by the Finance Committee on overseas investments is not reliable" — how that Committee shapes its advice is not important to supporting emergent process — it is simply a bad idea to seek their advice on overseas investment.

Managing, or rather supporting, emergent processes is rather more difficult than managing conventional production workflow [18]. Valuing some advice may be done objectively; for example, if a human agent is generally late in giving advice on some topic then this disturbance of the process flow may be reflected in the valuation of that agent's performance as an advice giver on that topic. Conversely, the valuation of some advice may be substantially subjective. All that matters to the process management system is that these valuations are available and their ontological context is at a sufficiently coarse level of granularity to feed a "Sim" function similar to that in Section 2.2. This requirement for a coarse model simplifies the computations.

The multiagent system described provides estimates of "trust" in an agents advice-giving ability as given by Equation 4. The term *trust* is used in line with the common meaning of the term. Its precise meaning is "expected valuation based on past performance"; that is, $\mathbb{P}(\tau_{\alpha\beta}(\hat{b}) = v)$ will be interpreted as the probability that agent β's advice to α within the ontological region $\hat{b}$ is v, where v is a member of the valuation space $\mathcal{V}$. Section 3.1 considers the selection of an agent for a specific piece of advice.

3.1   Selecting an Advice-Giver

Suppose the agent α requires advice on some topic within the semantic region $\hat{b}$. α has probability distribution estimates for the expected ability of each agent in the system to provide this advice as calculated by Equation 4. Let $\mathbb{P}_{\hat{b}}(\beta \gg)$ denote the probability that agent β is the best such choice. The question of whether one such probability distribution is "better than" another is essentially a subjective choice. For example, one agent may have a history of giving impeccable advice marred but the occasional disaster, and another my have a history of giving consistently reasonably good advice — the choice between these agents is subjective.

Let $\mathbb{P}_{\hat{b}}(\beta \gg \beta')$ denote the probability that β is a better choice for α than β' within the ontological region $\hat{b}$. Then if there are three agents to choose from:

$$\mathbb{P}_{\hat{b}}(\beta \gg) = \mathbb{P}_{\hat{b}}((\beta \gg \beta') \wedge (\beta \gg \beta''))$$
$$= \mathbb{P}_{\hat{b}}(\beta \gg \beta') \times \mathbb{P}_{\hat{b}}((\beta \gg \beta'') \mid (\beta \gg \beta'))$$

The difficulty with this expression is that there is no direct way of estimating the second, conditional probability. A reasonable way of finding an approximate solution to this problem is described in [5].

A selection strategy is a probability distribution $\{p_i\}_{i=1}^n$ that determines who from $\{\beta_i\}_{i=1}^n$ to ask for advice in some ontological region — we omit the region $(\hat{b})$ from the following to avoid overloading the notation. A greedy strategy *best* picks the "best" agent:

$$p_i = \begin{cases} \frac{1}{m} & \text{if } \beta_i \text{ is such that } \mathbb{P}(\beta_i \gg) \text{ is maximal} \\ 0 & \text{otherwise} \end{cases} \tag{5}$$

where m is such that there are m agents for whom $\mathbb{P}(\beta_i \gg)$ is maximal. This strategy is short-sighted in that it rewards success with work — although it is not uncommon in practice. Another strategy also favours high payoff, but gives all agents a chance to prove themselves, sooner or later:

$$p_i = \mathbb{P}(\beta_i \gg) \qquad (6)$$

A third strategy is equitable, and picks agents by:

$$p_i = \frac{1}{n} \qquad (7)$$

An *admissible* selection strategy has the properties:

$$\text{if } \mathbb{P}(X_i \gg) > \mathbb{P}(X_j \gg) \quad \text{then} \quad p_i > p_j$$
$$\text{if } \mathbb{P}(X_i \gg) = \mathbb{P}(X_j \gg) \quad then \quad p_i = p_j$$
$$(\forall i)p_i > 0 \quad \text{and} \quad \sum_i p_i = 1$$

So (5) and (7) are not admissible strategies but (6) is admissible. It the favoured strategy — it selects an agent with the probability that it is the best choice.

4   Working Relationships

The trust model described in Section 2.2 is a summary of the history of inter-action between α and β, $H_{\alpha\beta}$, augmented by reputation estimates. Trust is not the only way in which the interaction history may be usefully summarised. The *relationship model* contains summary estimates of the values of the information flows between individuals.

The model of working relationships measures the strength of relationships in terms of the free flow of communication. The idea being that two agents have a strong working relationship if they freely exchange information. The 'value' of information is measured in terms of the reduction of uncertainty to the listener using Shannon entropy that measures information gain as: $\mathbb{H}_{\text{prior}} - \mathbb{H}_{\text{posterior}}$. Su-perfluous information is automatically factored out by indexing the information over the ontology that is assumed to defined the region of general interest. These estimates require that all interaction be known to the system — in some situa-tions this may not be feasible. The formal representation of working relationships for emergent process uses the general principles of the LOGIC framework [12].

A *relationship* between two human or artificial agents is their *interaction his-tory* that is a complete record of their interactions evaluated *in context*. There is evidence from psychological studies that humans seek a *balance* in their working relationships. The classical view is that people perceive resource allocations as being distributively fair (i.e. well balanced) if they are proportional to inputs or contributions (i.e. equitable). However, more recent studies show that humans follow a richer set of norms of distributive justice depending on their *intimacy* level: equity, equality, and need. *Equity* is allocation proportionally to the effort (e.g. the profit of a company goes to the stock holders proportional to their in-vestment), *equality* being the allocation in equal amounts, and *need* being the allocation proportional to the need for the resource.

Section 2.1 focussed on the output of a dialogue — namely a piece of advice. We now drill down into the dialogues, where a *dialogue* is a set of related utterances. This section is concerned with *advice* that contains the implicit commitment that the advice given is sound. We assume that all dialogues take place in some or all of the following five stages:

1. the *prelude* during which agents prepare for the interaction
2. the *discussion* that may lead to
3. *requesting* advice b at time t
4. the *enactment* of the request b' at time t'
5. the *evaluation* at time t'' of the complete interaction process that is made when the value of the advice b' is known

A major issue in building models of dialogues and relationships is dealing with the reliability of the utterances made. For an information-based agent the *reliability* of an utterance is an epistemic probability estimate of the utterance's veracity. For example, if the utterance is an `inform` containing a proposition then its reliability is an estimate of the probability that the proposition is correct. If the utterance is an `opinion` then its reliability is an estimate of the probability that the `opinion` will in time be judged to be sound. The difficulty with estimating reliability is that it may take months or years for an agent to be able to say: "Ah, that was good advice". Reliability is a measure attached to an utterance, and integrity is a measure attached to a complete dialogue. A blanket estimation of the overall reliability of an agent was described in Section 2.2.

The LOGIC illocutionary framework [12] is a general framework classifying interactions. This framework is used to define one of the two dimensions of the relationship model described below, the second dimension being provided by the structure of the ontology as specified by a partial order $\leq$ defined by the is-a hierarchy, and a distance measure between concepts such as Equation 1. The five LOGIC categories for advice-based dialogues are quite general:

- *Legitimacy* contains *information* that may be part of, relevant to or in justification of advice that has been or may be requested.
- *Options* contains information about *advice* that an agent may be prepared to give.
- *Goals* contains information about the *objectives* of the agents — i.e. the use to which the advice may be put.
- *Independence* contains information about the agent's *outside sources* — i.e. sources of advice that may be external to the process management system.
- *Commitments* contains information about the *commitments* that an agent has to provide advice possibly to other agents.

and are used here to categorise all incoming communication that feeds into the agent's relationship model. This categorisation is not a one-to-one mapping and some illocutions fall into multiple categories. These categories are designed to provide a model of the agents' information as it is relevant to their relationships. They are *not* intended to be a universal categorising framework for all utterances.

Taking a more formal view, the LOGIC framework categorises information in an utterance by its relationship to:

L = $\{B(\beta)\}$, that is a set of β's *beliefs* on which its advice may be founded, and may be communicated by: **inform**.
O = $\{\text{Available}(\beta, \alpha)\}$, that is a set of *available advice* that β may offer to α.
G = $\{\text{Goal}(\beta)\}$, that is a set of β's process goals for which advice may be asked for with a: **request**
I = $\{\text{Can}(\beta, \text{Do}(p))\}$, that is a set of β's *capabilities*, communicated by: **canDo**.
C = $\{\text{Commit}(\beta, \text{Do}(p))\} \cup \{\text{Intend}(\beta, \text{Do}(p))\}$, that is a set of *commitments* to give advice communicated by: **commit** (for future promised advice), and **intend** (advice presently being delivered).

L, O, G, I and C are five predicates that recognise the category of an utterance. Information in an **inform** utterance is categorised as Goals, Independence and Commitments, otherwise it is categorised as Legitimacy.

Given a request for advice in category $\hat{b}$ and an agent β the variables $L_{\hat{b}\beta}^t$, $O_{\hat{b}\beta}^t$, $G_{\hat{b}\beta}^t$, $I_{\hat{b}\beta}^t$ and $C_{\hat{b}\beta}^t$ are aggregated from observations of how forthcoming β was during prior dialogues in the region of $\hat{b}$. They are then used to form α's expectation of β's future readiness to communicate across the five LOGIC categories. They are updated at the end of each dialogue using a linear form.

In the following a dialogue commences at time $t - s$ and terminates at time t when the five variables are updated. $t - d$ denotes the time at which these variables were previously updated. For convenience assume that $d \geq s$. The dialogue aims to satisfy a request for advice $b \leq \hat{b}$. All the estimates given below are for the effect of the dialogue requesting advice b on variables for a nearby need $\hat{b}$ for which $\eta' = \eta \times \text{Sim}(\hat{b}, b)$, η is the learning rate, and μ the global integrity decay rate.

$L_{\hat{b}\beta}^t$ measures the amount of information in β's Legitimacy **inform** utterances. The Shannon information in a single **inform** statement, u, is: $\mathbb{I}(u) = \mathbb{H}(\mathcal{M}^{t-1}) - \mathbb{H}(\mathcal{M}^t | u)$. It is defined in terms of the contents of $\mathcal{M}^t$, and so the valuation is restricted to 'just those things of interest' to α. During the dialogue Γ observe: $l = \sum_{u \in \Gamma, \mathsf{L}(u)} \mathbb{I}(u)$. Then update $L_{\hat{b}\beta}^t$ with:

$$L_{\hat{b}\beta}^t = \eta' \sum_{u \in \Gamma, \mathsf{L}(u)} \mathbb{I}(u) + (1 - \eta')\mu^d L_{\hat{b}\beta}^{t-d}$$

$O_{\hat{b}\beta}^t$ measures the amount of information β reveals about the advice he may be prepared to impart. Let random variable Y over advice space $\mathcal{C}$ denote α's beliefs that β is prepared and able to give advice. The information gain in Y during Γ is: $\mathbb{H}^{t-s}(Y) - \mathbb{H}^t(Y)$, and $O_{\hat{b}\beta}^t$ is updated by:

$$O_{\hat{b}\beta}^t = \eta' \left(\mathbb{H}^{t-s}(Y) - \mathbb{H}^t(Y) \right) + (1 - \eta')\mu^d O_{\hat{b}\beta}^{t-d}$$

$G_{\hat{b}\beta}^t$ measures the information β reveals about his process goals, and $I_{\hat{b}\beta}^t$ about his abilty to give advice. $G_{\hat{b}\beta}^t$ and $I_{\hat{b}\beta}^t$ are similar in that both **request** and canDo preempt the advice. Suppose β informs α that: request($\hat{b}$) and canDo(δ). If β is being forthcoming then this suggests that he has in mind an eventual request b in which $a \leq \hat{b}$ and $b \leq \delta$ (using $\leq$ from the ontology). Suppose that Γ leads to requesting the advice b then observe: $g = \mathrm{Sim}(b', \hat{b})$. Similarly, $i = \max_\delta \mathrm{Sim}(b, \delta)$, $\max_\delta$ is in case β utters more than one canDo(β, δ). $G^t_{\hat{b}\beta}$ is aggregated by:

$$G^t_{\hat{b}\beta} = \eta' \mathrm{Sim}(b', \hat{b}) + (1 - \eta')\mu^d G^{t-d}_{\hat{b}\beta}$$

Similarly: $I^t_{\hat{b}\beta} = \eta' \max_\delta \mathrm{Sim}(b, \delta) + (1 - \eta')\mu^d I^{t-d}_{\hat{b}\beta}$.

$C^t_{\hat{b}\beta}$ measures the amount of information β reveals about his commitments to give advice to others. These are measured just as for $L^t_{\hat{b}\beta}$ by aggregating the observation: $c = \sum_{u \in \Gamma, \mathrm{C}(u)} \mathbb{I}(u)$, and $C^t_{\hat{b}\beta}$ is updated by:

$$C^t_{\hat{b}\beta} = \eta' \sum_{u \in \Gamma, \mathrm{C}(u)} \mathbb{I}(u) + (1 - \eta')\mu^d C^{t-d}_{\hat{b}\beta}$$

In addition, if $\mathrm{val}_\alpha(\cdot)$ is α's evaluation function that is used to evaluate the overall increase in value of the interaction history

$$u^t(\Gamma) = \mathrm{val}_\alpha(H^t) - \mathrm{val}_\alpha(H^{t-s})$$

update the variable $U^t_{\hat{b}\beta}$ that estimates the overall value of the dialogue Γ:

$$U^t_\beta = \eta' \left(\mathrm{val}_\alpha(H^t) - \mathrm{val}_\alpha(H^{t-s}) \right) + (1 - \eta')\mu^d U^{t-d}_\beta$$

5   Discussion

Emergent processes are business processes whose execution is determined by the prior knowledge of the agents involved and by the knowledge that emerges during a process instance. This work addresses two issues: first, the management of the exchange of advice during a process instance, and second a quantified model of the strength of the working relationships between the players. Managing the exchange of advice is founded on estimates of the expected reliability of advice from a particular agent on a particular topic. The system achieves this by using ideas from information theory, and by using maximum entropy logic to derive integrity estimates for advice about which it is uncertain. All of this then feeds into strategies for selecting who to ask for what at any particular time. Managing advice is computationally feasible as it requires that the system know just: who asked who for what, and the subsequent valuation of the quality of the advice provided — all statements being categorised in terms of the ontology. The second issue, modelling the strength of relationships requires that all interaction pass through the system which may not be practical in some applications.

References

1. Mintzberg, H.: The design school: Reconsidering the basic premises of strategic management. Strategic Management Journal 11(3), 171–195 (1990)
2. Weske, M.: Business process management architectures. In: Business Process Management, pp. 333–371. Springer, Heidelberg (2012)
3. van der Aalst, W., van Hee, K.: Workflow Management: Models, Methods, and Systems. The MIT Press (2002)
4. Fischer, L.: The Workflow Handbook 2003. Future Strategies Inc. (2003)
5. Debenham, J.: An agent-based framework for emergent process management. International Journal of Intelligent Information Technologies 27(2), 30–48 (2006)
6. Kirchmer, M.: High Performance Through Process Excellence. Springer, Berlin (2011)
7. van den Hooff, B., Huysman, M.: Managing knowledge sharing: Emergent and engineering approaches. Information & Management 46(1), 1–8 (2009)
8. Smith, H., Fingar, P.: Business Process Management (BPM): The Third Wave. Meghan-Kiffer Press (2003)
9. Singh, M.: Business Process Management: A Killer Ap for Agents? In: Jennings, N., Sierra, C., Sonenberg, L., Tambe, M. (eds.) Proceedings Third International Conference on Autonomous Agents and Multi Agent Systems, AAMAS 2004, pp. 26–27. ACM (July 2004)
10. Lin, A., Hawryszkiewycz, I.T., Henderson-Sellers, B.: An agent-based collaborative emergent process management system. In: Bresciani, P., Giorgini, P., Henderson-Sellers, B., Low, G., Winikoff, M. (eds.) AOIS 2004. LNCS (LNAI), vol. 3508, pp. 1–18. Springer, Heidelberg (2005)
11. Sierra, C., Debenham, J.: Information-based agency. In: Proceedings of Twentieth International Joint Conference on Artificial Intelligence, IJCAI 2007, Hyderabad, India, pp. 1513–1518 (January 2007)
12. Sierra, C., Debenham, J.: The LOGIC Negotiation Model. In: Proceedings Sixth International Conference on Autonomous Agents and Multi Agent Systems, AAMAS 2007, Honolulu, Hawai'i, pp. 1026–1033 (May 2007)
13. Debenham, J., Sierra, C.: Robust trust: Prior knowledge, time and context. In: Huemer, C., Lops, P. (eds.) EC-Web 2012. LNBIP, vol. 123, pp. 1–12. Springer, Heidelberg (2012)
14. Sierra, C., Debenham, J.: Building relationships with trust. In: Ossowski, S. (ed.) Agreement Technologies. Law, Governance and Technology, vol. 8, pp. 485–510. Springer, Heidelberg (2013)
15. Halpern, J.: Reasoning about Uncertainty. MIT Press (2003)
16. van der Aalst, W., Hofstede, A., Kiepuszewski, B., Barros, A.: Workflow patterns. Distributed and Parallel Databases 14(1), 5–51 (2003)
17. Patel, N.: Deferred action: Theoretical model of process architecture design for emergent business processes. In: Simons, R. (ed.) Operations Management: A Modern Approach, pp. 29–56. Apple Academic Press (2011)
18. Orlikowski, W.J.: The sociomateriality of organisational life: considering technology in management research. Cambridge Journal of Economics 34(1), 125–141 (2012)

Understanding E-Government Development Barriers in CIS Countries and Exploring Mechanisms for Regional Cooperation

Lyudmila Bershadskaya[1], Andrei Chugunov[1], and Zamira Dzhusupova[2]

[1] St Petersburg National Research University of Information Technologies,
Mechanics and Optics, St Petersburg, Russia
chugunov@egov-center.ru, bershadskaya.lyudmila@gmail.com
[2] UN University - International Institute for Software Technology, Macau, China
zamira@iist.unu.edu

Abstract. This paper intends to fill the gap in the literature on electronic government (EGOV) development in Commonwealth of Independent States (CIS), which share similar problems in the process of transition from the hierarchical top-down control to effective governance systems. Based on the expert survey, we provide a better understanding of current practices and barriers for EGOV development in the region, and possible mechanisms for regional cooperation in EGOV implementation. The results show that collaborative efforts in developing institutional and human capacity and adoption of common policies, strategies and standards for electronic communication, cross-border information sharing and knowledge exchange could help to overcome the greatest barriers. As proven by the experience of other regions, cooperation in promoting and implementing ICT-enabled governance could facilitate integration and transition process. This, in turn, would foster intra-regional business and trade and help solve critical problems with migration and crime investigation, environmental and energy issues, as well as effective use of water and other natural resources.

Keywords : e-government, ICT-enabled transformation, regional cooperation, Commonwealth of Independent States, CIS region.

1   Introduction

Cross-border cooperation on promoting and implementing Electronic Government (EGOV) is emerging increasingly in light of the integration processes in various regions. Many regions demonstrate how countries from the same region could benefit from sharing knowledge and experience, developing regional strategies, polices and standards and implementing joint research development projects on ICT-enabled governance, cross- boundary information sharing and improvement of public services provided by their governments. The evidence of successful cooperation on EGOV development in European Union (EU) region is provided by numerous scholarly articles as well as ePractice.eu platform which involves practitioners from all 27 Member States, EU-member candidate states and EFTA countries. Various initiatives on regional

A. Kő et al. (Eds.): EGOVIS/EDEM 2013, LNCS 8061, pp. 87–101, 2013.
© Springer-Verlag Berlin Heidelberg 2013

collaboration in EGOV can be found in Middle East and North Africa (MENA) countries [1-2], Latin America and Caribbean countries [3], and Southeast Asia.

EGOV development in Commonwealth of Independent States (CIS) is an emerging phenomenon that should be examined in order to understand specific features, problems and issues typical to this region, and to offer possible solutions for solving them. Unfortunately, there is lack of studies on EGOV development in CIS member countries, which have historic ties and share similar problems in the process of transition from the hierarchical top-down control and the super-centralized system of resource allocation to effective public governance. According to UNDESA [4], the CIS region will most likely experience economic instability, or even a recession, in the near future. Having common history and legacy from Soviet Union and facing similar governance and socio-economic challenges after collapse, CIS countries recognize the importance of regional integration. In most cases, these countries have unique governance problems inherited from Soviet Union time. In this regard, cooperation in promoting and implementing ICT-enabled governance could facilitate the transition process and integration of CIS countries. This, in turn, will foster intra-regional business and trade and help solve critical problems with migration and crime investigation, environmental and energy saving issues, as well as effective use of water and other natural resources. As shown by regional cooperation experience in other regions, developing common policies, strategies and standards for electronic communication, cross-border information sharing, knowledge exchange and joint efforts in delivering shared e-services are essential for enabling effective integration.

Realizing the gap in the literature on EGOV development challenges in CIS region and importance of regional cooperation in facilitating ICT-enabled governance transformation, this paper intends to provide a better understanding of current practices on EGOV, critical challenges faced, and most importantly, to explore mechanisms for intra-regional collaboration in EGOV implementation. The rest of the paper is organized as follows. Section 2 presents literature review on challenges in developing EGOV that are common to many countries and the role of regional cooperation in this process. Section 3 introduces the context of the study and subsequently, Section 4 explains the research methodology adopted while Section 5 presents key findings. Section 6 includes a discussion about the findings, and Section 7 presents concluding remarks and some ideas for future work.

2   Literature Review

In this study, we have drawn on two streams of literature: (i) the literature on most common challenges of EGOV implementation; (ii) the literature on the role of regional cooperation in EGOV development.

2.1   Common Challenges of EGOV Implementation

Implementation of EGOV programs and projects in various countries and regions faces a variety of problems and challenges. However, it is noteworthy that studies conducted in different countries revealed some similar typical problems in EGOV development. For example, G.Strejcek and M. Theil [5] based on the materials of the EU countries emphasized the existing gap between the ambition of EGOV projects and their actual implementation. Chatrie and Wraight [6] considered the most critical issues of implementing EGOV in the 15 EU countries and came to the conclusion that most of them belong to one of the following subject areas: (i) governance, public administration; (ii) education, training programs; (iii) economy, e-commerce; and (iv) legislation. O.Signore, F. Chesi and M. Pallotti [7] identified and described key challenges that grouped around technical, economic and social perspectives. They claim that overcoming these challenges helps shifting to full vertical and horizontal integration. They suggest that use of W3C consortium's standards and goals could be a way to cope with these contradictions.

A large group of barriers are related to organizational factors, in particular, the lack of coordination between government agencies and different levels of government, as well as conflicting objectives of EGOV in the agencies and levels [8]. Problems associated with human capacity building are also hot on the agenda. This group of problems includes lack of public trust in government institutions [9], loss of public interest in the political process and governance procedures [10], problem of public apathy and frustration. In addition, there is a risk of reducing the authorities' responsibility in communication with citizens in electronic form, which would reduce the level of trust among the population and the state. Moreover, the problem of insufficient civil servants' qualification in the field of EGOV and e-services is still one of the major obstacles for EGOV development and coordination [11]. While this problem can be solved by developing training programs, there is a crucial concern how to make such trainings or educational programs effective, which level of staff should be targeted, which issues should be addressed most, etc [12].

2.2   The Role of Regional Cooperation in EGOV Development

Regional cooperation in various areas allows countries to facilitate the socio-economic development through consolidation of their efforts and resources to achieve common goals and objectives. It helps to improve efficiency of their industries through greater utilization of each country capability and harmonizing usage of natural resources in the region. In this regard, regional affiliation is determined by the similarity of development strategies, objectives and priorities and often supported by the common historical way of social organization. K. Bjoratn, while exploring the integration processes in the Third World, noted that, for example, "regional integration, in the form of lower transport costs, contributes to the regional balance of economic activity and income" [13]. In addition to economic and trade cooperation, common activities in international and regional cooperation are related to joining efforts to solving global climate change and environmental problems [14], problems of energy consumption and global economic growth [15]. Good practices of regional cooperation could be found on all continents. Asian "4 Tigers" including South Korea, Hong Kong, Chinese Taipei, and Singapore is an example of effective regional cooperation. The central feature of this cooperation is markets' development through the mechanisms of effective adaptation [16]. Despite the long-standing period of autocracy regime in this region, "Asian tigers" in a few decades were able to turn from the backward Asian countries into the advanced ones.

Internet technologies simplify the cross-country integration through the use of information systems and data exchange. Global ICT development programs become an expression of transnational movements to mobilization, representing a new form of governance. The researches identify a number of influential factors in this direction [17]: (i) the technologies being used are universal and public (Internet, Web sites); (ii) the values and goals of development are becoming universal; (iii) the institutions that implement these development strategies are also universal (eg, OECD, UN, World Bank, etc.).

There are a number of good practices on regional cooperation in EGOV in various regions like EU [18], Latin America and Caribbean [19], Southeast Asia [20], and MENA region [21-22]. For example, e-Practice [23] initiative of the European Commission offers a new service for the professional community of eGovernment, eInclusion, eParticipation and eHealth practitioners providing an online platform for knowledge sharing through the large collection of European experience and methodological resources. It is an interactive initiative that empowers its users to discuss and influence open government, policy-making and the way in which public administrations operate and deliver services. The EU e-Government Action Plan [24] contributes to knowledge based sustainable and inclusive economy for the European Union, as set forth in the Europe 2020 Strategy and supports and complements the Digital Agenda for Europe. The RED GEALC initiative provides a network of e-Government leaders of Latin America and the Caribbean created by Organization of American States and Institute for Connectivity in the Americas [3]. This virtual network helps to exchange expertise and share experiences, and lessons learned to facilitate capacity-building through the utilization of modern technology in the countries of the region. This initiative raised awareness on the EGOV potential for regional development, increased knowledge of government officials on the issues and challenges of EGOV implementation and laid the ground for stronger networking and collaboration on EGOV in the region. Another tool for the exchange and transfer of regional EGOV applications is eGobex, a portal that enables sharing of applications in areas such as mobile government or public attention. Moreover, EGOV interoperability in Latin America and the Caribbean is promoted as a common framework for regional action and discussion on ICT [25]. The e-ASEAN (Association of Southeast Asian Nations) Framework Agreement promotes cooperation to strengthen the competitiveness of the ICT sector and narrow the digital divide within and among member countries [26]. Within this cooperation framework, a number of EGOV and ICT training programs, workshops and seminars were conducted in member countries. Another example of cooperation in the Asia-Pacific region is establishing online community of ethnic Chinese, uniting people from China, Taiwan, Hong Kong and Singapore [27]. Thus, regional networks are becoming catalysts for innovation, investment stimulation, liberalization and privatization. Members of the Pacific Islands Forum have launched a number of initiatives, including the Forum Communications Action Plan, the Pacific Islands ICT Policy and Strategic Plan and the Pacific 14D Initiative, which identify priority areas for island countries, including telehealth, distance learning and universal access through community telecentres. One of the most notable initiatives of MENA countries is benchmark studies on EGOV development in the region and development of EGOV measurement framework [28].

As we can see from the literature reviewed in this section, regional cooperation in EGOV can help countries to address common challenges and overcome typical obstacles by joining efforts, sharing common solutions and bridging the digital divide between countries. It can help to solve critical issues of developing adequate infrastructure for EGOV with improved connectivity. Regional cooperation can support EGOV education, find new financing mechanisms, establish necessary legal and regulatory framework for cross-border public e-services and ultimately, improve governance through effective use of ICTs.

3   Context

There is growing general trend of multilateral cooperation in the economic and geographic areas of post-Soviet space. CIS is a regional organization established after the Soviet Union collapse. Currently there are 11 member states: Armenia, Azerbaijan, Belarus, Kazakhstan, Kyrgyzstan, Moldova, Russia, Tajikistan, Turkmenistan, Ukraine, and Uzbekistan. There are several reasons for greater interest in joint regional initiatives. They include (i) geographical proximity; (ii) legacy of old economic and cultural ties; (iii) common language of communication; (ii) majority of top-managers in the public sector, as well as in business are those who educated in Soviet Union.

Some economic communities are emerging in this region like Chambers of Commerce communities, Eurasian Union, Customs Union and others. The members of these organizations rely on the strength of the connections between the different agencies and enterprises established during the Soviet period and experience and memory of integrated economies and trade, coordination of resources in former USSR countries. Initially, EU integration model has been taken as a model for cooperation in CIS region. However, CIS integration appears fragmented while the EU integration has been promoted in a comprehensive way providing with a common platform for cooperation, polices, strategies and standards. Thus, the CIS integration model presents the mutual existence of separate regional sub-groups such as (i) the Eurasian community as a transnational association with an unified political, economic, military, customs, humanitarian, cultural space; (ii) the Custom Union with Belarus, Kazakhstan, Russia as members and Kyrgyzstan and Tajikistan expected to join in the nearest future; (iii) the Collective Security Treaty Organization; and (iv) the Organization for Democracy and Economic Development of Georgia, Ukraine, Azerbaijan and Moldova. The Custom Union represents the most intensive integration model among others. In the framework of this regional cooperation unit, some mechanisms of electronic interaction were developed, and the foundation of information security was provided so far. Regional Commonwealth in the field of Communications (RCC) intends to create a common information space. RCC developed the "Strategic lines of the Regional Commonwealth in the field of Communications activities 2012 – 2017" and RCC working groups and councils are developing proposals for introducing essential changes in national legislation, for the transition to innovative economy [29]. The model codes in ICT implementation are coordinated and approved in Inter-Parliamentary Assembly of Member Nations of CIS [30]. In light of such emerging trends in regional integration among CIS member countries and because of the fragmentation barriers, cooperation in EGOV development is getting more and more valuable.

4   Research Methodology

In this study, we apply both qualitative and quantitative research methods using primary data from the expert survey and secondary data from official reports of international organizations.

4.1   Research Method

The research methodology for the expert survey was developed in 2011 and applied by the authors for identifying key challenges in implementing EGOV in Russia [31]. In 2012, it was adopted for this exploratory study on EGOV development problems and solutions for cooperation in CIS region. The aim of the expert survey was to collect from experts opinions on (i) current EGOV practices in their countries; (ii) main problems in developing EGOV in CIS region; (iii) possible solutions for solving them; and (iv) mechanisms for regional intergovernmental cooperation in EGOV implementation.

The expert survey process includes three stages:

1.   Discussion with representatives of the government agencies responsible for EGOV development in CIS countries in order to select the range of possible problems identified from the literature review.
2.   Development of the questionnaire for the expert survey based on problem-oriented approach.
3.   Collection of expert opinions from the representatives of government agencies, public sector and academia from all eleven CIS countries participated in the survey.

Problem-oriented approach was applied for developing a survey questionnaire because the EGOV development in CIS countries is an emerging phenomenon not received sufficient attention from the research community so far. The problem-oriented approach concerns with the utilization of general knowledge for practical problems, which are not well-known and not structured according to disciplinary categories and delimitations [32]. The problem is mainly called a question with no single solution due to a degree of uncertainty [33]. The importance of this approach lies in the scientific community consolidation for discussing key problems, creating a common conceptual framework and for shaping solutions to the problems [34]. The initial list of problems was created in accordance with the most relevant issues revealed from the literature review. In addition to the proposed list, the experts stated other problems, which were of particular importance from their point of view.

4.2   Data Collection

The expert panel for collecting primary data was designed in accordance with the list of CIS representatives in RCC and also using professional contacts of the authors with representatives from educational, scientific and IT organizations. There was an intention to include representatives of government institutions involved in the formulation of EGOV policies and strategies, professionals from IT companies who provide EGOV solutions, as well as representatives of the scientific, educational community and non-governmental organizations (NGOs) involved in capacity building programs. The research expert panel consisted of 28 experts from government institutions (12), IT-companies (7) and scientific and expert organizations (9) involved in EGOV development in their countries. More than half of the experts worked on EGOV projects for over 5 years, 35% of them for over 10 years. Experts identified good practices and key problems of EGOV development in their own countries and suggested possible solutions for solving these problems including mechanisms for regional cooperation. The secondary data was collected from the latest UNDESA report on EGOV development.

5   Findings

5.1   Current EGOV Practices in CIS Countries

During the survey, the experts were asked to identify current practices of EGOV implementation in their countries. The survey revealed that most of the initiatives are related to e-portals, electronic document exchange and public e-services. Based on their purpose and services provided, the initiatives were distributed across three segments such as Government-to-Government (G2G), Government-to-Citizens (G3C), and Government-to- Business (G2B) as shown in Table 1. We revealed that over 60% of the projects were oriented on G2C interaction while 50% were associated with G2B segment and 42% covered the G2G segment.

Table 1. EGOV Practices in CIS Countries, 2012

	G2G	G2C	G2B
Armenia	Electronic document flow system	National identification system for citizens	
	Electronic document flows in the social sphere		
Azerbaijan	Establishment of the Agency on public services and social innovation under the President of Azerbaijan		
	The Ministry of taxes information system		

Table 1. (*Continued*)

Belarus	Secure e-mail in the authorities		
	e-Declaration system		
Kazakhstan	e-Government services portal		
	Official President portal		
Kyrgyzstan	Electronic resources to reduce corruption		
	State information system of real estate		
	Centers of citizens services development		e-Procurement portal
		Electronic tax reporting	
		Electronic services by Social Fund	
	Enquiry information system under State Registration Service		
	Web portal "Open budget"		
Moldova	Register for personal data control	Mobile digital signature implementation	
	e- Government services portal		
	Cloud Computing technologies implementation		
Russia			e-Procurement portal
	e- Government services portal		
Uzbekistan	Project "Learn your VAT number"		Electronic declaration for customs
	Documents forms on Government portal		
Ukraine	Open Government Partnership		
		Electronic accountability	
		Electronic system of vehicle registration, driver licence and testing	e-Customs system
Tajikistan	DHIS – application for management in the health sector	The Public Reception of Hudjad city	
	Electronic control system in education «OpenAdmin»		
	Mobile technologies to access social services		
		Online communities of a city	
	Program of targeted social assistance		
	Crowdsourcing web- platform		
Turkmenistan	Electronic document flow in the Ministry of Economy and Development		

5.2   Communication Channels between EGOV Stakeholders in CIS Countries

EGOV development depends on utilization of specific communication channels. Experts rated each communication channel on a 5-point scale (1- min, 5- max). Table 2 shows the most preferred channels of communication between government agencies, between government and citizens, and between government representatives and commercial companies. According to the expert opinions, the most preferred channels of communication between government agencies are a peculiar system for interagency communication, e-mail and hosted face-to face events. The majority of experts chose electronic communication channels like portals, e-mail, social networks as being the most preferred for communication between government and citizens. Public services web-portals were identified as the most preferred channel of communication between government representatives and commercial companies.

Table 2. Communication Channels in CIS Countries, 2012

Communication channel	G2G	G2C	G2B
Web-portals	3,6	4,1	4,3
E-mail	3,9	3,7	4,2
Telephone	3,4	3,1	3,1
System of Interagency Communication	4,2	2,1	2,9
Face-to-face communication	3,1	2,2	2,6
Social networks, blogs	2,3	3,4	2,9
Skype, ICQ	2,4	2,4	2,1
Videoconference	3,4	2,5	2,9
Events, meetings	3,7	2,7	2,9

5.3   EGOV Development Challenges in CIS Countries

The experts were asked to evaluate the list of EGOV development problems in order to identify the most pressing and critical among them. The experts' opinions were graded by points: 1 as minimum and 5 as maximum. Based on the results of the expert survey, a ranking of such problems was constructed as shown in Figure 1. As mentioned earlier, the initial list of problems was created in accordance with the most relevant issues revealed from the literature review. The survey results show that lack of civil servants' motivation (4.1) and lack of qualification (3.9) are the top ranked problems. However, according to the survey results, the CIS's experts showed less concern about the problem of unrealistic goals (2.8) and their achievement (2.9) as well as citizen's lack of confidence to technology (2.8) and lack of citizen's motivation.

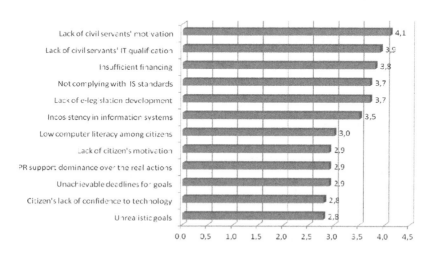

Fig. 1. EGOV Development Problems in CIS countries, 2012

In addition to the proposed list, the experts stated other problems, which were of particular importance from their point of view. The following problems were highlighted by the experts as most relevant: (i) EGOV projects do not focus on the real problems of citizens and business; (ii) lack of interest among government leaders in developing EGOV and their reluctance to promote and support EGOV initiatives; (iii) departmental orientation of state services at all levels and lack of information exchange between the different agencies and services; (iv) outdated data infrastructures; (v) the unattractive nature of EGOV projects to potential investors; (vi) lack of attention paid to market realities and possibilities afforded by the private sector.

5.4   Possible Solutions for Overcoming the Barriers

During the survey, experts suggested various solutions for solving EGOV problems identified by experts as being the most significant based on the experience of their own countries, as well as the experience of neighboring countries. The following table shows the proposed solutions to the problems (Table. 3).

Table 3. Possible Solutions for EGOV Problems in CIS

№	Problem/ solution
1	**Lack of civil servants' motivation**
	- a system of material and moral incentives for using innovative approaches, - staff change (full or partial)
2	**Lack of civil servants' IT qualifications**
	- development of mandatory training programs, - online platform for civil servants development, including eGov experience exchange and self-education, - CIO institution development
3	**Insufficient financing**
	- implementation of investment-attractive projects; - E-Governance Fund creation for organizing revenue from market products (license fee), - active fundraising, public-private partnership
4	**E-Government development does not comply with large information systems standards**
	- presence of a single coordinating body at the highest level; - project-based approach; - analysis of international best practices.
5	**Lack of e-legislation development**
	- mobilization of external experts; - consistency of regulations and retroactive implementation (as in the UK)

In addition, the majority of experts expressed the urgent need for international and regional cooperation in EGOV, joint activities towards integrated solutions and standards and also unified e-signature system.

5.5   Awareness about EGOV Development in CIS Countries

During the survey, experts were asked to list positive experiences of other CIS member countries in implementing EGOV and providing services through electronic channels. Most experts were aware with the experiences of Kazakhstan, Russia and

Moldova. The experts primarily listed the projects for developing state and municipal service web-portals development, an open data portal in Moldova, the creation of public access centers in Kazakhstan, efforts to harmonize the legislation in the field of electronic regulation, the implementation of a single portal of public services in Russia, and the project "Smart City" in Kazakhstan. The experts also mentioned E-Procurement web-portal in Kyrgyzstan, e-declaring system in Belarus, e-customs and open government projects in Ukraine, and mobile application for governmental services in Tajikistan. In addition to the initiatives in CIS region, the experts also highlighted some achievements of non-CIS post-Soviet countries such as eVoting and X-road in Estonia, standardized documentation centers in Georgia, and e-Justice in Lithuania. Most experts positively evaluated the idea of a unified e-signature system in the CIS as shown in Figure 2.

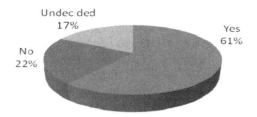

Fig. 2. Need for a unified e-signature system in the CIS

In support of this system experts listed the vast potential of e-commerce, simplification of migration and customs processes' registration. They argue that citizens could benefit from these e-services. The following statements were also highlighted: (i) not all of CIS member countries are equally prepared for this process; (ii) obstacles associated with proper policy decisions.

5.6   Mechanisms for Regional Cooperation on EGOV in CIS Countries

The experts suggested possible mechanisms for intergovernmental regional cooperation that could improve the implementation of EGOV programs in CIS countries. They include:

1. Creating a platform for knowledge sharing and experience exchange.
2. Defining regional strategies, policies, common information exchange standards, regional coordination structures to enable shared services in customs, border management, law enforcement, immigration, etc.
3. Establishing joint working groups for developing common IT solutions and platforms.
4. Implementing joint research and development projects on specific EGOV development issues.
5. Promoting regional public-private partnership, outsourcing, use of open source software and learning from private sector experience.

6. Organizing joint conferences and thematic forums as a platform for networking and knowledge sharing.
7. Facilitating a mutually beneficial exchange of scientific and technical information and documentation.
8. Promoting joint ventures, associations, companies and firms working on innovative solutions and development of new technologies.
9. Developing a regulatory framework for regional cooperation in EGOV and harmonizing national legislation.
10. Establishing joint framework for measuring and monitoring EGOV progress in CIS countries and benchmark studies.

5.7   CIS Countries in Global EGOV Studies

The development progress in utilizing ICTs in public administration and governance in CIS is different from country to country. Thus, according to the latest UN E-Government Development Index [35], Russia was rated in the world ranking as 27 out of 183, Kazakhstan – 38, Belarus – 31, Ukraine – 68, Moldova – 69, Uzbekistan – 91, Armenia – 94, Azerbaijan – 96, Kyrgyzstan – 99, Tajikistan – 122, and Turkmenistan – 126. Kazakhstan, particularly, has improved its global ranking by around eight positions in 2012 and became one of the top leaders in e-participation sharing with Singapore the second position. This was resulted from significant efforts in modernizing the public sector including technology-based reform of administrative governance systems. Russia became the leader in Eastern Europe advancing 32 positions in the world rankings. Moldova improved its ranking, started implementation of a Strategic Programme for Technological Modernization of the Government supported by the World Bank. The aim is ICT-enabled institutional reform to increase access to government information, improve public administration and services. Unfortunately Azerbaijan, Kyrgyzstan, Uzbekistan, and Turkmenistan were ranked lower than in the previous global UN EGOV ranking while Armenia and Tajikistan have not demonstrated significant improvements.

There are numerous factors influencing the EGOV progress in the region including the socio-economic situation, political instability, leadership, public administration reform, investment policies, regulation and legislation, institutional and human capacity, national culture, access to external funds, etc.

6   Discussions

This research shows that the level of EGOV development in CIS countries is not the same and highly dispersed. More developed countries, like Russia and Kazakhstan, demonstrate significant progress in implementing EGOV initiatives while governments in other CIS member countries are making slow progress. Based on the research findings, we can claim that the key barriers in EGOV development in CIS region are associated mostly with the lack of qualification and motivation among civil servants and weak support from top management. We believe that the greater attention must be paid to the development of institutional capacity and human re-sources in government agencies. We argue that capacity building programs on EGOV for civil servants in some CIS countries supported by the international organizations like UNDP, World Bank, and European Commission are not well coordinated and cannot be provided on a regular base. However, high quality educational programs delivered by the local academic institutions in collaboration with regional and interna-tional partners and probably supported by donor organizations at the initial phases would ensure sustainability of such programs and most importantly, systematic way of developing both institutional and human capacity in the public sector organizations.

Concerning communication channels for facilitating citizen's participation and democracy in CIS countries, the majority of experts pointed out social networking as the most preferred. Moreover, a large number of experts referred to social networking as in-demand communication channel between government agencies, citizens and businesses community. In this regard, rich experience of EU in exchanging expe-rience, good practices, and lessons learned from the projects as well as innovative solutions on e-services, e-participation, e-inclusion, e-democracy, etc through the e-Practice platform and its journal could be useful for facilitating EGOV development in the CIS region.

The intra-regional cooperation in EGOV strengthened by establishing joint work-ing groups, developing common policies, strategies, and standards, and implementing unified systems like e-signature, and supported by the partnership in developing ca-pacity of public sector workforce could help to overcome the barriers. CIS countries could learn from good practices and lessons from the regional cooperation in ICT-enabled government transformation in EU, Latin America, Southeast Asia, and MENA regions. Attention must be paid also on how to use the private sector's expe-rience in developing and delivering online services like, for example, secure Internet banking services or e-commerce transactions. As shown by the successful cooperation experiences in other countries, particularly, smaller and poorer countries should un-dertake regional EGOV alliances that would allow them to pool resources and gain greater efficiency at building their infrastructure. Such collective efforts give citizens in the region opportunity to find information or get services that cut across individual nations [36]. International cooperation experience and use of common standards and solutions should be a good example for developing EGOV in CIS region avoiding "the reinventing the wheel".

7   Conclusion

This exploratory study attempts to fill the gap in the literature about EGOV develop-ment trends in CIS countries providing a better understanding of current practices and key implementation problems. The research findings suggest that consolidated efforts of the countries in the region could facilitate the progress in EGOV implementation and help solve common problems and facilitate both integration and transition processes. Unfortunately, this study has some limitations in terms of the number of experts involved in the survey, representation from the government and non-government organizations, and also limited scope of the questionnaire. These limitations are directly related to the lack of resources for conducting more comprehensive research and funding mechanisms for such projects in CIS region. However, there is an urgent need to extend research on various aspects of EGOV implementation in CIS member countries through benchmark studies, comparative analysis and action research.

References

1. Materials of the 6th Meeting of the Working Group 2 on E-Government and Administrative Simplification (2010), http://www.oecd.org/mena/governance/6thmeetingoftheworkinggroup2one-governmentandadministrativesimplification.htm#Meeting
2. Customer- Centric E-Government. Modernizing the MENA Region's Public Sector. Booz Company Report (2009), http://www.booz.com/media/uploads/Customer-Centric_E-Government.pdf
3. Regional cooperation is an important tool for the development of e-government. eLAC2010 Monitoring (2010), http://www.cepal.org/cgi-bin/getProd.asp?xml=/socinfo/noticias/noticias/8/41578/P41578.xml&xsl=/socinfo/tpl-i/p1f.xsl&base=/socinfo/tpl-i/top-bottom.xsl
4. World Economic Situation and Prospects: UN Report (2013), http://www.un.org/en/development/desa/policy/wesp/wesp_current/wesp2013.pdf
5. Strejcek, G., Theil, M.: Technology push, legislation pull? E-Government in the European Union. Decision Support Systems 34, 305–313 (2002)
6. Chatrie, I., Wright, P.: Public strategies for the information society in the Member States of the European Union. DG Information society. Brussels (2000), http://ncsi-net.ncsi.iisc.ernet.in/cyberspace/nd/IS_Public_Strategies_update.pdf
7. Signore, O., Chesi, F., Pallotti, M.: E-Government: Challenges and Opportunities. In: Proceedings of the 19th Annual Conference CMG, Italy (2005)
8. Jaeger, P., Thompson, K.: E-government around the world: lessons, challenges, and future directions. Government Information Quarterly 20, 389–394 (2003)
9. Millard, G., Nielsen, M., Smith, S., Macintosh, A., Dalakiouridou, E., Tambouris, E.: D5.1a: eParticipation recommendations- first version. European participation consortium (2008), http://www.epractice.eu/files/ePractice-Journal-Volume-7.pdf
10. eGovernment for the people: eParticipation. European Commission (2008)
11. Joia, L.A.: Connecting the Americas through an E-Government capacity- building network. In: Proceedings of the Americas Conference on Information Systems, AMCIS, pp. 139–149 (2006)
12. Biasiotti, M.A., Nannucci, R.: Teaching e-Government in Italy. In: Traunmüller, R. (ed.) EGOV 2004. LNCS, vol. 3183, pp. 460–463. Springer, Heidelberg (2004)
13. Bjorvatn, K.: Third World regional integration. European Economic Review 43(1), 47–64 (1999)
14. Gupta, J.: Climate change and development cooperation: trends and questions. Current Opinion in Environmental Sustainability 1, 207–213 (2009)
15. Yoo, S.-H., Lee, J.-S.: Electricity consumption and economic growth: A cross-country analysis. Energy Policy 38(1), 622–625 (2010)

16. Park, Y.J.: Regime formation and consequence: The case of internet security in the East-Asia "Four Tigers". Government Information Quarterly 26(2), 398–406 (2009)
17. Navarra, D., Cornford, T.: Globalization, networks and governance: Researching global ICT programs. Government Information Quarterly 26, 35–41 (2009)
18. Nixon, P., Koutrakou, V., Rawal, R.: Understanding E-Government in Europe Issues and Challenges. Routledge, P.G. (ed.), p. 324 (2010)
19. Padget, J.: E-Government and E-Democracy in Latin America. IEEE Intelligent Systems 20(1), 94–96 (2005)
20. Holliday, I.: Building e-government in East and Southeast Asia: Regional rhetoric and national (in)action. Public Admin. Dev. 22, 323–335 (2002), doi:10.1002/pad.239
21. OECD, "Achievements in E-Government", in OECD, Progress in Public Management in the Middle East and North Africa: Case Studies on Policy Reform. OECD Publishing (2010), doi: 10.1787/9789264082076-12-en
22. Saidi, N., Yared, H.: eGovernment: Technology for Good Governance, Development and Democracy in the MENA countries. Published by The Economic Research Forum (2002)
23. Real life good practice cases, submitted by the ePractice members (2013), `http://epractice.eu/en/cases/`
24. European eGovernment Action Plan 2011-2015, `https://ec.europa.eu/digital-agenda/en/european-egovernment-action-plan-2011-2015`
25. ECLAC, Opportunities for regional cooperation and integration (2008), `http://www.eclac.org/publicaciones/xml/7/36907/Opportunities_regional_cooperation_integration_chapter_III.pdf`
26. UNESCAP, Meeting the challenges in an era of globalization by strengthening regional development cooperation (2004), `http://www.unescap.org/pdd/publications/regcoop/ch5.pdf`
27. Ching, H., Huang, K.: Using the Internet as a Catalyst for Asia-Pacific regional economic cooperation: an example of new Chinese networks. Technology in Society 20, 131–139 (1998)
28. Reddick, C.: Comparative E-Government. Springer (2010)
29. Strategic lines of the Regional Commonwealth in the field of Communications activities 2007-2012, `http://www.en.rcc.org.ru/index.php/rcc/strategic-lines-of-activities`
30. CIS Program of Long-term Cooperation for the Promotion of Information Society till 2015, `http://www.iacis.ru/eng/activities/long_term_plan/`
31. Bershadskaya, L., Chugunov, A., Trutnev, D.: Monitoring Methods of e-Governance Development Assessment: Comparative Analysis of International and Russian Experience. In: Gil-Garcia, J.R., Helbig, N., Ojo, A. (eds.) Proceedings of the 6th International Conference on Theory and Practice of Electronic Governance, ICEGOV 2012, pp. 79–82. ACM Press, New York (2012)
32. Conrad, J.: Limitations to Interdisciplinarity in Problem Oriented Social Science Research. The Journal of Transdisciplinary Environmental Studies 1(1) (2002)
33. Avouris, N., Dimitracopoulou, A., Komis, V.: On analysis of collaborative problem solving: an object- oriented approach. Computers in Human Behavior 19(2), 147–167 (2003)
34. Goldstein, H., Susmilch, C.: The problem-oriented approach to improving police service (1981), `http://www.popcenter.org/library/researcherprojects/DevelopmentofPOPVolI.pdf`
35. UNDESA, United Nations E-Government Survey (2012)
36. West, D.: Improving Technology Utilization in Electronic Government around the World (2008), `http://www.brookings.edu/research/reports/2008/08/17-egovernment-west`

The Synchronized Functional Project (SFP)
of Public Administration

Iván Futó

National Tax and Customs Administration
1054 Széchenyi u. 2, Hungary
futoivan@t-online.hu

Abstract. In the Public Administration (PA) a great number of projects are in late, their results are not the expected ones, participants consider them over administrated, and the work of employees participating in isn't transparent. The origin of most of these problems is the conflicting coexistence of the project organization and that of the highly hierarchical Institution of the Public Administration (functional organization).

In the paper a new project management method - the Synchronized Functional Project Management (SFPM) - is introduced which eliminates the above mentioned problems by mapping the activities of the project into the daily routine work of the Institution's functional units without setting up a project organization.

SFPM was successfully used in a project at the National Tax and Customs Administration (NTCA) when IT applications of the former Tax Office and that of Customs had to be integrated. During the project the majority of the tax and some of the large IT applications of the Customs were modified, more than 300 specialists were involved in the integration and more than 1100 activities were synchronized.

Keywords: project management, project, Public Administration, functional organization.

1   Introduction

Each profession has its own procedures how to proceed to achieve its goals. In the case of ICT - for the development of applications - the projects are the appropriate frames. Projects follow a given methodology described by the project management principles.

Software development methods basically could be characterized as **predictive** and **adaptive** methods.

Predictive methods focus on planning the future in "full" details (for e.g. the "waterfall" approach). A productive team announces exactly what features are planned for the entire duration of the development process. They look forward typically for more

A. Kő et al. (Eds.): EGOVIS/EDEM 2013, LNCS 8061, pp. 102–111, 2013.

than 3 months. The plan is derived from the original objectives, and productive teams have difficulty changing direction.

The most popular **adaptive methods** are the **agile** ones (for e.g. XP [1], FDD [2], Scrum [3]). An adaptive team will have difficulty describing what features are planned for the entire duration of the development process. Their planning looks forward for 3 months or less. Adaptive methods focus on easily adapting projects to frequent changes.

The National Tax and Customs Administration is a large functional organization [4], [12]. The reference project of this paper is the integration of the IT systems of the former Tax Office and that of Customs. This integration is mission critical and hundreds of specialists are involved in.

In [5], risk analysis is used to estimate the best matching use cases for predictive and agile methods. It is stated that if the functions are critical, the team size is large and the culture is centralized decision making, than the appropriate approach is the predictive one[1].

In our case it meant that the right method to be selected had to be a predictive and not an adaptive one.

According to PMBOK [4] projects in a functional organization generally do not cross the borders of the functional units of the organization.

However in our case we had to coordinate the work of several functional units of NTCA.

In Hungary the official project management method for the Public Administration is a tailored version of PRINCE – Projects in Controlled Environment [7]. Originally it was developed in 1986 by the Central Computer and Telecommunications Agency [8] which was part of HM Treasury and the centre of information systems policy in the British government. The method was further upgraded to PRINCE2. It is in use in the Public Administrations all over the world [9].

Earlier already the question arose, are the conventional project management methods fully adequate for the IT projects of the Public Administration [9]? At that time the problem was treated in detail, but no solution was given.

The aim of this paper is to introduce a new project management methodology – the Synchronized Functional Project Management (SFPM) – which was successfully used at the National Tax and Customs Administration (NTCA) during the integration of IT systems of the former Tax Office and that of Customs.

The notion Synchronized Functional Project (SFP) refers to the fact, that the method **synchronizes the activities** of the **functional units** of the institution. The units involved form the varying **virtual organization of SFP.** No parallel project organization is created.

In our reference project the majority of the former Tax Office and some of the large IT applications of the Customs were affected, more than 300 specialists were involved in the integration and more than1100 activities were synchronized.

---

[1] To be correct, several successful agile PA projects are mentioned in [6].

2   What are the Problems with the PRINCE-Like Projects?

At the first glance we can summarize the problems in the followings:

1. Rigid organizations working in parallel (Institution, project)
2. Competition for the human resources.
3. Problems in managing the "bolt from the blue" effects.

2.1   Rigid Organizations Working in Parallel (Institution, Project)

PRINCE and similar methodologies solve the task to be absorbed – the development of an application or system – by the creation of a well separated and well structured project organization.

The project decides about the task assignments, task execution, monitoring, controlling and deployment.

In the Project Initiation Document (PID) the structure and hierarchy of the project is defined, the participants are enumerated together with their duties and competences. For the participants the ratio of working in the project compared to their working hours is fixed.

In an appropriately working organization the IT applications have **owners**. The owner normally is a "business" department. In the paper we will call it also professional department in contrast to the IT departments.

Development, modification of an IT application is possible only if the owner department authorized or initialized it.

Even in the case of a green-field application it has an owner and the new application is to be deployed not in a vacuum, but in an already working environment. This will affect other applications, which should be modified and they also have their own owners.

In organizations having the above property the professional department and the ICT are in a **procurer – supplier** relation and only **ordered** activities could be performed.

The project organization interrupts this relationship, separating the professional and the IT departments, see Fig.1.

The contours of the project organization are marked with continuous lines.

The project develops its product – the application – within its scope, already receiving at advance all the necessary resources and competences and not obliged to ask permissions from the owners for modification of the concerned applications.

The project organization is well circumscribed and works rather independently inside the organization of the Institution, as it is shown on the figure above.

This is one of the reasons why the business considers the project that it goes outside of its scope of authority.

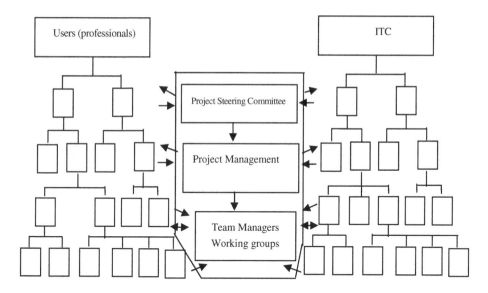

Fig. 1. Project organization inside the Institution [7]

2.2   Competition for the Human Resources

In the project organization, the Team Manager controls the work of a working team, the smallest unit of the project organization. The TM is responsible for a deliverable and for its delivery for due time. Then the Project Manager itself is responsible for all the deliverables of the project.

Consider first the case, when an already existing application should be re-designed and rewritten. In this case, the old applications also should be maintained, until the new applications are finished. Generally those IT people, who developed the original applications, are the best experts of the applications. That means they could be only partly dedicated to the project.

As the delegation is only partial, the team members also belong to a department of the organization. The result is that the team members have two "bosses", the Project Manager and the head of department.

This is what we call competition for the human resources between the organization and the project.

2.3   Problems in Managing the "Bolt from the Blue" Effects

Contrary to the private sector, managers in the Public Administration do not control totally the working of their Institution.

The government or the legislative in any moment can make decisions, even without any prior consultation, which affect the functioning of the Institution.

This intervention it is independent from the subjects, non predictable but deeply influences their work.

Naturally the market can also behave in a non predictable way, but important, sudden and frequent changes are rare.

Such changes generate hardly executable tasks for the business and the IT of the Institution because to be compliant to the regulations the necessary modifications of the IT applications should be performed within in a very short time limit.

These tasks generally have higher priority than the projects and as the Project or Team Leaders are not the head of departments owning the affected applications, they don't feel responsible for the project's deadlines and products. (They consider the Project Manager to be the primary responsible which is in principle true). The result is that they call back more easily their employee from the projects.

The result is that the project will lack of human resources, starts to be in late and cannot make an appropriate schedule for the deliverables.

3   The Synchronized Functional Project – SFP

As starting point we have to declare, that the organization of Public Administration's institutions is functional.

Functional structures are generally useful for big organizations. Employees within the functional structure are differentiated to perform a specialized set of tasks (in our case: declaration processing, audit, tax account management, etc.) This specialization leads to operational efficiencies where employees become specialists within their own realm of expertise. The problem is that communication within the institution is rather rigid, making the organization slow and inflexible.[12]

Functional structures are often characterized by large degree of formalization, making each function reliant on standard ways of operating. Decision-making power is centralized [12].

It is a well-known problem, how difficult to organize projects in a functional organization.

Generally such projects do not cross the border of a functional unit of the institution and the communication between functional units not under the supervision of the same executive is long and complicated [4].

Normally the role of a project organization is to dissolve this hierarchical obstacle, putting together the necessary competences to solve the given task.

However in the previous section of the paper we showed why the popular project management method – PRINCE – used by most of Public Administrations isn't really adequate for the functional environment of PAs.

In the next paragraphs a different method – Synchronized Functional Project Management (SFPM) – is introduced which better takes into account the specialties of functional organizations.

The notion Synchronized Functional Project (SFP) refers to the fact, that the method **synchronizes the activities** of the **functional units** of the institution. The units involved form the varying **virtual organization of SFP.**   No parallel project organization is created.

3.1   The Organization of SFP

A basic principle of the method is that each IT application should have an **owner**.

The second important pillar is that the "business" (profession) and the IT should be in **procurer – supplier** relation. This means that each modification in an application should be preceded by an **order** from the owner of the application.

Organizations not fulfilling in their everyday functioning the above conditions cannot use in its original form the SFP methodology.

The first step to start an SFP is the creation of a working team whose task is the preparation of a feasibility study. The feasibility study should contain a time schedule of the high level tasks which later will be worked out in detail.

When the feasibility study is ready, the next step is the appointment the 1st level (see later) members of the SFP organization.

Then the first task of the 1st level is to set up the 2nd level (see later) of the SFP.

The organization of the SFP - on the level of the Institution - is **basically a virtual** one:

1. The SFP doesn't have named participants only on the managing levels.
2. There are two managing levels:
   (a) The 1st is the level of **Management** (M). Here are present the managers – members of the management of the Institution - supervising the business and IT fields interested in the SFP - together with the **Chief-Coordinator** (Cc).   (The 1st level could be considered more or less to be similar to the PSC of PRINCE)
   (b) The 2nd is the level of **Operational Management** (OM) (more or less equivalent to the PM of PRINCE, but with stronger involvement). Here are the owners of the applications affected by the SFP. Also on this level we can find the **Operative Manager** (Om). He/she is the responsible for the coordination of business and IT activities of the SFP. His/her work is supported by the administrative team. Problems not solved on this level are escalated to the 1st level (this occurs very rarely).
3. The real work is done by the working teams (3rd **virtual** level). To the activities of the original scheduling, Team Managers are assigned. Basically they are the owners of the applications in question. The members of the teams will be the (business) experts and the IT specialists of the application. The organization of the teams and the creation of a detailed schedule of activities are the task of Team Managers.

Working teams are formed and dissolved when needed, depending on how the SFP advances. The teams have no pre-assigned members, but the formation of a stable core is possible.

Fig. 2. shows the place of SFP in the hierarchical structure of the Institution.

The parts with continuous line are fixed and defined in advance (1st and 2nd level), while the elements with dotted line contour are the virtual, dynamic ones.

The task of the administrative team, present in the fix part of the structure, is to follow and control the activities of the SFP by the use of a project management tool (MS
Project in our case).

The virtual part includes some of the elements of the Institution's structure (departments), whose activities are in connection with the SFP. The execution of these
activities **remains within the Institution's organization**, contrary to the PRINCE
based projects, where they are performed inside the project organization.

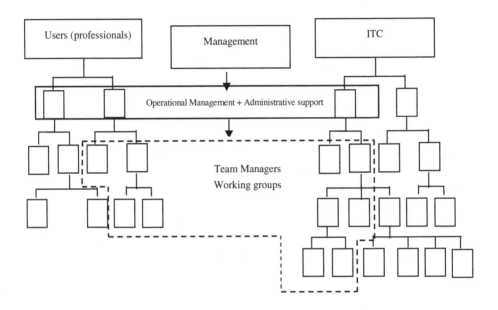

Fig. 2. The SFP in the hierarchical structure of the Institution

3.2   The Working Process of SFP

As it was already mentioned earlier that to set up an SFP first a working group is
formed whose task is to work out an initial feasibility study.

The feasibility study should contain a task list (activity list) with the expected
dead-lines. Naturally the study should be as detailed possible.

To the tasks of the feasibility study responsible departments – functional units - the
owners of the applications involved, are assigned. (The Task Managers will be the
representatives of the owner functional unit).

The Task Managers set up the appropriate working groups and they continue de-
composing the tasks to elementary units of actions. The resulted basic actions are
loaded into the project management tool. Their interdependencies are also defined and
treated there.

The elementary activities are executed by the functional units of the SFP **following
the daily routine** of the Institution.

The Operative Manager periodically, depending on the size and dead-lines of the SFP, receives status reports from the Team Leaders (every two weeks in our case).

Based on the status reports the schedule of the SFP is updated. The possible conflicts are resolved on the next status meeting. If it there is no consensus the problems are escalated to the 1st level (this is quite rare).

It can be seen that the SFP influences the daily routine of the Institution only by the **synchronization** of certain activities following the periodic status meetings.

At the first glance it seems that the coordinators responsible for the quality assurance and security are missing.

In reality they are present on the 2nd level. The Institution should have defined IT quality indicators and standards, and also it should have IT security regulation as well as departments supervising them. Leaders of these departments are members of the 2nd level and during the existence of the SFP their departments do they business as usual. It is possible to do so, because the everyday and usual modification of the IT system isn't done in the frame of projects. This means that there are procedures to handle these events routinely. In the case of the SFP these procedures should be followed too when the orders – products of the working groups - are sent by the owner departments to the IT.

The communication among the participants of the SFP is fully electronic.

The SFP has no Project Initiation Document (PID), only a short Regulation of a few pages. It defines the documents to be used, their locations, how could be they produced and accessed.

The maintenance of documents is the duty of the Administrative support.

The SFP is initiated by the formation of the working group responsible for the feasibility study and after by the nomination of the 1st level.

4   Conclusions

In the paper we shortly described a new project management method suitable for the Institutions of Public Administration (and in general for functional organizations). It was successfully used in the first phase of the integration of IT systems of the former Tax Office and that of Customs at the National Tax and Customs Administration (Hungary).

In the SFP practically all the large applications of the former Tax Office and some of the Customs were modified or canceled, more than 1100 activities were synchronized and controlled, the number of participants was over 300.

The summary of differences between the PRINCE like projects and that of the SFP is given bellow.

4.1   The Question of Responsibility

In the case of a traditional project, the accomplishment of the project's goals is the responsibility of the Project Manager and the Team Managers.

In the SFP certainly the (Chief)Coordinator is the ultimate responsible for the success, but his/her responsibility is immediately broken down to the owners of the applications. It isn't the same situation when the owners of the applications are members of the Project Steering Committee (no direct responsibility). It is very rare that the owners of the applications are at the same time the Team Leaders in a traditional project.

In the case of projects in the Public Administration it is always a problem the accountability of the employees delegated into the project. When, and for what extent they should be available for the project and for the everyday tasks.

In the case of SFP the work of the participants gets into their everyday routine activities, as the task accomplished by them is part of the duties of their bosses.

Everybody works as if the SFP didn't exist. As a consequence, the owner of the application at the same time responsible for the tasks related to his/her application. The allocation of human resources to the SFP or to the daily routine tasks depends on his/her decision.

4.2   The Place of a SFP in the Structure of the Institution

The second important difference is that the organization of the SFP is not separated from the organization of the Institute.

The SFP exists only **on the level of coordination** (synchronization of the activities); its functioning gets into the everyday work of the Institution.

4.3   Communication and Documentation

The third difference is that communication and documentation is limited to the minimum.

The most important difference however is that leaders participating in the SFP feel that they should spend as much energy to the SFP as they think to be appropriate within their competence and duties.

They don't have to "battle" with responsibles of another organization that is of the project.

References

1. Beck, K., Andres, C.: Extreme Programming Explained: Embrace Change, 2nd edn. Addison-Wesley Professional (November 2004)
2. Palmer, S.R., Felsing, M.: A Practical Guide to Feature-Driven Development. Pearson Education (2001)
3. Schwaber, K., Beedle, M.: Agile Software Development with Scrum. Prentice Hall PTR, Upper Saddle River (2001)
4. PMI: PMBOK A Guide to Project Management Body of Knowledge, Project Management Institute, USA (2004)
5. Turner, B., Turner, R.: Balancing Agility and Discipline: A Guide for the Perplexed. Addison-Wesley Longman Publishing Co., Inc., Boston

6. Wernham, B.: Agile Project Management for Government, Maitland and Strong (2012)
7. Molnár B: Projektirányítás módszertana (PRINCE), Budapest (1997)
8. CCTA: PRINCE Project in Controlled Environment, NCC Blackwell (1990)
9. Buttrick, R.: PRINCE2 and the National and International Standards, The Stationery Office (2012)
10. Futó, I.: Are the traditional IT PM-methods fully adequate for the Public Sector? IPMA. World Congress on Project Management, Budapest, June 19-20 (2004)
11. OGCIO: Practitioner Guide On Prince [G38] Version : 3.10 Office of the Government Chief Information Officer, Government of the Hong Kong Special Administrative Region (January 2012)
12. http://www.businessmate.org/Article.php?ArtikelId=184

Transparency and Social Control via the Citizen's Portal: A Case Study with the Use of Triangulation

Lislaine Krupek Braz de Oliveira and Cristiano Maciel

Universidade Federal de Mato Grosso – Av. Fernando Correa da Costa, 2367,
Boa Esperança – Cuiabá – MT – Brazil
cmaciel@ufmt.br, lis.kk@hotmail.com

Abstract. Public transparency is made evident by the dissemination of the acts practiced by the Public Administration, aiming at social control and at citizens' participation. As provided in Art. 37 of the Constitution of the Federative Republic of Brazil, "Public Administration must follow the principles of lawfulness, impersonality, morality, publicity and efficiency" [5]. Faced with such principles, our aim is to verify the perception of municipal managers, software developers and citizens concerning the transparency and the control of public accounts via the Citizen's Portal of the State of Mato Grosso (Brazil), comparing data in a triangular way. For this, a comprehensive review of the literature in the area is made, as well as the collection and qualitative analysis of data with the use of the triangulation method, which allowed comparison of the opinions of the subjects involved in the research.

Keywords: Public Accounts, Transparency, Citizen Portal, Social Control, Citizens.

1 Introduction

Public accounts, in public administration, are represented by a set of accounting, financial and budgetary data and information, making their dissemination and publication necessary for society to follow the investment of public resources. This dissemination is what allows the transparency of public spending.

For the CGU ("Office of the Federal Controller General"), "public resources are a set of the assets and rights composing the public assets, such as money, estates (hospital and school buildings), vehicles, tables and chairs, etc" [12].

The control of public accounts in Mato Grosso (Brazil) can be electronically conducted via the Citizen's Portal. However, the question is whether the portal actually provides citizens with transparency, ease of use and clarity in the dissemination of public accounts, being satisfactory to citizens. In this context, the work mentioned proposes to verify the perception of municipal managers, software developers and citizens concerning the transparency and the control of public accounts via the Citizen's Portal of the State of Mato Grosso using triangulation to compare data.

A. Kő et al. (Eds.): EGOVIS/EDEM 2013, LNCS 8061, pp. 112–124, 2013.

The research conducted comprehends an inductive data survey and qualitative research. As a case study, the Municipal Government of Nova Mutum was used in 2011 having as a base the information available at the Citizen's Portal, accessed by means of the site of the Mato Grosso State Audit Court. So as to widen the research, questionnaires were applied by population sampling in Nova Mutum, and interviews were made with municipal managers and a software manager. The triangulation method was utilized for data analysis.

After this introduction, this article presents the methodology, a brief theoretical referential based on a bibliographical survey, the analysis of the field research data and the presentation of the results obtained in the study followed by the conclusions.

1.1   Methodology

This research is composed of two stages, the first of which is a bibliographical and experimental survey and the second is a qualitative and triangulational analysis of data from a case study.

For the case study, from the Municipal Government of Nova Mutum in 2011, the basis was the digitalized public account auditing system (APLIC), accessible on the website of the Mato Grosso State Audit Court (TCE-MT, www.tce.mt.gov.br).

For the population sample, 300 questionnaires were applied which represents 1% of the population of this municipality. The sampling method used was probable random including representatives from a variety of locations in the town with information from different classes and social levels.

Individual interviews were held with the municipal manager and software manager using a non-structured interview enabling the interviewees to speak freely on the topic. For the case study a data triangulation method was used which integrates the combination and cross-referencing of a variety of points of view to obtain better understanding of the problem to be researched.

Triangulation is a qualitative research procedure that uses a technique that contrasts different sources, perspectives and circumstances of data collection of the same phenomenon. The aim of triangulation is not to replicate results but to check the validity of the results collected by verifying the consistency and coherence of different interpretations [29]. Therefore, to conclude the survey of transparency and control of public accounts, data triangulation becomes a necessity. According to Denzin [16], "data triangulation" refers to the collection of data from different sources whereby one possibility is the use of different individual opinions, as adopted in this study.

The data triangulation was divided into three important categories: interviews with the municipal manager, interview with the software manager and the application of the 300 questionnaires to citizens. The results of this study enabled visualization of how the citizens check on the public authorities and if the tools for such checking meet the objectives of the public authority in terms of citizens` dissemination and participation in the application of public resources

2   Transparency of Public Accounts

What is "transparency"? Rosendorff and Vreelandde (2006, p.06) "define transparency as the dissemination of regular and accurate information. Simply put, a transparent political regime is one that provides accurate information about itself, its operations, and the country as a whole, or permits that information to be collected and made available". [26]

Through its pioneering surveys in recent years, the Transparency International (TI) has tried to gauge the extent of corruption in different countries, identify Government departments where corruption appears to be most rampant, and establish some reasons why it seems to grow.

Two major factors that contribute to the growth of corruption are the low probability of discovery, and perceived immunity against prosecution. Secrecy in government, restrictions on access to information by citizens and the media, ill defined/complex and excessive rules, procedures and regulations can all lead to a low chance of discovery. A lack of transparency in the functioning of the government agencies can make it easy for the perpetrators to cover their tracks and unearthing corruption becomes very difficult [9].

Transparency and the right to access government information are now internationally regarded as essential to democratic participation, trust in government, prevention of corruption, informed decision-making, accuracy of government information, and provision of information to the public, companies, and journalists, among other essential functions in society [3].

Public spending transparency is an essential factor for strengthening the relationship between society and public managers. The disseminated information must be clear, understandable and easy to access.

On this topic, the CGU says "It is every public entity's duty to clearly inform the population on how it spends money (the budget) and to render accounts of their acts. This information has to be provided in clear language that can be understood by citizens in a simple way. Likewise, public entities must stimulate popular participation in the discussion of the strategies used to put public policies into practice, in the elaboration of their planning and of their budgets" [11].

It can be argued however that transparency not only incorporates the rather passive right of every citizen to have access to information (if they activate that formal legal right) but also the much broader and more pro-active duty of the administration itself to ensure that information about its policy and actions is provided in an accessible fashion [15]. Moreover, the stimulus to public transparency must be one of Public Administration goals, once it contributes to strengthening democracy, valuing and developing citizens, as provided in LRF 101/2000.

For this, the Fiscal Responsibility Law establishes public finance standards directed towards responsibility in fiscal management, Public Administration being incumbent with abiding by the goals and constraints provided in Art. 1, and detailed in its § 1: "Fiscal management responsibility presupposes planned and transparent actions, in which risks are prevented and deviations capable of affecting the balance of public accounts are corrected, in compliance with result goals between revenues and expenses and by obeying constraints and conditions concerning waiver of revenues, generation of expenses with personnel, of social security and others, consolidated and bond debts, credit operations, including those for deferred revenue, guarantee granting and inclusion in Amounts to be Paid" [4].

However, it is crucial that Public Administration publishes and disseminates its public acts, promoting popular participation in public spending control, requiring the adequate use of the collected resources deriving from taxes, fees and services, making Public Administration transparent in function of a democratic society.

The CGU clarifies that, "The government should provide citizens with the possibility of understanding the management mechanisms, so that they can influence the decision-making process. The citizens' access to simple and understandable information is the starting point for greater transparency" [11].

According to Shah and Schacter, "Increasing transparency can strengthen the lines of accountability between government and citizens. When citizens are informed about government performance, they are in a better position to put pressure on public officials to perform their duties in the public interest." [27]

The LRF states that "Fiscal management transparency instruments imply the wide dissemination of public documents, including electronic means of access for citizens. Moreover, the use of the Internet and of information and communication technology, favors the improvement of public services rendered, providing the interaction of citizens with the Electronic Government, increasing the transparency of public accounts" [4]. The concept of Electronic Government (e-Gov), in the view of Maciel, is "the use of Information and Communication Technologies to meet citizens' needs of obtaining information (it makes the presentation of government information viable)" [20].

As well as this, there is also the "concept of Open Government Data (OGD) which includes all the information produced, archived and distributed by government organizations, published on the internet in open and primary formats in a non-proprietary, full and non-discriminatory way, free of licensing and accessible both to citizens and computers." [22]. According to Karna, "Open Government is to be seen in the context of citizens' rights: the right to actively participate in the process of agenda-setting and decision-making". [19]

Certainly, in order to have an effective exercise of social control, it is necessary that all citizens have access to the information. However, both parties must be committed to making this control of public resources, once, if the government makes information available, citizens are incumbent with looking for them and using them in their ambit.

3   Information Systems

So as to meet the needs of Public Administration, information systems are in increasing evolution. The demand for more complete software that meet the requirements imposed by laws and by the supervising bodies, leads to investment in the Electronic Government are, aiming at greater social control.

Maciel et al point out that "Electronic Government fundamentally means the strategies used by the government for using Information and Communication Technologies (ICTs) resources, with the intention of modernizing the administrative apparatus and of meeting citizens' needs" [21].

Current Information and Communication Technologies (ICTs) have made it possible to enhance traditional participation procedures by electronic means, introducing in this way the concept of electronic Participation (eParticipation). eParticipation "refers to efforts to broaden and deepen political participation by enabling citizens to connect with one another, with civil servants, and with elected representatives using ICTs". [25]

It is worth emphasising that the technological tools must provide citizens with easy and rapid interaction, enabling the public to contribute to the definition of how public resources are applied, as stated by Anjos and Ezequiel: "The use of new technologies by public administration may allow for an uncontestable opening of the state to the general public widening access to the digitalized databases. Access to these databanks to obtain information and services directly, without intermediaries, can be considered an important contribution to exercising of citizenship. However, obtaining access does not mean understanding the information obtained"[2].

The use of technology can contribute positively to the dissemination and guidance given to citizens providing usability methods are implemented that facilitate the use of the information by citizens as according to the following author:

"Usability is a quality attribute related to the easiness of using something. More specifically, it refers to the quickness with which users can learn to use something, their efficiency in using them, how much they remember of it, their degree of propensity to errors and how much they like to use it" [23]. Custodio adds that, "Usability can be understood as a capacity, in human functional terms, of a system to be used easily and efficiently by the user" [14]. Maciel et al (2005) corroborate this statement, ratifying that "usability is traditionally associated with the attributes: easiness of use, easiness of learning, memorability, user's satisfaction, productivity and flexibility" [20]. Therefore, it is found that web information systems have to provide ease of use, clarity and comprehensibility of the information available, aiming at citizens' participation and interaction with the government.

3.1   The Audit Court and the Citizen's Portal

The Mato Grosso State Audit Court is a public institution of external control accounting for inspecting the legality, legitimacy and economics of public spending deriving from the State or from the Municipalities that have to render accounts about public spending [24].

In accordance with Organic Law 269/2007, of the Mato Grosso State Audit Court, in articles 35 and 36, inspection has the aim of verifying the legality, legitimacy, efficiency and economy of administrative acts in general as well as compliance with fiscal management norms in order to ensure effective external control and to instruct trials within the ambit of the court. The activities of organs and entities that come under the jurisdiction of the Audit Court will be inspected selectively and concomitantly based on information obtained from official press sources, audits and inspections, and reports and complaints [8].

The TCE-M's vision is "To be acknowledged in society as an essential and referential institution for the external control of the management of public resources". The TCE-MT's external control actions are guided by technical areas (exercised by the Court), internal areas (exercised by public administrators) and social areas. The latter refers to the active participation of society in the management of public resources based on constitutional and infra-constitutional fundaments that offer administrations some reflection on the values that are behind the running of the institution in the view of those being inspected and especially that of society, such as: commitment, ethics, transparency, quality, agility and innovation.

The CGU states that "the State Audit Courts conduct verifications and audits, on their own initiative or as proposed by the Prosecution Office, besides examining and judging the regularity of the state and municipal public managers' accounts" [11].

In order to strengthen itself institutionally, the TCE-MT has sought to widen its channels of communication with the entities being inspected, citizens, partners, NGOs, civil and organised society and others. The aim of this is to distribute information in order to encourage citizens to exercise their citizenship.

Among its actions, bearing in mind the need for greater control of public management, the State Audit Court developed a computerized system denominated Digitalized Public Accounts Auditing (APLIC), aimed at conveying the rendering of accounts via internet in a fast and easy way, aiding the timely inspections of public acts.

According to the Audit Court, the Digitalized Public Accounts Auditing (APLIC) aims to strengthen the constitutional role, widening its work of external control and contributing to the strengthening of the internal controls of those under the court's jurisdiction." [24].

The Digitalized Accounts system was developed to enable internet transmission of all the information that is of public interest including: financial and accounting statements, budgets, bidding processes, public contests and personnel acts. All of these are published for citizens on the Citizen's Portal in compliance with the Law on Access to Public Information no. 12.527/2011 of 18th November 2011 [7].

According to Occar et al. "accountability: the appropriate open datasets properly mashed up can provide several views on information about the performance of the government to achieve its public policy goals" [1]. Thus, the Citizen's Portal provides citizens with a follow up of public acts, making it possible to assess whether the initial goals proposed by the Public Administration are being attained by Municipal managers.

4   Case Study

The results obtained from the survey will be presented according the research methodological proposal, considering the analysis of the information obtained in the interviews with municipal managers about the dissemination and transparency of public accounts; the analysis of the survey data together with the software managers; and the analysis of the data obtained from the survey with citizens. Lastly, the triangulated data are analyzed according to the categories proposed in this study.

4.1   Municipal Managers

By means of the information collected in the interviews with two municipal managers, it is possible to verify the perception and understanding about the dissemination and the transparency of public accounts via Digitalized Public Accounts Auditing. It is worth stressing that the two municipal managers believe that the State Audit Court does not properly guide the Public Administration, demands a lot and provides little information on how to act so that the managing unit can meet the expectations of the inspection body.

The Digitalized Public Accounts Public model was developed to guide and strengthen the constitutional role, expanding the work of external control and contributing to strengthening the internal control of those under its authority [24].

For manager one, the inspection of public spending is positive to public administration as it prevents errors from being committed in the future. In turn, manager two points out that inspection partially prevents errors or irregularities from occurring, as the rendering of accounts take long to occur.

Dropa adds clarification: "Transparency is the only way of preventing certain public administration acts from being corrupted or masked, allowing the population to know how their representatives are operating the public machine, and whether they abide by the basic principles of honesty, impartiality, legality and loyalty" [17].

However, for the public managers, the information provided in the Citizen's Portal is transparent, yet difficult to be understood by citizens, as it is technical information and its interpretation depends on specific knowledge about the accounting area.

Dropa states that "information technology is a great ally of the citizen's in this process, offering innumerable possibilities to facilitate access to information"[17].

Furthermore, the two managers believe that by having an effective social control, citizens should follow up public accounts and give opinions on them. Yet, they lack guidance as to how to access this information, or when they access such information it is not clear or understandable.

The CGU adds that it is the municipal government's duty to clearly inform the population about how public money is spent [10].

It should be emphasized that the Digitalized Public Accounts Auditing, in the conception of manager one, has made processes more difficult due to adaptation, since before the implementation of the on-line auditing modality, the municipal government used to send the balance sheets via post, and had the opportunity of checking the information before sending.

Currently in electronic media, there are many flaws in the management systems, which implies sending inconsistent information.

Also, in the view of manager two, the implementation of the on-line auditing facilitated the work routine with the use of layout and norms, allowing clearness and improving the performance of functions in each department.

It is worth stressing that the information systems used by the municipal government are constantly updated, yet, the software updating does not manage to timely follow the constant changes in rules specified in layout made available by the TCE-MT. Therefore, the Software manager's views on the same topics as those of the municipal managers were sought, as seen as follows.

4.2   Software Manager

Considering the interview conducted with the representative of the software company for the public area, responsible for keeping the systems updated with versions that meet the TCE-MT requirements, it is possible to understand the difficulties met by the company in its search for fast and effective solutions.

As states the software manager, "the timely inspection and dissemination of public accounts allow greater transparency, contributing to social control, as the inspection via an on-line system makes its execution easier; should there be irregularities in the public acts, it loses its balance".

Dropa says that, "Social control has to be exercised so that the community is aware that the public administrator actions are being conducted abiding by the law" [17]. The manager stresses "that the Audit Court requirements allowed greater control on public administration, ordering public processes, mainly in the purchase and in the competitive bidding sector, since prior to this goods and services were purchased and hired and only then would the acts be regularized; with the auditing implementation, information is timely, that is, it has to be legalized at the moment of purchasing or of hiring services".

As ensured by the provisions of Bidding Law, and detailed in its Art. 14, "no purchase will be made without the adequate characterization of its object and indication of the budgetary resources for its payment, under the penalty of nullifying the act and making the person who has caused it to account for the deed" [6].

Moreover, according to the manager "so as to meet the Public Administration needs, the information systems have to be improved concerning the control on estates, stock, vehicles and on the planning of the PPA, LDO, LOA goals; at the moment, the software company lacks tools to effect these controls". Nonetheless, the software manager "believes that any citizen sufficient skills to access and to interpret the information available in the Internet, since the Internet is at anyone's reach, but they just lack the interest to research the information available".   •

We then resorted to the citizens' opinions in an attempt to identify whether the social control is being exerted by means of the visualization of the public information in the Citizen's Portal.

4.3   Citizens

To complete the data analysis, 300 citizens' opinions were collected, representing 1% of the Nova Mutum population in 2011.

The survey conducted used sampling with random collection of public opinion due to it being impossible to expand the survey globally. Therefore, information was analyzed from different social classes and education levels ensuring data collection from all representatives of the population.

Public participation in the control of public accounts via the Citizen's Portal can be seen by the results obtained in the survey. In relation to the citizen's profile, the survey achieved 66% participation by women and 34% by men.

From this survey, it was found that half of the citizens interviewed had an intermediate level of knowledge and skill in computer use and the internet which was a positive result for this survey bearing in mind the main focus of the study is public participation in the inspection of public accounts via the Digitalized Accounts System.

Yet, this number drops in relation to the use of technological means to access the information available in the Citizen's Portal; only 23% of those surveyed know the Citizen's Portal, access the information disseminated and use it to follow up on their municipal manager's actions. Graph 1, as follows, shows the reasons that make

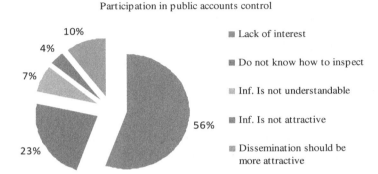

Fig. 1. Research data, year

citizens fail to participate in public accounts control, causing the small number of accesses to the information by society. The full analysis of the citizens' data can be found in [30].

Hence, by means of the survey, most citizens were found to not be the targets of this knowledge, as they cannot follow or understand the information available in the Citizen's Portal. "One overall responsibility is to ensure the fundamental right as democracy, openness and transparency, privacy and to improve citizen's quality of life" [18]. Therefore, such data deserve the implementation of a public policy that puts the citizen in the role of the main player. Due to the richness of the data obtained via the survey with citizens, the data were detailed by the authors.

5   Triangulation

The analysis of results by means of data triangulation will be performed under the three important categories identified in the speech of the three types of subjects investigated, that is, understandability of public statements; citizens' interest in controlling public accounts; and the usability of information systems. According to Cohen et al, "Triangulation is an attempt to map out, or explain more fully, the richness and complexity of human behavior by studying it from more than one standpoint, by using quantitative and qualitative data" [13].

5.1   Understandability of Public Statements

The understandability of public statements is of paramount relevance for social control, aiming at the popular participation in the control of the actions performed by public managers.

According to the two municipal managers, the information must be clearer and more understandable, facilitating citizens' understanding, regardless of their knowledge or skills. In this sense, it was found that 71% of the citizens consider that the information available on the Citizen's Portal makes use of technical terms, making it impossible to understand that information. In turn, the software manager believes that the information available in the Citizen's Portal is easy to understand and it allows citizens to interact with the municipal government. This opinion may be due to the high digital literacy level the manager has.

In general, it is found that it is necessary to improve the information available in the Citizen's Portal, making it more attractive and more easily understandable by society, by developing statements that allow easy and clear interpretation of the information published, using, for example, graphs, glossaries and explanatory notes.

5.2   Citizens' Interest in Public Accounts Control

According to municipal manager one, "citizens are not able to understand the information published, as it is technical information" and depend on specific knowledge about the accounting area. Again, municipal manager two "believes that it is important for citizens to follow up public acts, but they lack guidance on how to access this information".

Further, the software manager "believes that citizens are fully exercising their citizenship, being capable of accessing and of understanding the information available". Nevertheless, 56% of the citizens interviewed were found not to have an interest in inspecting public acts, as many of them are untrusting of public policies, or do not trust the data available, believing that the transparency programs only generate more expenses, since they do not reach their main target, "the citizens". Therefore, the need for the Public Administration to stimulate popular participation is evident, to show that all citizens are inspectors, and should participate in the control of public accounts.

In turn, citizens have to participate and to demand better results in the allocation of public resources, which is a vital factor for public control and transparency.

5.3   Information Systems Usability

According to the two managers "it is important for the citizens to manage to access the information available with ease; nonetheless, it is worth stressing that the two managers consider that the Audit Court information systems do not provide ease of use for those accessing it".

The software manager states that "the citizen portal information system provides citizens with ease of use". It should be stressed that, in the manager's understanding, all citizens, regardless of their knowledge and skills, are able to access and to interpret the information available.

However, 49% of the citizens who know the Citizen's Portal consider that the system does not provide ease of use, since they believe that the site is confusing, causes queries and difficulties in the search for the required information.

Hence, it can be said that improvements in the Citizen's Portal information systems are required, with the aim of achieving easy and fast access by citizens, providing the required social control and public transparency.

In this sense, the recommendation is that inspections and usability tests are conducted in the systems, using acknowledged techniques in the area, so as to provide improvements in the citizens' use of these systems [23].

6   Conclusion

The citizen's portal of the Mato Grosso State Audit Court is an instrument that aims to guarantee citizens' rights, as it allows public managers' actions to be followed up by all citizens, thus ensuring the government constitutionality and transparency.

The correct allocation of public resources and the dissemination of public information is crucial, not only to meet the legislation in force, but to be accessible to all citizens who have the right to know how public money is being used. In this sense, the use of computational resources for such end is beneficial to society. According to the research data, the public body effort to promote the dissemination and to provide publicity to public acts before society, aiming at the transparency in public accounts is perceptible. Yet, the effort is not resulting in a real profit from the data by society, according to the data collected in the interviews with both managers and citizens.

By means of triangulation, it was also noticed that the way in which systems have been developed, from the interfaces and from the information visualization point of view, has even more hindered citizens to understand data. It is thus found that the dissemination of public accounts via web information systems still has to undergo improvements. In this sense, Public Administration must implement new techniques for disseminating public acts, aiming at better results of interaction between citizens and the Electronic Government. Social networks nowadays exert a strong power of acceptance by society; with this in mind, such social networks can be used positively so as to stimulate social participation, thus contributing to better public transparency.

According to Shneiderman "The dramatic success of social medias, such as Facebook, Twitter, YouTube, blogs and discussion groups enables individuals to become active in local and global communities" [28]. Here, information sharing is a powerful communication resource among users, and may be useful in relation to dissemination and discussion of public issues.

It is hence necessary to expand studies directed to electronic government, in terms of its usability in websites, social interaction between citizens and government and means to make public transparency effective.

There is, therefore, a great challenge for countries due to the lack of training of the development teams in terms of methodologies and techniques and the public are not ready to deal with the large amount of information made available by the state making it difficult to identify what is relevant and how this can be better presented to citizens.

Acknowledgement. We would like to thank the Information Technology Project at Mato Grosso State Audit Court (TCE-MT) and UFMT/UNISELVA for all the support to develop and publish this research.

References

[1]   Accar, S., Alonso, J., Novak, K. (eds.): Improving Access to Government through Better Use of the Web. W3C Interest Group (2009), Disponível em: http://www.w3.org/TR/egov-improving (access February 04, 2013)

[2]   Anjos, G.M.A.A., de Castro Ezequiel, V.: Cidadania Virtual: O espetáculo do Governo Eletrônico (2011) (in Portuguese), Disponível em: http://seer.fclar.unesp.br/estudos/article/view/3887/3569 (access February 08, 2013)

[3]   Bertot, J.C., Jaeger, P.T., Grimes, J.M.: Government Information Quarterly. Using ICTs to create a culture of transparency: E-government and social media as apenness and anti-corruption tools for societies, pp. 264–271. Elsevier (2010)

[4]   Brasil. Lei Complementar n° 101, de 4 de maio de 2000. Estabelece normas de finanças públicas voltadas para a responsabilidade na gestão fiscal (in Portuguese), Disponível em: http://www.planalto.gov.br/ccivil/leis/lcp/lcp101.htm (access February 20, 2012)

[5]   Brasil. Constituição. Constituição da República Federativa do Brasil: promulgada em 5 de outubro de 1988 (1988) (in Portuguese), Disponível em: http://www.planalto.gov.br/ccivil_03/Constituicao/Constitui%C3%A7ao.htm (access January 28, 2012)

[6]   Brasil. Lei n° 8.666, de 21 de junho de 1993. Estabelece normas gerais sobre licitações e contratos administrativos pertinentes a obras, serviços, inclusive de publicidade, compras, alienações e locações no âmbito dos Poderes da União, dos Estados, do Distrito Federal e dos Municípios (in Portuguese), Disponível em: https://www.planalto.gov.br/ccivil_03/leis/l8666cons.htm (access November 01, 2011)

[7]   Brasil. Lei Complementar n° 12.527, de 18 de novembro de 2011. Regula o acesso a informações (in Portuguese), Disponível em: http://www.planalto.gov.br/ccivil_03/_ato2011-2014/2011/lei/l12527.htm (access June 03, 2013)

[8]   Brasil. Lei Complementar n° 269/2007, atualizada até janeiro de 2013. Dispõe sobre a Lei Orgânica do Tribunal de Contas do Estado do Mato Grosso (in Portuguese), Disponível em: http://jurisdicionado.tce.mt.gov.br/legislacao?categoria=4 (access June 05, 2013)

[9]   Bhatnagar, S.: Transparency and Corruption: Does E-Government Help? (2003), Disponível em: http://unpan1.un.org/intradoc/groups/public/documents/unpan/unpan035963.pdf (access February 01, 2013)

[10] Controladoria Geral da União. Olho Vivo no dinheiro público. 1ª ed. Brasília (2009) (in Portuguese)

[11] Controladoria Geral da União. Controle Social – orientações aos cidadãos para participação na gestão pública e exercício do controle social. 2° ed. Brasília, p. 17 (2010) (in Portuguese)

[12] Controladoria Geral da União. Recursos Públicos (2011) (in Portuguese), Disponível em: http://www.portalzinho.cgu.gov.br/sala-de-leitura/glossario/recursos-publicos (access November 01, 2011)

[13] Cohen, L., Manion, L.: Métodos de Investigación Educativa. Triangulación. Editorial La Muralla, Madrid (1990)

[14] Custodio, D.M.: Usabilidade na web: o usuário como agente-facilitador no desenvolvimento de interfaces de home pages. Bauru, 106f. Dissertação (Mestrado em Desenho Industrial) - Universidade Estadual Paulista (2007) (in Portuguese)

[15] Curtin, D., Meijer, A.J.: Does transparency strengthen legitimacy? A critical analysis of European Union policy documents, pp. 109–122. IOS Press (2006)

[16] Denzin, N.K.: The Research Act. Prentice Hall, Englewood Cliffs (1989)

[17] Dropa, R.F.: Transparência e Fiscalização na Administração Pública. Revista âmbito jurídico (in Portuguese), Disponível em: http://www.ambito-juridico.com.br/site/index.php?n_link=revista_artigos_leitura&artigo_id=3917 (access November 01, 2011)

[18] Jansen, A.: The Understanding of ICTs in Public Sector and Its Impact on Governance. In: Scholl, H.J., Janssen, M., Wimmer, M.A., Moe, C.E., Flak, L.S. (eds.) EGOV 2012. LNCS, vol. 7443, pp. 174–186. Springer, Heidelberg (2012)

[19] Karna, S.R.: The Largest Democracy (India) Poised for Eletronic Government and Electronic Democracy. In: CeDEM 2012, Conference for E-Democracy and Open Government, Austria (2012)

[20] Maciel, C., Nogueira, J.L.T., Garcia, A.C.B.: g- Quality: um método para avaliação da qualidade dos sítios de e-Gov. In: VIII Escola de Informática do SBC – centro-oeste, Cuiabá. SUCESU-MT. PAK Multimídia, Cuiabá (2005) (in Portuguese)

[21] Maciel, C., Garcia, A.C.B., Roque, L.: E-Democracy: Concepts, Experiences and Challenges. In: Herrmann, P (Org.) Democracy in Theory and Action, pp. 51–92. Nova Science Publishers, Inc., New York (2010)

[22] Maciel, C., Filho, J.V., Breitman, K.: Governo Brasileiro no Futuro. Transparência Pública e Dados Abertos Governamentais. Cubzac editora, São Paulo (2012) (in Portuguese)

[23] Nielsen, J., Loranger, H.: Usabilidade na web: projetando websites com qualidade, 409 p. Elsevier, Rio de Janeiro (2007) (in Portuguese)

[24] Portal do Tribunal de Contas do Estado do Mato Grosso (in Portuguese), Disponível em: http://www.tce.mt.gov.br/ (access October 28, 2011)

[25] Panopoulou, E., Tambouris, E., Tarabanis, K.: European Journal of ePractice - eParticipation initiatives: How is Europe progressing? p. 16 (2009), Disponível em: http://www.epractice.eu/journal (access November 28, 2012)

[26] Rosendorff, P.B., Vreeland, J.R.: Democracy and data Dissemination: The Effect of Political Regime on Transparency (2006), Disponível em: https://ncgg.princeton.edu/IPES/2006/papers/Rosendorff_Vreeland_S200_2.pdf (access February 11, 2013)

[27] Shah, A., Schacter, M.: Combating Corruption: Look Before You Leap. A lack of progress in eradicating corruption could be due to misguided strategies, Disponível em: http://www.12iacc.org/archivos/WS_6.2_CLIFF_ANWAR_SHAH_AND_MARK_SCHACTER.pdf (access January 30, 2013)

[28] Shneiderman, B.: Technology-Mediated Social Participation: The Next 25 Years of HCI Challenges. In: Jacko, J.A. (ed.) Human-Computer Interaction, Part I, HCII 2011. LNCS, vol. 6761, pp. 3–14. Springer, Heidelberg (2011), http://hcil.cs.umd.edu/trs/2011-03/2011-03.pdf (access January 29, 2012)

[29] Souza, C.S., Leitão, C.F.: Semiotic Engineering Methods for Scientific Research in HCI. Morgan &Claypool Publishers (2009)

[30] Oliveira, L.K.B., Maciel, C.: Interaction with public accounts via citizen portal: a case study. In: 4th IFIP ePart Conference, Kristiansand (Norway). Electronic Government and Electronic Participation, vol. 39, pp. 231–239. Trauner Verlag, Osterreich (Áustria) (2012)

Assessing the Suitability of Current Smartphone Platforms for Mobile Government

Thomas Zefferer, Sandra Kreuzhuber, and Peter Teufl

Secure Information Technology Center - Austria,
Inffeldgasse 16a, 8010 Graz, Austria
{thomas.zefferer,sandra.kreuzhuber,peter.teufl}@a-sit.at
http://www.a-sit.at

Abstract. Smartphones offer a great opportunity to improve governmental procedures and services in terms of efficiency and user acceptance. Unfortunately, the heterogeneity of current smartphone platforms such as Apple iOS, Google Android, or Microsoft Windows Phone 8 renders the integration of smartphones into such governmental procedures and services difficult. The choice of the most appropriate smartphone platform is crucial for the security and success of smartphone based procedures and services. Making the correct choice is a difficult task as smartphone platforms are continuously evolving. Furthermore, requirements that need to be fulfilled by the chosen platform heavily depend on the particular use case.

To overcome this problem, this paper identifies use cases, in which smartphones can be used to improve governmental procedures and services. From these use cases, relevant platform properties are derived. These properties are then analyzed on current versions of the three smartphone platforms Android, iOS, and Windows Phone 8. Based on the results of this analysis, the platforms' suitability for the identified use cases is assessed. This way, the paper provides responsible decision makers from governments and public administrations with a profound basis for choosing the correct smartphone platform for a given use case.

Keywords: Mobile government, Smartphones, Security, Android, iOS, Windows Phone 8.

1   Introduction

During the past years, smartphones have emancipated from traditional end-user devices such as desktop computers and laptops. Nowadays, smartphones are an integral part of the typical western always-on society and frequently used to access information and services everywhere and at any time. For governments and public administrations, the recent emergence of smartphones offers new opportunities, but also raises new challenges. So far, the integration of information and communication technologies (ICT) in the context of e-government solutions has mainly focused on traditional end-user devices. With the recent emancipation of mobile end-user devices, governments and public administrations are

A. Kő et al. (Eds.): EGOVIS/EDEM 2013, LNCS 8061, pp. 125–139, 2013.

requested to take the step from electronic government (e-government) towards mobile government (m-government) and to integrate smartphones into governmental applications and solutions [1].

The need to open governmental applications and solutions to smartphones and similar mobile devices raises several problems. Most of these problems are related to the choice of appropriate smartphone platforms, for which governmental applications should be provided. During the past years, a rather heterogeneous ecosystem of different smartphone platforms has evolved. Currently, Google Android[1] and Apple iOS[2] represent the most popular smartphone platforms. However, also other platforms such as Microsoft Windows Phone 8[3] or BlackBerry[4] hold market shares and can be expected to gain relevance in future.

Unfortunately, current smartphone platforms differ significantly in terms of provided functionality and implemented security features. Hence, responsible decision makers must decide for each platform separately, for which applications this platform is suitable. This decision depends on the particular application's requirements regarding security and functionality, and on the particular platform's capability to meet these requirements. The choice of appropriate smartphone platforms is further complicated by their fast and continuous evolution. New versions of mobile operating systems and new features are introduced frequently and make it difficult to keep track of the current state of the art.

At the same time, taking wrong decisions can have severe consequences. This is for instance illustrated by an attack mounted in December 2012 on SMS based authentication mechanisms of European e-banking portals. By employing the capability to intercept SMS messages on Android, US\$47.000.000 have been stolen from bank accounts [2]. This incident illustrates that detailed knowledge of application requirements and capabilities of smartphone platforms is crucial to make correct decisions regarding the choice of appropriate smartphone platforms. The comparison of different smartphone platforms has been the topic of several scientific publications [11]. The capabilities of different smartphone platforms for different fields of application have also been assessed in literature [12]. However, few publications have focused on the special field of e-government so far.

In this paper, we provide decision makers from governments and public administrations a basis for correct decisions regarding the choice of appropriate smartphone platforms for security-critical governmental applications and solutions. We start by identifying general use cases that allow for an integration of smartphones into governmental applications and solutions. For each use case, we derive a set of research questions that potentially need to be answered by responsible decision makers. Furthermore, we discuss potential threats for the identified use cases and derive a set of platform properties that influence a smartphone platform's capability to fend off these threats. Subsequently, we analyze current versions of the three popular smartphone platforms Google Android,

---

[1] http://www.android.com/

[2] http://www.apple.com/ios/

[3] http://www.windowsphone.com

[4] http://www.blackberry.com

Apple iOS, and Microsoft Windows Phone 8 according to the identified platform properties. Based on the obtained results of this analysis process, we finally assess the suitability of the three smartphone platforms for governmental use cases by answering the predefined research questions.

2 Use Cases

Smartphones have the potential to improve governmental processes in various ways. In general, two potential use cases can be distinguished. First, smartphones can be used by governments and public administrations to improve internal processes. Second, smartphones can be used by citizens to remotely access provided m-government services. These two general use cases are discussed in the following subsections in more detail. For each use case, research questions are derived that are potentially relevant for responsible decision makers.

2.1 Internal Usage

Efficiency has become one of the most important requirements for governments and public administrations [3]. During the past years, the integration of ICT and the application of e-government has significantly improved the efficiency of internal governmental processes. Nowadays, smartphones offer great opportunities to further improve efficiency by providing employees of governments and public administrations access to internal infrastructures and data anywhere and at any time. In most cases, smartphones are issued by the employer to its employees. However, recently a new trend called bring-your-own-device (BYOD) has emerged [5]. BYOD means that employees are allowed to use their own private smartphones to access corporate infrastructure and data. This saves costs for employers and is hence also interesting for public bodies that need to save money. However, BYOD also raises several security challenges as employers typically have no or only limited control over used smartphones.

In any case, the internal use of smartphones by employees raises several challenges for governments and public administrations. If responsible decision makers decide to allow employees to access internal infrastructures and data with smartphones, they need to find answers to the following questions.

- *Q1:* Which smartphone platforms should be chosen when equipping employees with smartphones?
- *Q2:* Which smartphone platforms should be supported in BYOD scenarios?
- *Q3:* Which smartphone platforms are in general beneficial in terms of security and functionality?

2.2 Citizen Applications

Smartphones are gradually replacing established end-user devices such as desktop computers or laptops and are evolving to the most preferred end-user devices for accessing information and services. To react to this trend, governments and public administrations are requested to provide e-government services also for mobile end-user devices. Considering the current heterogeneous ecosystem of smartphone platforms, governments and public administrations have to decide for which platforms to provide mobile e-government applications. In particular, application providers need to find answers to the following research questions.

- *Q4:* Which smartphone platforms should be supported by provided m-government applications?
- *Q5:* Which level of security can be assumed for different smartphone platforms?
- *Q6:* Which smartphone platform provides most functionality for m-government applications?

3   Threat Analysis

To answer the above-defined research questions, different criteria can theoretically be taken into account. For instance, the choice of an appropriate smartphone platform can be based on platforms' current market shares or the price of respective end-user devices. However, for governmental applications, security is usually one of the most important criteria. In this section, we first elaborate on threats that potentially compromise the security of smartphones used in the above-mentioned use cases. From these threats we then derive a set of platform properties that are relevant for the security of a smartphone platform.

3.1   Assets and Threats

Data being stored and processed on smartphones represents the basic asset of smartphone based governmental applications. This applies to scenarios, in which employees of governments and public administrations access internal data with their smartphones, and also to scenarios, in which citizens use their smartphones to execute provided m-government applications and consume m-government services. The capability to protect data being processed and stored on mobile end-user devices is hence the main quality measure for smartphone platforms.

On current smartphone platforms, the security of the asset data is potentially compromised. Security issues on current smartphone platforms have been discussed in [4] and [6]. In general, an attacker can follow two strategies to gain access to data on the mobile device. These two strategies represent the main threats for confidential data on smartphones and are listed and discussed below.

- *Theft:* Due to their mobile nature, smartphones are more prone to loss and theft than stationary end-user devices such as desktop computers. By stealing the smartphone, attackers can potentially gain access to confidential data being stored on the device.

- *Malware:* Compared to traditional mobile phones, smartphones allow users to install additional software. Attackers can use this feature and make users to install malware on smartphones in order to gain access to stored data. Recent reports show that smartphone malware is indeed a growing issue [7].

3.2   Security-Relevant Platform Properties

The security of confidential data stored or processed on smartphones is potentially compromised by the threats theft and malware. A smartphone platform's capability to fend off these threats depends on several properties of the particular platform. Security-relevant platform properties are identified and discussed in the following subsections. We will later use these properties to analyze and assess the security of current smartphone platforms and their appropriateness to be used in the context of governmental use cases.

Data Protection: The capability to reliably protect data even if the device gets lost or stolen is a key criterion for the assessment of a smartphone platform's suitability for governmental use cases. The capability to reliably protect data in the case of loss or theft depends on the following aspects.

- *Access protection:* This aspect covers the platform's support for access-protection features. These features assure that only legitimate users are able to access the smartphone's GUI and data stored on the device. Typical implementations of access-protection mechanisms on smartphones rely on password based authentication schemes. When assessing the security of a smartphone platform, the set of supported access-protection methods and their resistance against known attacks need to be considered.
- *Encryption:* Encryption is a cryptographic method that assures the confidentiality of data. Current smartphone platforms typically support different types and methods of encryption. An important aspect of encryption systems is the secure derivation and storage of encryption keys that are used to encrypt confidential data. The set of supported encryption methods and implemented key-derivation functions are hence main aspects that need to be considered when assessing the security of smartphone platforms.
- *Secure storage of credentials:* PINs, passwords, or cryptographic keys that grant access to protected data or services are usually subsumed under the term credentials. Credentials represent highly confidential data that need to be appropriately protected when being stored on smartphones. Some smartphone platforms provide especially protected storage locations for credentials. The availability of such storage locations and their capability to protect credentials are important aspects that need to be considered when assessing the security of smartphone platforms.
- *Mobile device management:* Supported security features such as access protection or encryption are typically optional and need to be manually enabled by the user. Experience has shown that users often refrain from activating

these features for convenience reasons. Mobile device management (MDM) has recently evolved as a potential solution to this problem, as it allows for a central management and configuration of smartphones. Furthermore, MDM allows for remote execution of tasks and routines on smartphones. This way, data stored on smartphones can for instance be remotely deleted (remote wipe) when the device gets lost or stolen. MDM is mainly applied in professional environments, where smartphones are for instance issued by an employer to its employees. In these scenarios, the employer being the owner of the issued smartphones has the legal and organizational power to centrally control and configure these devices. For scenarios, in which users use their own private smartphones, MDM is usually not an option. Still, the support for MDM solutions is a relevant aspect that needs to be considered when assessing the security of smartphone platforms.

Malware Resistance: The resistance against malware is another key criterion for the assessment of a smartphone platform's suitability for security-critical governmental use cases. The resistance against malware mainly depends on the following aspects.

- *API and IPC:* Basically, malware has access to the same application programming interfaces (APIs) and capabilities for inter-process communication (IPC) as ordinary smartphone applications. IPC capabilities and the provided API are hence important aspects for an assessment of the platform's security. If a platform provides fewer capabilities to access system functionality through provided APIs, also malware on this platform is less powerful as it simply has no access to system functionality. The same basically applies for IPC and similar capabilities provided by the smartphone platform.
- *Resistance against rooting:* To improve the capabilities of malware on targeted smartphones, attackers often try to exploit known security flaws of smartphone platforms in order to gain root access to the smartphone's operating system. This is a major threat as attackers with root access to a smartphone can potentially circumvent implemented security measures. The resistance against rooting is hence an important aspect that needs to be considered when assessing the security of smartphone platforms.
- *Integrated security features:* Smartphone platforms implement various features to improve the security of smartphones and to fight malware. These features range from restrictions of potential application sources, over security measures on operating-system level, to sophisticated permission systems that restrict capabilities and access rights of installed applications. The availability of such security features and their implementation are hence also relevant aspects that need to be considered when assessing the security of smartphone platforms.
- *Availability of updates:* Frequent security updates are an important mechanism to fix discovered security flaws and to keep systems up to date. Outdated and unfixed versions of operating systems typically contain more known security flaws and are hence more prone to malware based attacks.

The availability of frequent updates is hence an important aspect that needs to be considered when assessing the security of smartphone platforms.

4   Platform Analysis

Based on the identified relevant system properties, we analyse current versions of the three popular smartphone platforms Apple iOS, Google Android, and Microsoft Windows Phone 8 in this section. BlackBerry has not been considered in detail, as this platform is currently less popular in private and non-corporate scenarios. The conducted analysis has been based on literature research, Web research, and on information provided by the platform vendors.

4.1   Apple iOS

Apple smartphones (iPhone) and the mobile operating system Apple iOS have significantly contributed to the development and current popularity of smartphones. In this section, we analyze the platform's capabilities to protect security-critical data and to resist malware.

Data Protection: Access protection, encryption, secure storage of credentials, and mobile device management have been identifed as relevant aspects regarding the protection of confidential data on smartphones. These aspects are investigated on Apple iOS in the following in more detail.

- *Access protection:* Access to iOS devices can be protected by means of numeric PINs or more complex passphrases that contain also alphanumerical and special characters. However, access protection is disabled by default and needs to be enabled either by the user or by an MDM solution in place.
- *Encryption:* Apple iOS supports a comprehensive and powerful encryption system. Actually, this encryption system consists of two separate subsystems. The first subsystem allows for the encryption of the entire file system. The second subsystem can be used by smartphone applications to encrypt files individually. For each file, a protection class needs to be selected that defines the encryption method, the used key, and the underlying key derivation method. Depending on the chosen protection class, a secure element is integrated into the key-derivation process, which significantly improves the resistance against brute-force attacks. In general, it can be stated that iOS provides application developers with a powerful encryption system to protect confidential data. However, it is in the responsibility of the application developer to appropriately use and employ the provided encryption mechanisms.
- *Secure storage of credentials:* A so-called KeyChain is available on iOS smartphones. The KeyChain is an especially protected container that can be used by application developers to store security-critical credentials on the mobile device. Similar to the encryption system, developers are responsible to correctly use functionality provided by the KeyChain.

– *Mobile device management:* Apple iOS provides broad support for MDM. An appropriate MDM client is integrated directly into the mobile operating system. From a technical point of view, iOS is well suited for the deployment of appropriate MDM solutions, as it allows for a central configuration (e.g. enable file encryption and access protection) and control (e.g. remote wipe) of iOS devices.

Malware Resistance: Aspects of the Apple iOS platform that are relevant for the platform's resistance against malware are discussed in the following in more detail.

– *API and IPC:* Compared to Google Android, iOS provides only a reduced API for the implementation of third-party applications. The provided API does not support access security-critical system functionality such as SMS processing. Additionally, iOS does not provide broad support for background services and multitasking. While this reduces the power of applications, it also limits the capabilities of malware residing on the smartphone.
– *Resistance against rooting:* Rooting or jailbreaking has become very common on iOS devices. Users typically jailbreak their smartphones in order to allow for the installation of more powerful applications that circumvent restrictions of the original operating systems. There are several tools available, that ease the jailbreaking of iOS devices and that facilitate the rooting of smartphones also for technically inexperienced users.
– *Integrated security features:* Apple iOS follows a sandboxing based approach to separate different applications from each other and to avoid that installed applications negatively influence each other. Additionally, iOS implements a permission system that restricts applications' capabilities to access system functionality. Access to certain functionality has to be requested by the application and granted by the user. Furthermore, iOS allows the download and installation of applications from the official Apple AppStore only. Applications offered through this AppStore are subject to reviews and quality-assurance mechanisms. This complicates the distribution of malware for the iOS platform and can hence be seen as a security feature.
– *Availability of updates:* Updates are available for iOS based devices frequently. At this point, iOS is clearly advantageous compared to Google Android. Main reason for the satisfactory situation regarding updates is the fact that there is only one vendor for hardware and software. The limited number of different devices and operating-system versions facilitates the provision of updates on a regular basis.

4.2   Google Android

During the past years, Android has evolved to the most popular smartphone platform in terms of market share. We analyze Android's capabilities to protect confidential data and to resist malware in this section.

Data Protection: Compared to Apple iOS, Android follows slightly different approaches to protect confidential data. Details of supported methods and mechanisms are discussed in the following.

- *Access protection:* Android support various different access-protection methods. Users can define simple PINs or more complex alphanumerical passwords to protect access to their device. Alternatively, access to Android smartphones can also be protected by means of a secret pattern. However, this approach has turned out to be less secure due to reduced entropy compared to password based access-protection methods. Current versions of Android also support biometric access-protection methods based on photos of legitimate users (face unlock). Also this method has recently turned out to be insecure. All access-protection methods are disabled by default and need to be enabled by the user or an MDM solution in place. Hence, the user (or a MDM solution) is in charge of selecting appropriate methods and of choosing secure passcodes.

- *Encryption:* Encryption is supported on Android since version 3.0 (Honeycomb). Similar to access-protection methods, encryption is disabled by default and needs to be manually enabled. In contrast to Apple iOS, Android does not support file based encryption. If encryption is enabled, the entire file system is encrypted using AES. The encryption key is derived from a passcode defined by the user. A secure element is not involved in the key derivation. Hence, brute force attacks on the passcode (and hence on the encryption key) can also be carried out off the smartphone.

- *Secure storage of credentials:* Current versions of Android provide application developers with an API to a special data structure in order to securely store credentials. Similar to Apple iOS, this data structure is called KeyChain. The Android KeyChain encrypts stored credentials using AES and an encryption key derived from the user's access-protection passcode. A passcode based access-protection method is hence a mandatory prerequisite of the Android KeyChain. Again, the derived key does not depend on a secret stored in a secure element, which eases the implementation of brute-force attacks.

- *Mobile device management:* Compared to Apple iOS, Android supports only very limited MDM capabilities. Only few system properties can actually be defined by MDM solutions. Several smartphone vendors tackle this problem by enhancing Android with proprietary MDM capabilities. This has led to a significant fragmentation, which in turn complicates the deployment of MDM solutions and the support of different Android devices. Another limitation of the Android platform regarding the use of MDM is the lack of integrated MDM clients. Using MDM on a smartphone requires the installation of a separate app that acts as MDM client and enforces defined MDM policies. As this app is subject to the same potential security flaws as any other app on the smartphone, this approach raises additional security issues.

Malware Resistance. Recent reports show that Android is more prone to malware than other smartphone platforms. Reasons for this vulnerability are discussed in more detail below.

- *API and IPC:* Compared to other platforms, Android offers application developers a much richer API that allows third-party applications access to various system features. Additionally, Android provides a wider support for inter-process communication and allows the implementation of arbitrary background services. While a rich API and wide support for IPC is beneficial for the implementation of powerful applications, it also allows for the development of more powerful malware. On Android, malware is able to implement functionality that would require root access to the operating system on other smartphone platforms.
- *Resistance against rooting:* The rooting of Android devices is quite common nowadays. Several tools exist that allow even technically inexperienced users to easily and quickly gain root access to the operating system of their mobile phone. Similarly, various malware exists that employs known security flaws to gain root access to the attacked smartphone's operating system. In general, Android's resistance against rooting must be rated as rather poor.
- *Integrated security features:* Similar to other smartphone platforms, Android follows and implements a sandboxing approach to separate third-party applications from each other. This assures that one application cannot access data that belongs to another application installed on the same smartphone. The probably most relevant security feature of Android is its permission system [9]. Access to resources and functionality of a smartphone (e.g. access to stored contacts, access to GPS functionality, etc.) requires appropriate permissions. For instance, if an application wants to make use of e.g. GPS functionality, it has to request assignment of the respective permission. Requested permissions have to be granted by the user upon installation of the application. Hence, the user is responsible for assigning requested permissions and for defining access rights and capabilities of installed applications. This is also the main problem of Android's permission system. Users are often not aware of implications of granted permissions and often do not understand this security feature [10].
- *Availability of updates:* Android suffers from fragmentation. Several smartphone vendors supply their devices with modified versions of the Android operating system. In these cases, vendors are responsible to supply customers with appropriate system updates. As the provision of system updates causes effort but does not directly produce profit, updates are often provided on an irregular basis only.

4.3   Microsoft Windows Phone 8

Microsoft has launched its new smartphone platform Windows Phone 8 (WP8) in late 2012 with the aim to catch up with the currently leading platforms Google

Android and Apple iOS. In order to analyze its security and suitability for governmental use cases, this section discusses identified security-relevant properties of Windows Phone 8 devices.

Data Protection: Relevant properties that influence WP8's capability to protect confidential data are discussed in the following in more detail.

- *Access protection:* Windows Phone 8 supports the definition of 4 to 16 digit numeric PINs to protect access to the device. Interestingly, a first analysis shows that alphanumeric passphrases can only be used in conjunction with an MDM solution being in place.
- *Encryption:* According to the official documentation, the Windows Phone 8 platform uses the BitLocker technology for full file-system encryption [8]. The used encryption keys are stored in a trusted platform module (TPM) that is mandatory for each Windows Phone 8 device. Integration of the TPM into the encryption system assures that only trusted boot components verified by an UEFI Secure Boot environment are able to decrypt the file system. Interestingly, file-system encryption can only be activated by MDM policies but not by individual end users.
- *Secure storage of credentials:* To securely store confidential data as well as credentials in the application's isolated storage, data can be encrypted using WP8's data protection API. The used decryption keys are unique for each application and generated at the first start of an application. The keys are derived using the TPM, the user's credentials, and an application identifier.
- *Mobile device management:* WP8 supports basic MDM policies to centrally define access protection mechanism, enable disk encryption, and to apply a remote wipe of the device. MDM is fully integrated in the operating system. Thus, when configuring devices using Microsoft Exchange ActiveSync or Windows Intune, no additional MDM client is required.

Malware Resistance: We have also analyzed WP8's capabilities to resist malware. Results of this analysis are discussed in the following.

- *API and IPC:* Compared to Android, the WP8 platform provides a restricted API and very limited IPC capabilities for third-party applications only and is hence basically comparable to Apple iOS. Also, WP8 provides no wide support for the definition of background tasks. For instance, voice recording and the use of the smartphone camera are not possible in background tasks. This avoids the feasibility of spyware.
- *Resistance against rooting:* WP8 devices include UEFI Secure Boot for verifying the integrity of the operating system. Each software component loaded at boot time is verified and checked for a valid signature. As each component has to be signed by Microsoft, modified versions of the operating system or alternative boot components, which grant root access to the device, cannot be executed in theory. In practice, the situation with WP8 appears to be

advantageous compared to Android or iOS. However, WP8 is still a quite new platform and time will show if it is indeed more resistant against rooting than other platforms.

- *Integrated security features:* Similar to Android and iOS, WP8 follows a sandboxing approach (so-called chambers) to avoid that applications influence each other negatively. WP8 also implements a permission system (so called capabilities) that allows users to define the available functionality for an application. As an additional security feature, WP8 does not allow applications to share data. Each application can only access its own isolated storage. Similar to iOS, applications for Windows Phone 8 can only be installed from the Windows Phone Store or being distributed via a company account to employees. Thus, users cannot install applications from e.g. e-mails or untrustworthy download locations. To prevent malware, Microsoft applies a rather strict review process for third-party applications distributed through the Windows Phone Store.

- *Availability of updates:* Although Windows Phone 8 devices are distributed by multiple hardware vendors, Microsoft is in full control of the Windows Phone 8 platform. Except for some small extensions on Nokia devices, all WP8 handsets run the original version of the operating system. Feature updates, bug fixes, and firmware updates from hardware vendors are distributed directly by Microsoft and should be available frequently.

5   Assessment

The results obtained from the conducted platform analysis build the basis for a concrete assessment of the investigated smartphone platforms' suitability for m-government related use cases. In particular, we assess the two previously defined concrete use cases by answering the research questions that have been defined in Section 2. We finally use the results of this assessment to rank the investigated platforms according to their suitability for mobile government.

5.1   Internal Usage

This use case covers scenarios, in which governments and public administrations allow their employees to use smartphones in order to improve the efficiency of internal processes. Either these smartphones are issued by the employer, or employees are allowed to use their own private smartphones following the BYOD approach. The integration of smartphones into internal processes raises several challenges for governments and public administrations. These challenges are reflected by the research questions *Q1* to *Q3* defined in Section 2.

Considering the results of the conducted platform analysis, research question *Q1* can be answered as follows. As for all analyzed platforms access protection and encryption is optional and needs to be manually enabled, the availability of appropriate MDM solutions is obviously an important requirement. The conducted platform analysis has shown that MDM is rather difficult to implement and use on Android. Main reasons are the need for additional client software and the increasing fragmentation of this platform. Another important point is Android's weak resistance against malware compared to other platforms. Summarizing, in order to answer research question *Q1*, we can state that Android should not be chosen when supplying employees with smartphones. Apple iOS and WP8 appear to provide a similar level of security and suitability for this use case. However, while much experience is already available for the iOS platform, WP8 is still a rather new platform and still has to prove its practicability.

Similar considerations apply to research question *Q2*. However, if employees are asked and allowed to bring their own devices, slightly different requirements need to be considered. The most important aspect in this case is fragmentation, as employees usually own and use a broad spectrum of different end-user devices. Again, the conducted analysis has shown that Android is disadvantageous in this context as it shows the highest degree of fragmentation of all evaluated smartphone platforms. To answer research question *Q2*, we can hence state that the support of Android cannot be recommended in BYOD programs. Again, WP8 and iOS are more suitable to meet given requirements and are thus more suitable when following BYOD approaches.

Considering research question *Q3*, the conducted platform analysis has revealed that Android provides definitely more functionality than the rather restrictive platforms iOS and WP8. However, the drawback of this increased functionality is a higher vulnerability against malware and attacks. The selection of an appropriate platform hence has to be made subject to security and functionality requirements of the given scenario. In any case, decision makers need to be well aware of the given trade-off between security and functionality.

In summary, reliance on the smartphone platforms iOS and WP8 is suggested for this use case. The use of Android cannot be recommended due to the platform's security vulnerabilities and its increasing fragmentation. If decision makers still decide to rely on Android due to its improved functionality, they need to be well aware of potential security-reducing consequences.

5.2   Citizen Applications

This use case describes scenarios, in which public administrations provide citizens with smartphone applications for a more efficient and convenient conduction of governmental procedures. This use case raises several challenges that are reflected by research questions *Q4* to *Q6* defined in Section 2. Although these research questions cover different aspects, they can be condensed to one central question: Which is the most suitable smartphone platform for this use case?

Considering the demand to reach as many citizens as possible, Google Android and Apple iOS definitely need to be considered as potential target platforms. However, market share is not the only criterion that needs to be considered. The choice of an appropriate target platform also depends on the context and on the requirements of the smartphone application that is to be provided to citizens. If functionality is the most important criterion, Google Android is definitely a good choice as it allows for more powerful applications than iOS or WP8. However, in many cases, m-government applications process security- and privacy-critical data. Hence, security is often a key requirement that needs to be met. For such applications, Android is often not the best choice due to the platform's vulnerability to malware. For security-critical applications, Apple iOS and Microsoft WP8 should be chosen as target platform instead.

5.3 Platform Ranking

We have used the obtained results of the conducted platform assessment to rank the investigated smartphone platforms according to their capabilities to meet requirements of e-government use cases. For each defined research question, we have ranked the three platforms accordingly.

	Google Android	Apple iOS	Microsoft WP8
Q1	3	1	2
Q2	3	1	2
Q3 – Security	3	2	1
Q3 – Functionality	1	2	3
Q4 – Security-critical applications	3	1	2
Q4 – Non-critical applications	1	2	3
Q5	3	2	1
Q6	1	2	3

Fig. 1. Ranking of the assessed smartphone platforms according to identified research questions

As shown in Figure 1, Apple iOS turns out to be the overall winner when directly comparing all rankings of all platforms. Google Android is successful especially in use cases and scenarios, in which functionality is more important than security. For security-critical scenarios, Android is not an option. After a first analysis, Microsoft Windows Phone 8 can be assumed to be closer to iOS than to Android in terms of functionality and security. However, being a relatively new platform, WP8 still has to prove its capabilities to provide an appropriate level of security and functionality in practice.

6   Conclusions

In this paper, we have assessed the capabilities of the three popular smartphone platforms Google Android, Apple iOS, and Microsoft Windows Phone 8 to be used in different use cases related to e-government and mobile government. For this purpose, we have identified relevant security properties of smartphone platforms. We have then analyzed the above-mentioned platforms according to these security properties. Based on the results of this analysis process, we have finally assessed the platforms' suitability for m-government use cases.

Results show that there is a trade-off between the provided functionality of a smartphone platform and its security. Considering the fact that m-government use cases very often define strict security requirements, especially the platforms Apple iOS and Microsoft WP8 have turned out to be suitable for m-government use cases. Although Google Android can be an option in special cases, the use of Android can in general not be recommended due to various unsolved security issues of this platform.

By identifying strengths and weaknesses of different smartphone platforms, this work supports responsible decision makers of governments and public administrations to make the correct decisions and to choose appropriate target platforms when deploying smartphone based solutions. This way, this work enhances the development of secure and useful m-government applications at an early stage and helps to employ the potential of smartphones to further improve governmental services.

References

1. Zefferer, T., Teufl, P.: Opportunities and Forthcoming Challenges of Smartphone-based m-Government Services. Megatrends in eGovernment - European Journal of ePractice (2011)
2. Schwartz, M.: Zeus Botnet Eurograbber Steals $47 Million. InformationWeekSecurity (2012), http://www.informationweek.com/security/attacks/zeus-botnet-eurograbber-steals-47-millio/240143837
3. Yanqing, G.: E-Government: Definition, Goals, Benefits and Risks. In: Management and Service Science MASS 2010 International Conference, pp. 9–12 (2010)
4. Enck, W., Ongtang, M., McDaniel, P.: Understanding Android Security. IEEE Security Privacy Magazine 7, 50–57 (2009)
5. Woods, S.: Bring Your Own Device (BYOD) Increasingly Important to Small Business Budgets. Technorati (2013), http://technorati.com/business/small-business/article/bring-your-own-device-byod-increasingly
6. Enck, W., Octeau, D., Mcdaniel, P., Chaudhuri, S.: A Study of Android Application Security. USENIX Security, 935–936 (August 2011)
7. Lookout Mobile Security: 2011 Mobile Threat Report (2011), https://www.lookout.com/resources/reports/mobile-threat-report
8. Microsoft: Windows Phone 8 security and encryption (2013), http://www.windowsphone.com/en-US/business/security
9. Barrera, D., Kayacik, H., Mcdaniel, P., van Oorschot, P., Somayaji, A.: A methodology for empirical analysis of permission-based security models and its application to android. In: Proceedings of the 17th ACM Conference on Computer and Communications Security, pp. 73–84 (2010)
10. Felt, A.: Android Permissions: User Attention, Comprehension, and Behavior. Science and Technology, 1–16 (2012)
11. Rogers, M., Goadrich, M.: A hands-on comparison of iOS vs. android. In: Proceedings of the 43rd ACM Technical Symposium on Computer Science Education, SIGCSE 2012, pp. 663–663. ACM, New York (2012)
12. Renner, R., Moran, M., Hemani, Z., Thomas, E., Pio, H.S., Vargas, A.: A comparison of mobile GIS development options on smart phone platforms. In: Proceedings of the 2nd International Conference on Computing for Geospatial Research & Applications, COM.Geo 2011. ACM, New York (2011)

Towards Mobile Government: Verification of Electronic Signatures on Smartphones

Thomas Zefferer, Fabian Golser, and Thomas Lenz

Institute for Applied Information Processing and Communications
Graz University of Technology
Inffeldgasse 16a, 8010 Graz, Austria
{thomas.zefferer,thomas.lenz}@iaik.tugraz.at,
fabian.golser@student.tugraz.at

Abstract. Electronic signatures are a crucial concept for transactional e-government services. Beside the secure creation of electronic signatures, the reliable verification of electronically signed documents is of special importance. Various tools, which allow verification of electronic signatures, have been introduced during the past years. However, most of these tools have been tailored to the requirements of classical end-user devices such as desktop computers or laptops and cannot be conveniently used on smartphones. This is problematic, since smartphones and related mobile end-user devices are gradually replacing classical end-user devices. To overcome this issue, we present a signature-verification solution for smartphones in this paper. The presented solution is based on a platform-agnostic architectural design, which can be applied on arbitrary smartphone platforms such as Google Android or Apple iOS. The practical applicability of the proposed solution has been evaluated by means of a concrete implementation. This implementation shows that the presented solution provides convenient means to verify electronically signed documents on smartphones and hence paves the way for the realization of transactional e-government services on mobile end-user devices.

Keywords: Electronic signatures, Mobile Government, Smartphones, Signature verification.

1 Introduction

Electronic signatures are an important cryptographic concept for transactional e-government solutions [6]. Electronic signatures are based on asymmetric cryptographic methods and algorithms such as RSA [1] or ECDSA [2]. These cryptographic algorithms are usually applied together with a public-key infrastructure (PKI), which is used to unambiguously link a signer's cryptographic key to his or her identity by means of electronic certificates. This way, the cryptographic concepts of electronic signatures and PKIs can be used to reliably assure data integrity and non-repudiation or origin. These properties make electronic signatures especially suitable for the

A. Kő et al. (Eds.): EGOVIS/EDEM 2013, LNCS 8061, pp. 140–151, 2013.

realization of transactional e-government solutions that require a digital alternative to hand-written signatures.

In Europe, the importance of electronic signatures and related concepts has been recognized by legislative bodies of the European Union. In particular, the use of electronic signatures has been defined and regulated in the Directive 1999/93/EC of the European Parliament and of the Council of 13 December 1999 on a Community framework for electronic signatures (hereinafter referred to as EU Signature Directive) [3]. The EU Signature Directive defines different types of electronic signatures. For e-government use cases, especially qualified electronic signatures are of relevance, as they are defined to be legally equivalent to hand-written signatures by the EU Signature Directive. This way, qualified electronic signatures are perfectly suitable for transactional electronic procedures and help to avoid media breaks by rendering the print-out of documents and the application of hand-written signatures unnecessary [6].

During the past years, electronic signatures have become an integral component and key concept of various e-government services and solutions all over the world [11]. This includes solutions for the creation of electronic signatures as well as for the validation of an electronic signature. Most of these solutions have been mainly designed for classical end-user devices such as desktop computers and laptops. However, during the past years, smartphones and tablet computers have emancipated from these classical end-user devices and are nowadays frequently used to access information and services. Governments and public administrations are required to face this recent development and to provide e-government services and applications also for mobile end-user devices [16].

Appropriate concepts and solutions to implement electronic signature based procedures on mobile end-user devices have already been introduced and discussed in literature. For instance, a smartphone app for Google Android[1] that allows users to electronically sign arbitrary PDF documents on their mobile devices has been introduced in [4]. Together with other similar solutions, this work has shown that electronic signature based solutions on smartphones are basically feasible. Interestingly, most of the proposed solutions focus on the creation of electronic signatures on smartphones, but do not provide appropriate means to verify electronic signatures on mobile end-user devices. A smartphone user, who received an electronically signed document, has therefore no opportunity to conveniently and reliably verify the obtained signature on his or her smartphone. Due to the lack of appropriate signature-verification tools on smartphones, smartphone users are not able to employ the key advantage of electronic signatures compared to hand-written signatures, i.e. their unambiguous verifiability.

To close this gap, we present a signature-verification solution for smartphones in this paper. This solution is tailored to the special requirements and properties of current smartphones and related mobile end-user devices. Considering the current heterogeneous ecosystem of different smartphone platforms and mobile operating systems, we first introduce a platform-agnostic architectural design for the proposed solution. We evaluate the applicability and practicability of this platform-agnostic

---

[1] http://www.android.com/

architectural design by means of a concrete implementation for the Google Android platform and show that our solution is basically ready for productive operation.

2   Related Work

The importance of electronic signatures for e-government is evident and has been discussed extensively in scientific work such as [6]. Their relevance becomes also evident when analyzing e-government infrastructures and solutions of different countries [5][14]. In most cases, electronic signatures are a key concept used to reliably authenticate users, to protect the integrity of data in online processes, and to obtain written consent from users in electronic procedures.

Besides e-government, electronic signatures can actually also be useful in other fields of application from the corporate and the private sector. For instance, experience has shown that companies frequently make use of electronic signatures e.g. to sign invoices that are electronically sent to customers. Similarly, electronic signatures are increasingly used also by private persons e.g. to sign contracts in electronic form. In this context, especially PDF signatures have recently gained importance. Beside the well-known PDF signature format introduced by the company Adobe[2], solutions that allow private, public, and corporate users to create qualified electronic signatures on PDF documents are available in several countries [6].

With the growing importance and increasing spread of electronic signature based solutions, also the need for and the importance of appropriate signature-verification tools has increased. Such tools are crucial as they allow receivers of electronically signed documents to verify the validity of the obtained document's signature. During the past years, different verification tools for electronic signatures have been introduced. For instance, a publicly available Web based signature-verification tool called WebNotarius[3] has been provided by Unizeto Technologies SA[4]. WebNotarius supports the verification of different document and signature formats including PCKS#7 [7], CMS [8], S/MIME [9], and XMLDSig [10]. The German company signagate[5] provides a similar Web based signature-verification tool. In contrast to WebNotarius, this tool is however limited to the PDF file format. Web based signature-verification tools for the verification of signed XML and PDF files are also provided by the two companies ascertia[6] and SecuredSigning[7].

Another powerful signature-verification tool has been introduced by Lenz et al. [11]. Similar to the above-mentioned solutions, also the tool proposed by Lenz et al. follows a Web based approach and allows for the verification of different document and signature formats. However, access to this tool's functionality is not limited to the

---

[2] http://www.adobe.com/products/acrobat/
    electronic-signatures-e-signatures.html
[3] http://www.webnotarius.eu
[4] http://www.unizeto.pl/
[5] http://www.signagate.de/
[6] http://www.ascertia.com/
[7] http://www.securedsigning.com/

Web interface. Additionally, the tool features a web-service interface that can be used by external entities to communicate with the tool and to access its functionality programmatically. This way, external entities such as Web applications can send signed documents, which should be verified, to the signature-verification tool and retrieve results of the conducted verification process.

This brief survey on existing signature-verification tools shows that most existing solutions currently follow a Web based approach and that these tools are mainly tailored to the needs of classical end-user devices such as desktop PCs and laptops. These solutions allow users to upload signed documents to a central Web application through a Web based interface and display verification results in the used Web browser. Even though Web based interfaces can also be accessed from smartphones, this is actually less practicable due to the limited input and output capabilities of smartphones. For smartphones, a dedicated app that allows the verification of electronic signatures would be beneficial, since smartphones apps can be tailored to the special input and output capabilities of smartphones. We propose a general architectural design for signature-verification tools for smartphones in the next section.

3   Architectural Design

The verification of electronic signatures is a complex task that involves the application of cryptographic methods to technically verify the validity of a given signature and the communication with external PKI entities to determine the validity of used signing certificates. Even though the computational power of smartphones is constantly increasing, it is usually reasonable to outsource complex operations to server components in order to speed-up processes and to save smartphone resources at the same time.

The signature-verification tool for smartphones that we present in this paper follows this approach and relies on functionality provided by a central server component. This is illustrated in Figure 1. A smartphone app provides the user means to verify arbitrary signed documents. Basically, the app allows the user to choose documents, which should be verified, and displays results of the verification process. However, the app does not implement the signature-verification process itself, but accesses a central server component for this purpose. This way, the smartphone app can be kept lightweight. Furthermore, additional functionality can be added to the signature-verification process easily without requiring users to update their local smartphone apps.

Fig. 1. General architecture of the proposed signature-verification solution for smartphones

According to the general architecture shown in Figure 1, the proposed solution consists of a server component and a smartphone app. We propose and discuss the architectural designs of these two core components in the following subsections.

3.1   Server Component

While the smartphone app is kept lightweight, the server component implements most functionality required to verify electronic signatures and electronically signed documents. This includes the determination of the format of the provided document, the verification of the provided document's signature(s), and the verification of the used signing certificate's validity. From these requirements, the architectural design shown in Figure 2 can be derived.

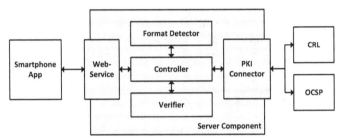

Fig. 2. Architectural design of the server component

In general, the server component consists of the following core components.

— *Controller:* The Controller represents the central component of the server component. It controls the entire process flow that starts with the reception of a signed file to be verified and finally leads to the verification of the provided document.
— *Web Service:* The Web Service represents the interface to the smartphone app. The smartphone app can use the provided Web Service to hand over documents to be verified and to retrieve verification results. Reliance on a Web service based interface guarantees that the functionality of the server component can be accessed by arbitrary external components.
— *Format Detector:* The Format Detector implements the first step of the verification process. Any document or file to be verified is sent to the Format Detector first, in order to determine the provided document's format. Based on the result of the format-detection process, the appropriate verification module is selected by the Controller.
— *Verifier:* The Verifier checks the cryptographic validity of the provided document's signature(s). The Verifier implements appropriate verification modules for each supported document format. The correct module is selected by taking into account the result of the format-detection process. The selected verification module verifies the cryptographic validity of the provided document's signature.
— *PKI Connector:* The PKI Connector verifies the validity of the used signing certificate by accessing appropriate certificate revocation lists (CRL) or external entities

implementing the online certificate status protocol (OCSP). This way, the PKI Connector represents the interface to external public-key infrastructures.

Following the architectural design outlined in Figure 2, the server component encapsulates all functionality that is required to verify electronically signed documents. Access to this functionality is provided through a Web-service interface. This way, the server component can be used by arbitrary external entities including smartphone apps. The architectural design of a smartphone app that uses signature-verification functionality provided through this Web-service interface is presented in the following subsection.

3.2   Smartphone App

As shown in Figure 1, a smartphone app represents the second core component of the proposed signature-verification solution for smartphones. The smartphone app basically takes over two core tasks. First, it implements a graphical user interface (GUI). Through this GUI, the user can select signed files, which should be verified, and define various parameters related to the verification process. Additionally, the GUI is used to display verification results. Second, the smartphone app communicates with the server component through the provided Web-service interface in order to transmit signed documents and to retrieve the corresponding verification results.

Based on these two core tasks, we have developed an appropriate architecture for the smartphone app. This architecture has been designed such that it is applicable on arbitrary smartphone platforms and not restricted to a certain platform such as

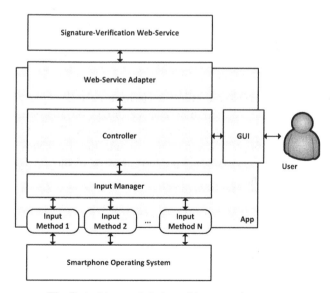

Fig. 3. Architectural design of the smartphone app

Apple iOS[8] or Google Android[9]. The resulting platform-agnostic architecture is shown in Figure 3.

Similar to the server component, also the smartphone app is composed of several core components that implement the app's functionality. These components are introduced in the following in more detail.

- *Controller:* The Controller represents the central element of the smartphone app. This component implements the app's business logic and controls other components and building blocks of the app.
- *Graphical User Interface (GUI):* The GUI represents the interface to the user. It allows the user to select arbitrary signed files for verification and displays obtained verification results.
- *Input Manager:* The Input Manager represents the main interface to the underlying smartphone platform and its mobile operating system. The Input Manager is used to retrieve files to be verified from the operating system. Different smartphone platforms provide apps different methods to retrieve files from the operating system. For instance, direct access to the smartphone's file system is available on Google Android devices, but forbidden on smartphones running the Apple iOS operating system. To cope with this situation, the Input Manager follows a modular approach. This is also illustrated in Figure 3. Depending on the particular smartphone platform, the Input Manager supports different input methods, which allow the retrieval of signed files from the underlying operating system.
- *Web-Service Adapter:* The Web-Service Adapter implements the communication to the Web-service interface provided by the server based signature-verification tool. This way, the Web-Service Adapter basically represents the gateway to the signature-verification functionality. The app's Controller component uses the Web-Service Adapter to send signed files selected by the user through the GUI and retrieved from the smartphone's operating system by the Input Manager to the server based signature-verification tool and to retrieve the results of the signature-verification process.

The app's architecture and its core components have been designed in a platform-agnostic way. Hence, this architecture can be used for appropriate signature-verification solutions for all current smartphone platforms. We have assessed the applicability and practicability of the proposed architecture by means of a concrete implementation for the Google Android platform. Details of this implementation are provided in the next section.

4   Evaluation

In order to assess and evaluate the practical applicability of the proposed architecture, we have developed a signature-verification solution for Google Android smartphones

---

[8] http://www.apple.com/ios/
[9] http://www.android.com

according to the proposed architectural design. The Google Android platform has been chosen, as this platform is currently the world market leader and can be assumed to remain one of the most important platforms in the future [15].

According to the architectural design discussed in Section 3, our implementation consists of a server component and a smartphone app. Further implementation details of these two components are presented in the following subsections.

4.1   Server Component

For the server component, our implementation relies on the Web based signature-verification tool introduced by Lenz et al. in [11]. As this tool already provides an appropriate Web-service interface, it is perfectly suitable to act as server component for our implementation.

Details of the implementation of the server component are provided in [11]. For our smartphone based signature-verification solution, the design of the server component's Web-service interface is of special importance. The provided Web service uses the SOAP protocol [12] to transmit data in the form of XML based SOAP messages between the server component and external entities. HTTP [13] is used on the underlying layer and acts as carrier for exchanged SOAP messages.

SOAP requests being sent to the server component need to comply with a well-defined XML schema that is shown below. While the element *Document* is mandatory and contains the signed document to be verified, the element *FileID* is optional and can be used to identify the signed file.

```
<xsd:element name="VerifyDocumentRequest">
   <xsd:complexType>
      <xsd:sequence>
         <xsd:element name="Document"
                      type="xsd:base64Binary"/>
         <xsd:element name="FileID" type="xsd:token"/>
      </xsd:sequence>
   </xsd:complexType>
</xsd:element>
```

Upon reception of a schema compliant request, the server component starts the signature-verification process and verifies all electronic signatures of the received document. Results of the verification process are collected and assembled into an XML based verification report. This verification report is finally electronically signed by the server component in order to guarantee its authenticity and integrity. The signed verification report is embedded into a SOAP message that complies with the XML schema shown below. This SOAP message represents the response that is finally returned to the calling smartphone app.

```
<xsd:element name="VerifyDocumentResponse">
   <xsd:complexType>
      <xsd:sequence>
```

```
            <xsd:element name="VerificationReport"
                         type="tns:VerificationReportType"/>
            <xsd:element name="Signature"
                         type="dsig:SignatureType"/>
         </xsd:sequence>
      </xsd:complexType>
</xsd:element>
```

The provided Web-service interface allows external entities to easily access the server component's signature-verification functionality. For more details on the implemented signature-verification process itself, the interested reader is referred to [11].

4.2   Smartphone App

The smartphone app represents the second basic building block of the architectural design proposed in Section 3. According to the proposed design shown in Figure 3, the smartphone app needs to implement an appropriate GUI as well as appropriate means to select documents to be verified. Finally, the smartphone app also needs to implement means to communicate with the Web service provided by the server component.

Fig. 4. File selection   **Fig. 5.** File handler

Our implementation relies on the Google Android platform to realize a smartphone application that is able to meet these requirements. Considering the special capabilities and specifics of this smartphone platform, our implementation of the smartphone app allows users to select documents for verification in two different ways. First, user can use the GUI shown in Figure 4 to open a file-selection dialogue and to choose the document to be verified from the smartphone's file system. Second, the smartphone app also registers a file handler for supported file formats in the operating system. This way, the smartphone app can be easily selected from a dialogue that appears when the user attempts to open one of the supported file types. This is illustrated in Figure 5.

Fig. 6. Start of signature-verification process

When the document to be verified has been selected using one of the two supported methods, the signature-verification process can be started using the Send File button as shown in Figure 6.

After touching this button, the selected document is sent to the server component's Web-service interface using a schema compliant SOAP request. Upon completion of the signature-verification process, the verification result is returned to the smartphone application. The smartphone application evaluates the obtained verification results and displays them to the user as shown in Figure 7.

For each verified document, the smartphone app displays related information such as the filename, the hash value of the document, its size, and the type of the detected signature. Furthermore, verification results of all signatures that have been found in the document are presented to the user. As shown in Figure 7, for each detected signature, the verification result of the signature (S), the signing certificate (C), and the manifest (M) are shown. This way, the validity of the found signatures becomes apparent immediately.

As an additional feature, the implemented smartphone app provides the user with a history of recently verified documents. This is illustrated in Figure 8. Users can review their recent verification results by clicking on the respective file. Entries in this history list can be deleted using the recycle-bin icon located next to the file name.

Fig. 7. Result illustration

Fig. 8. Result history

5   Conclusions

In this paper we have proposed a signature-verification solution for smartphones. This solution tackles the problem that most currently available signature-verification tools have been designed for classical end-user devices such as desktop PCs or laptops and hence lack an appropriate level of usability on smartphones and related mobile devices. The architecture of the proposed signature-verification solution has been designed in a platform-agnostic way in order to assure that the solution is applicable on arbitrary smartphone platforms.

The general applicability and practicability of the proposed solution and of the presented architectural design has been successfully evaluated by means of a concrete implementation for the Google Android platform. This implementation shows that the proposed solution is capable to provide easy and usable means to verify electronically signed documents on smartphones. Although the implemented Android application is already fully functional, it is still in a prototypical state. We are currently working on several improvements in order to prepare our solution for publication and distribution in the Google Play store. Similar implementations of the proposed solution on other smartphone platforms such as Apple iOS or BlackBerry are also regarded as future work.

Summarizing, the solution presented in this paper provides users the opportunity to conveniently verify electronically signed documents on smartphones and related mobile end-user devices. This way, the presented solution represents a significant step towards the mobile processing of transactional mobile procedures and helps to pave the way for future mobile government solutions.

References

1. Jonsson, J., Kaliski, B.: Public-Key Cryptography Standards (PKCS) #1: RSA Cryptography Specifications Version 2.1, RFC 3447, RFC Editor, United States (2003)
2. National Institute of Standards and Technology (NIST): FIPS-186-2: Digital Signature Standard (DSS) (January 2000)
3. The European Parliament and the Council of the European Union: Directive 1999/93/EC of the European Parliament and of the Council of 13 December 1999 on a Community framework for electronic signatures (2000), http://eur-lex.europa.eu/LexUriServ/LexUriServ.do?uri=OJ:L:2000:013:0012:0020:EN:PDF
4. Zefferer, T., Tauber, A., Zwattendorfer, B., Stranacher, K.: Qualified PDF signatures on mobile phones. In: Electronic Government and Electronic Participation - Joint Proceedings of Ongoing Research and Projects of IFIP EGOV and IFIP ePart (2012)
5. Leitold, H., Hollosi, A., Posch, R.: Security Architecture of the Austrian Citizen Card Concept. In: Proceedings of 18th Annual Computer Security Applications Conference, ACSAC 2002, Las Vegas, December 9-13, pp. 391–400. IEEE Computer Society (2002) ISBN 0-7695-1828-1, ISSN 1063-9527
6. Leitold, H., Posch, R., Rössler, T.: Media-break resistant eSignatures in eGovernment: An Austrian experience. In: Gritzalis, D., Lopez, J. (eds.) SEC 2009. IFIP AICT, vol. 297, pp. 109–118. Springer, Heidelberg (2009)
7. RSA Laboratories: PKCS#7: Cryptographic Message Syntax Standard, RSA Laboratories (1993)
8. Housley, R.: Cryptographic Message Syntax (CMS), RFC 5652 RFC Editor, United States (2009), http://www.ietf.org/rfc/rfc5652.txt
9. Ramsdell, B., Turner, S.: Secure/Multipurpose Internet Mail Extensions (S/MIME) Version 3.2 Message Specification, RFC 5751, RFC Editor, United States (2010)
10. World Wide Web Consortium: XML Signature Syntax and Processing (Second Edition), W3C (2008b), http://www.w3.org/TR/xmldsig-core/
11. Lenz, T., Stranacher, K., Zefferer, T.: Towards a Modular Architecture for Adaptable Signature-Verification Tools. In: 9th International Conference on Web Information Systems and Technologies (2013)
12. Gudgin, M., Hadley, M., Mendelsohn, N., Moreau, J.-J., Nielsen, H.F.: Soap version 1.2 part 1: Messaging framework, W3C (2007)
13. Fielding, R., Gettys, J., Mogul, J., Frystyk, H., Masinter, L., Leach, P., Berners-Lee, T.: Hypertext transfer protocol – http/1.1, RFC 2616, RFC Editor, United States (1999), http://www.ietf.org/rfc/rfc2616.txt
14. Posch, K.C., Posch, R., Tauber, A., Zefferer, T., Zwattendorfer, B.: Secure and Privacy-preserving eGovernment – Best Practice Austria. In: Calude, C.S., Rozenberg, G., Salomaa, A. (eds.) Rainbow of Computer Science. LNCS, vol. 6570, pp. 259–269. Springer, Heidelberg (2011)
15. Jones, C.: Android Solidifies Smartphone Market Share. Forbes (2013), http://www.forbes.com/sites/chuckjones/2013/02/13/android-solidifies-smartphone-market-share/
16. Zefferer, T., Teufl, P.: Opportunities and Forthcoming Challenges of Smartphone-Based m-Government Services. European Journal of e-Practice, Megatrends in E-Government (2011), http://www.epractice.eu/files/European%20Journal%20epractice%20Volume%2013%20-%2004%20-%20Megatrends%20in%20eGovernment.pdf

Open Government Data Catalogs:
Current Approaches and Quality Perspective

Jan Kučera[1], Dušan Chlapek[1], and Martin Nečaský[2]

[1] University of Economics, Prague, Czech Republic
{jan.kucera,chlapek}@vse.cz
[2] Charles University in Prague, Czech Republic
necasky@xrg.cz

Abstract. Open Government Data (OGD) is seen as a key factor of Open Government initiatives. However, government data is often scattered across various government websites which makes them difficult to find. OGD catalogs serve as a single point of access to open government datasets and thus support discovery and use of OGD. In this paper we define the term Open Government Data and present current OGD activities in the Czech Republic. Number of the OGD catalogs has been established over the past years, but recent experience shows that the quality of the catalog records might affects the ability of users to locate the data of their interest. Therefore we discuss the quality of the catalog records and we propose relevant techniques for its improvement. In addition to the academic perspective authors reflect the experience they gained as coauthors of the Open data cataloging strategy of the Czech public administration.

Keywords: Open Data, Open Government Data, Data Catalog, Data Quality, Catalog Record Quality, Data Analysis, datacatalogs.org, Czech Republic.

1 Introduction

Open Government is a movement that aims at more transparent and more democratic government which enables close cooperation among public administration, politicians and representatives of industry and general public [2]. Several countries have already demonstrated their commitment to Open Government by joining the Open Government Partnership (OGP) [31]. The aim of the Open Data initiative is to make data free to use, reuse and redistribute by anyone. Open Data principles support free access to the government information and their reuse and therefore Open Data is seen as a key enabler of Open Government [2].

Open Government Data not only supports transparency of the government but its reuse in products and services can result in economic benefits as well [40]. However, government data are often scattered across various government websites which makes them difficult to find [5]. An ability to easily discover the relevant data is a prerequisite to unlocking the potential of OGD. Creating a catalog of available Open Government datasets is a way how to make these datasets more accessible and thus easier to

A. Kő et al. (Eds.): EGOVIS/EDEM 2013, LNCS 8061, pp. 152–166, 2013.

reuse. Several countries have already started their data cataloging activities. The USA [38] and Great Britain [21] are just two examples of such countries.

In this paper we illustrate the scope of current OGD cataloging activities. We analyze Open Data catalogs registered at the datacatalogs.org. We also briefly introduce the OGD activities in the Czech Republic. Our experience and current experience from some other countries show that the quality of the catalog records might be an important factor that affects ability of the OGD catalog users to locate the data of their interest. We therefore discuss the concept of catalog record quality and we propose relevant techniques for its improvement. In addition to the academic perspective we also reflect our experience with the topic gained as coauthors of the Open data cataloging strategy of the Czech public administration [10].

This paper is structured as follows. First we define the term Open Government Data and we present the current OGD activities in the Czech Republic. Then we present the results of the datacatalogs.org analysis. In the following section we focus on the quality of the catalog records and we propose some techniques and tools that can be used to improve the quality of the data catalog records. Concluding remarks are presented at the end of this paper.

2   Open Government Data

Open Government Data is a specific subset of data which lies at the intersection of two domains: Open Data and government data. In general Open Data is *"data that can be freely used, reused and redistributed by anyone – subject only, at most, to the requirement to attribute and share-alike"* [35]. Open Data shall be open both technically and legally.

Legal openness of the data is achieved by publishing the data under an appropriate license or terms of use. The Open Definition [32] sets eleven requirements that Open Data should conform to where most of these requirements are related to the licensing of the data. Due to the space limitation we will not discuss these requirements in detail but it is important to mention that according to the Open Definition the terms of use of Open Data must allow reuse and redistribution of the data, it must not discriminate any person and it must not restrict use of the data in a specific field of endeavor. Therefore restricting profit motivated use of the data is not allowed [35].

According to [35] Open Data is technically open if it is available as a complete set in an open, machine readable format and if it is *"priced at no more than a reasonable cost of reproduction."* Complete dataset means that the entire content of a database or a register is made available. Open data format is a format that is *"platform independent, machine readable, and made available to the public without restrictions that would impede the re-use of that information"* [18]. Adapting the definition of machine readability from [13], data in a machine readable format can be defined as data that is *"sufficiently structured for software applications to identify reliably individual statements of fact and their internal structure."* Machine readable format allows easy manipulation with the data in software applications and openness of this format allows it to be implemented in different applications and thus it reduces the risk of vendor lock-in. Finally, Open Data should be made available to the users at a minimal possible cost because the cost or fees are seen as a barrier in access to the data. Preferably it should be made available as a free download from the Internet [35].

In this paper government data is any data that is created by a public sector body. We will use the definition of the public sector body from the Directive 2003/98/EC on the re-use of public sector information (PSI Directive) where it is defined as *"the State, regional or local authorities, bodies governed by public law and associations formed by one or several such authorities or one or several such bodies governed by public law."* [16]

Open Government Data is a government data created and published in a way that it meets the Open Definition, i.e. it is technically and legally open. Since Open Data is meant to be freely used and reused, not every government data can be published as Open Data. For example access to some datasets is restricted for national security reasons and thus it cannot be made publicly available for reuse.

According to [7] one of the differences between private and public sector is that the public sector is more limited by the legal and formal constraints. Legislation can have a significant impact on Open Government Data as it can place restrictions on some categories of data. However, it can support the OGD initiatives as well. Personal information is an example of domain where legislation often restricts how the data should be handled. In the European Union the protection of personal information is harmonized by the Directive 95/46/EC [17]. On the other hand, Freedom of information laws constitute the basic right of citizen on access to the information provided by the public sector bodies [30]. Freedom of information laws or legislation supporting reuse of public sector information (e.g. the Directive 2003/98/EC) can help the OGD initiatives because it might constitute the basic principles of access and reuse of the government data. Revision of the Directive 2003/98/EC has been proposed which introduces obligation to publish government data in machine-readable formats together with its metadata [13]. According to Mouzakitis, et al. [28] some public sector bodies have already proposed their own OGD policy or guidelines.

2.1   Open Government Data in the Czech Republic

The Czech Republic is the EU member state with the Free Access to Information Act No. 106/1999 Coll. This act also implements the requirements of the PSI Directive. In 2011 the Czech Republic joined the Open Government Partnership [41]. In its Action Plan the Czech Republic made its commitment to improve access to the public sector data and information through the use of the Open Data principles [20]. 10 datasets were identified for opening up but only the election statistics was published as OGD by the Czech Statistical Office by the end of 2012 [11].

Experimental unofficial catalog of the Czech government data `cz.ckan.net` was established in 2011 as a result of an academic initiative. According to [25] none of the 1470 cataloged government datasets represented Open Data because of a missing license or terms of use.

One of the Czech OGP commitments is to build the official Open Government Data catalog [20]. Although this catalog has not been launched yet, requirements and the architecture of this catalog have been described in the Open data cataloguing strategy of the Czech public administration [10].

3   Open Government Data Catalogs

Open Government Data has a great potential for reuse but in order to turn this potential into actual benefits it is necessary for potential users to be able to easily find the data of their interest. Open Government Data catalog (OGD catalog) is a tool that can significantly improve discoverability of the Open Government datasets. According to [8] data catalog is "*a collection of catalog records*". These records consist of metadata describing a dataset which represent "*a collection of information in a machine-readable format*" [8]. OGD catalog is therefore a data catalog which contains records about Open Government Data.

3.1   OGD Catalogs Around the World

Datacatalogs.org is a catalog of the Open Data catalogs around the world [1]. By 1st February 2013 it contained 285 catalog records. We have analyzed these catalog records in order to get a high level overview of the current OGD cataloging initiatives. Distribution of the catalogs registered at the datacatalogs.org into public sector and non-public sector groups is presented in the Table 1.

Table 1. Types of catalogs in the datacatalogs.org

Catalog type	Number
Public sector catalogs	220
Non-public sector catalogs	59
Undetermined	2
Duplicate entries	3
Datacatlogs.org catalog record	1
Total	**285**

Our analysis of the datacatalogs.org was based mainly on the information provided in the catalog records. Web sites of the catalogs were consulted only in case that the information in the catalog records was not sufficient to determine the type of the catalog. The results of this approach might not be completely precise but we deem it sufficient to provide a high level overview. The data catalog was considered to be a public sector catalog if it is owned by a public sector body. This was determined either by the description in the catalog record or by the home page of the catalog. If the homepage belonged to the domain of some public sector body, the catalog was marked as the public sector catalog. In some cases the public sector catalogs have their own domain (e.g. http://datasf.org). If the description of the catalog indicated that a catalog might actually be a public sector catalog but the homepage was not in the domain of the public sector body, the website of the catalog was consulted for clarification.

Due to the broken homepage links it was not possible to determine the type of the data catalog in two cases. Three duplicate entries in the `datacatalogs.org` were also identified and these were not calculated into the total number of public sector and non-public sector data catalogs. `Datacatalogs.org` contains a catalog record describing itself so this record was not included in the analysis.

Not all of the catalogs registered at the `datacatalogs.org` are OGD catalogs. The group of the non-public sector catalogs contains various catalogs maintained by their community members or by some private entities, e.g. universities, non-profit organizations. There are also company-owned Open Data catalogs, for example the power company Enel Open Data catalog [12].

Public sector data catalogs are good candidates for OGD catalogs. Out of the 220 public sector catalogs 123 have the term *"open data"*, *"opendata"* or *"open govern-ment data"* in their name, description or homepage URL. We consider these catalogs to be official OGD catalogs. After visiting web pages of the remaining catalogs we added another 68 catalogs into this category because they were described as OGD catalogs or they provided at least one openly licensed dataset. This makes a total of 191 OGD catalogs. The rest of the public sector data catalogs remained undetermined because they were not clearly described as OGD catalogs. More detailed analysis would be necessary in order to properly determine their category.

Public sector bodies at different levels have established their data catalogs [9]. Based on the level of the owning public sector body or by the focus of the data cata-log we divided the public sector data catalogs into the following groups:

- local – data catalog owned by cities or towns or with only city/town coverage,
- regional – data catalogs owned by a regional authority (i.e. county government or federal state government) or with regional coverage,
- national – data catalog owned by a central government body or with nationwide coverage,
- international – data catalog owned by an international institution or with the inter-national coverage.

Distribution of the public sector data catalogs into local, regional, national and inter-national groups is presented in the Table 2.

Table 2. Public sector data catalogs by focus

Focus	Type	Number
Local	OGD catalog	80
	Undetermined	5
Regional	OGD catalog	72
	Undetermined	15
National	OGD catalog	36
	Undetermined	9
International	OGD catalog	3
	Undetermined	0
Total		**220**

Our analysis also shows that there are public sector data catalogs from 37 countries registered at `datacatalogs.org`. There are 3 public sector data catalogs with international focus: Open Data Portal of the European Commission [15], Semic.eu portal (now part of the Joinup portal) [14] and the Open Energy Info portal which is sponsored by the U.S. Department of Energy but has international focus [39]. The number of public sector data catalogs per country is presented in the Table 3.

Table 3. Number of public sector data catalogs per country

Country	Catalogs	Country	Catalogs	Country	Catalogs
USA	50	Chile	3	Morocco	1
Canada	35	China	3	Norway	1
UK	18	Ireland	3	Peru	1
Spain	17	Uruguay	2	Portugal	1
France	16	Argentina	1	Russia	1
Italy	16	Bahrain	1	Saudi Arabia	1
Australia	6	Belgium	1	Singapore	1
Austria	6	Denmark	1	Slovak Republic	1
Netherlands	6	Greece	1	South Korea	1
Finland	5	India	1	Thailand	1
Brazil	4	Kenya	1	United Arab Emirates	1
Germany	4	Lithuania	1		
Sweden	4	Moldova	1		

3.2   Conclusions and Limitations

The analysis presented above shows that there are government data and OGD cataloging activities in number of countries around the world. OGD catalogs exist at different levels of public sector and their focus goes from local to international. While the most of the analyzed countries have only one public sector data catalog registered at the `datacatlogs.org`, there are also countries with more than ten registered data catalogs. Although it is not evident from the analyzed data, in countries with more OGD catalogs some kind of integration or cooperation of the OGD cataloging activities might be necessary in order to provide the users with the access to the open government datasets across more levels of the public sector. Example of such governance structure can be found in the study Open Government Data Germany [24].

The analysis of the `datacatalogs.org` catalog records presented above has also some limitations that can affect the precision of the results. First, the analysis is based mostly on the metadata in the catalog records. Home pages and about pages of the data catalogs were consulted only in cases when the metadata in the catalog records was insufficient. Correctness of the provided metadata was not checked.

Second, whether the public sector data catalog is OGD catalog or not was determined by the catalog's name, description or homepage. Detailed analysis of the terms of use of the cataloged data and analysis of their technical openness would be necessary in order to distinguish between Open Government Data and non-open government data catalogs more precisely. Actually, descriptions of some of the analyzed data catalogs indicated that they are mixed catalogs containing records about both open and non-open government datasets. In our analysis these mixed catalogs were marked as OGD catalogs because at least some of the open government datasets were registered in them. However, it might be interesting to know what percentage of catalog records in the mixed public sector data catalogs describes Open Government Data.

There is also one finding related to the `datacatalogs.org` itself. Although we were able to classify and analyze most of the registered catalogs, it was not possible to perform the analysis using solely the information provided in the catalog records. The portion of the problematic records was relatively small but we would like to point out that sometimes there was missing information about the author of the data catalog, missing description, or both. In some cases even if the description was provided it did not provide us with enough information to make a sound judgment about the particular data catalog. We consider these issues as examples of possible data catalog record quality issues and we will discuss this topic in more detail in the next section.

4   Quality of the OGD Catalog

The OGD catalogs should make the search for the Open Government datasets easier. However, if the OGD catalog contains incomplete, inaccurate or misleading information about the data, it will not serve as a reliable source of information about OGD. This can also result in the poor use of the OGD catalog.

According to the National Audit Office report [29] on the `data.gov.uk` "*descriptive information about each data release is currently not standardised and incomplete. Users will therefore find it difficult to identify data sets that may be most useful.*" More than four-fifths of the users leave the `data.gov.uk` without accessing any of the provided links to the data [22]. Inconsistent classification of the data and difficult website navigation are mentioned as two possible causes [22]. In order to solve these problems an upgrade to the UK data portal was made and a clearer standard taxonomy of the information was designed [29].

We will not discuss the usability of the web based applications in this paper. We will focus on the data catalog record quality because we see the inconsistent classification of the data as a quality issue. Furthermore, awareness of the need to ensure the data catalog (metadata) quality starts to be evident. For example the Berlin Open Data Strategy proposes quality assurance measures [6]. The Study on Open Government in Germany discusses responsibilities with regard to the assurance of the metadata quality and it suggests that metadata standards should be issued [24].

Although the concept of quality is cross-disciplinary, there is no single agreed upon definition of quality [37]. In this paper we define the quality of OGD catalog as the degree to which the catalog fulfills requirements. As it was stated above the data catalog is a collection of catalog records describing datasets [8]. Quality of the catalog records will affect the quality of the OGD catalog as a whole. Because the OGD catalog records represent a category of data, this allows us to build upon the practices of the data quality methodologies where it is a common approach to measure the quality of data in several dimensions representing certain requirements on its quality.

4.1   OGD Catalog Quality Dimensions and Requirements

Quality dimensions differ among the data quality methodologies but the accuracy, completeness, consistency and timeliness can be found in majority of works [3]. These dimensions can be applied to a single OGD catalog records as well as the whole OGD catalog contents, i.e. set of OGD catalog records. Definition of the OGD catalog quality dimensions and description of the quality requirements are provided in the Table 4. In the following text we reference the quality requirements by their IDs.

Table 4. OGD catalog quality dimensions and requirements

Quality dimension		Quality of the OGD catalog record		Quality of the OGD catalog contents	
		ID	Description	ID	Description
Accuracy	Definition		Extend to which a catalog record correctly describes the data.		Portion of the catalog records correctly describing the data.
	Requirements	QR1	All information in a catalog record should correspond to the data described by the record.	QC1	All the catalog records in the catalog should be accurate.
Completeness	Definition		Portion of the filled in mandatory attributes of a catalog record.		Portion of the open government datasets registered in the catalog.
	Requirements	QR2	All mandatory attributes of the record should be filled in.	QC2	All published open government dataset should be registered in the catalog but there should be no duplicate catalog records.
Consistency	Definition		Conformance of a catalog record to the set of semantic rules.		Conformance of the catalog records to the set of semantic rules applied to the catalog as a whole.
	Requirements	QR3	There should be no contradiction or discrepancy between the facts in the catalog attributes.	QC3	There should be no contradiction or discrepancy between related catalog records.
				QC4	Same terms or concepts should be used to classify data of the same type or category.
				QC5	Unknown or missing information should be handled in the same way across the whole catalog.
				QC6	All the catalog records should be consistent.
Timeliness	Definition		Extend to which a catalog record is up-to-date.		Portion of up-to-date catalog records in the catalog.
	Requirements	QR4	All information in the catalog record should be up-to-date.	QC7	All the catalog records should be up-to-date.

All of the catalog records in the OGD catalog should correspond to the data they describe (QR1, QC1). Otherwise they do not provide correct information about the data to the users. For example inaccurate information about the terms of use might lead to unintentional violation of these terms. Invalid links to the datasets make the datasets inaccessible through the OGD catalog.

The OGD catalog records should be kept up-to-date (QR4, QC7). For example if a dataset is moved during a redesign of some government agency's website, its catalog record should be updated with the new location of the dataset.

OGD catalog should be complete (QR2, QC2) because datasets which are not registered in the OGD catalog cannot be located using the catalog. Open Data cataloging strategies and policies (e.g. [6], [10]), might specify which datasets should be cataloged. In this case completeness of the OGD catalog should be measured against the threshold defined by the policy.

Contents of the OGD catalog should be consistent (QR3, QC3-6). Inconsistent classification of the data might lead to the situation in which not all relevant datasets from a certain category can be easily located.

4.2   OGD Catalog Quality Improvement Techniques

In this section we propose a set of techniques which can be used to improve the OGD catalog quality. According to [3] two types of strategies for improvement steps can be found in the data quality methodologies: data-driven and process-driven. Data-driven techniques directly modify the values of data and thus they are used to improve the quality of existing data. Correction of invalid data values or data normalization is an example of data-driven techniques. Process-driven techniques aim at redesign of the data creation and modification processes in order to identify and eliminate the root cause of quality issues. Implementation of data validation step into the data acquisition process is an example of process-driven technique.

In the Table 5 we propose a set of data-driven and process-driven techniques that can be used to improve the quality of the OGD catalog. Process-driven techniques are included because they might help to prevent the OGD catalog quality issues. Role of the catalog editor is discussed in [6] and [10]. Furthermore, [10] describes responsibilities of the catalog editor with regard to the review of the catalog record. We also reflect our experience with the experimental cataloging of the Czech OGD during which the data cataloguing methodology proved to be a key element [25]. Based on [36] we propose automatic metadata authorship as a possible way how to achieve more consistent metadata in the catalog records.

However, information in the catalog records might get obsolete over time. In this case data-driven techniques might help to locate and correct existing inaccurate catalog records.

Identification and correction of the quality issues can be both manual and automatic (DT2-5). According to [6] users of the OGD catalog might be a valuable source of feedback about the quality of the catalog because they can notify the OGD catalog editors or custodians about catalog records with missing, incomplete or inaccurate information. Sometimes even a correct description of a dataset might be obscurely written. This is another area where user feedback might help. Therefore this feedback should be systematically gathered and analyzed (DT1). For example Berlin Open Data platform allows registered users to post questions or feedback to the portal or to the registered data [4].

Table 5. Examples of the OGD catalog quality improvement techniques

Category	Technique	ID
Data-driven	**Identification of the quality issues**	
	Analysis of user feedback	DT1
	Manual review of the catalog records	DT2
	Automatic identification using software tools	DT3
	Correction of the quality issues	
	Manual correction	DT4
	Automatic correction	DT5
Process-driven	**Validation of the catalog records**	
	Manual review	PT1
	Automated validation	PT2
	Automatic metadata authorship (integration with other systems)	PT3
	Use of controlled vocabularies	PT4
	Use of the data cataloging methodology	PT5

Validation of newly created or edited catalog records can prevent the quality issues. This validation might involve checking if the classification of the data is correct and consistent or if the links to the data sources are valid. We provide details about the review process proposed for the official Czech OGD catalog in the next section.

Automation of the validation is possible (PT2) but it probably has some limitations. For example validation of correctness of the free text data description will probably require an action of a qualified person (PT1). However, the data cataloging tool might still provide features that can help to automate the validation, e.g. checking if the required attributes are non-empty or if the provided links are not corrupted.

In Table 4 consistent classification of the data in the OGD catalog was mentioned as one of the quality requirements. According to [23] one way how to achieve higher quality of metadata is to use controlled vocabularies for the metadata attribute values instead of free words (PT4). Although the referenced article discusses the metadata quality in different context than the OGD catalog, controlled vocabularies can be used in this type of catalog as well. A controlled vocabulary is *"any kind of knowledge organization structure, from simple lists of valid terms to more sophisticated structures thesaurus and ontologies"* [23]. Use of controlled vocabularies can help to prevent the situations in which multiple similar terms are used for the same category of data. For example EUROVOC taxonomy is proposed as classification taxonomy for the publicdata.eu portal [5].

In order to achieve consistent classification of the data the concepts of the controlled vocabularies must be applied in a consistent way by those who create and update the OGD catalog records. Some kind of guidelines might help to unify the data classification approach. These guidelines can be a part of the data cataloging methodology (PT5) that can provide recommendations and guidelines for other areas as well.

During our experimental cataloging of the Czech OGD we formulated simple cataloging methodology that provided guidelines on how to describe data, how to classify datasets with CZ-NACE and the Integrated Public Sector Vocabulary (IPSV), or how to structure packages in CKAN software [25]. As different people created the catalog records during this cataloging activity, the methodology proved to be a key element that unified the approach to the catalog records creation.

OGD catalogs might contain significant number of catalog records. According to [29] "*the number of data sets catalogued within www.data.gov.uk has grown from 2,500 in January 2010 to 7,865 in December 2011*". Large number of data catalog records might require automation of the quality improvement techniques. There are number of data quality tools on the market that offer functionality like data profiling, standardization and cleaning [19]. Applicability of these tools in the OGD catalog context should be analyzed. However, the quality related functionality can be implemented in the data cataloguing tools as well. For example, there is a CKAN cataloging tool extension which allows identification of the invalid data source URLs [33].

According to [36] automatic metadata authorship may result in more consistent metadata even though it can be less descriptive. If the metadata for Open Government datasets is already available in some of the existing systems, integration of these systems and the OGD catalog should be considered (PT3). For example CKAN cataloging software provides features for harvesting records from other systems [34]. However, the full automation of the catalog record authorship might not be always possible because it seems desirable to provide highly descriptive characteristics of the data.

4.3   Quality Approach in the Official Czech OGD Catalog

Although the official Czech OGD catalog has not been put into operation yet, in this section we introduce the proposed approach to the quality of this catalog described in the Open data cataloging strategy of the Czech public administration [10].

Approach to the quality of the official Czech OGD catalog is based mostly on the process-driven techniques. There are 8 workflows that describe how users of different roles should interact with the Czech OGD catalog. The most important process-driven technique is a review process (PT1). Therefore the review steps are part of the workflows for data catalog creation and editing. In addition to the review process it is recommended to use the controlled vocabularies and the data cataloging methodology (PT4-5).

Every newly created or updated catalog record in the Czech OGD catalog must undergo a review before it can be published in the catalog. The review is performed by the catalog editor who is commissioned by the owner of the Czech OGD catalog (a public sector body that has the responsibility for the catalog).

During the review process the catalog editor checks:

- relevance of the catalog record – the record must describe OGD published by the Czech public sector bodies,
- completeness of the catalog record – all the required attributes of the record must be filled in,
- validity of the data source URI,
- correspondence of the description with the data,
- correctness and consistency of the data classification,
- validity of references to the Data Elements Information System and to the Public Sector Information Systems Register.

Data Elements Information System (DEIS) [26] and the Public Sector Information Systems Register (PSISR) [27] are two existing cataloging systems of the Czech public administration. DEIS serves as a register of data elements used across the public sector information systems and it contains definitions of common entities, e.g. address, person etc. If some of these data elements are used in the cataloged Open Data, references to the respective elements in the DEIS should be included in the catalog record.

Role of PSISR is similar to DEIS. It is a register of existing public sector information system (PSIS). If the cataloged Open Data comes from one of PSIS, reference to the PSISR should be included in the catalog record.

Catalog record that passes the review is published in the Czech OGD catalog and the users of the catalog can access it. If the catalog editor identifies some issues in the catalog record, it is returned to the publisher of the data who can correct it and resubmit it to the Czech OGD catalog. The review process is repeated until the catalog editor publishes the catalog record in the Czech OGD catalog.

The data cataloging tool should provide features for automation of the record validation steps (PT2). There should be features for automatic validation of the data format and the data source URI. It is also proposed to assess the possible future use of the machine learning methods for automatic classification of the data or for automatic identification of the duplicate catalog records.

In [10] it is also recommended to use the controlled vocabularies for data classification, namely EUROVOC and the CZ-NACE classification of the economic activities. It is recommended to develop a data cataloging methodology that should provide guidelines on how to apply these controlled vocabularies as well as on other aspects of the Open Data cataloging process.

Analysis of the user feedback (DT1) is another proposed technique for the Czech OGD catalog quality assurance. Therefore the data cataloging tool must provide features that will allow users to provide the feedback. However, no specific technology (e.g. email) is recommended in [10].

5   Conclusion

Data catalog is an important tool that facilitates exploitation of OGD. Based on the descriptions provided at the `datacatalogs.org` portal we identified a total number of 220 government data catalogs and out of this number we classified 191 catalogs as OGD catalogs. Despite the fact that we performed no in-depth analysis of the individual data catalogs, our analysis indicates that in some countries there is more than one data catalog. There are OGD catalogs established by central government agencies, however in some countries cities and regional governments have established their OGD catalogs as well. There are also international OGD catalogs, e.g. Open Data Portal of the European Commission.

In our analysis we focused on the Open Data catalogs established by the public sector bodies. However, public sector is not the only domain in which Open Data cataloging is being conducted. There are Open Data catalogs established and maintained by their community members, universities, non-profit organizations or companies as well.

Number of existing data catalogs is quite high and their focus is diverse. A catalog of data catalogs like `datacatalogs.org` might help users to locate the data catalogs with information about the data of their interest. Therefore catalog owners should consider registration of their data catalog at the `datacatalogs.org`.

OGD catalogs should foster OGD reuse but if the OGD catalog contains records with incomplete, incorrect or misleading information, users might find it difficult to identify datasets they need. Recent experience shows that alongside the quality of OGD itself, the quality of the OGD catalog records requires attention of the OGD practitioners.

Individual OGD catalog records as well as the OGD catalog as a whole should be accurate, complete, consistent and up-to-date. Based on our experience and the literature review we identified several data-driven and process-driven techniques for OGD catalog quality improvement. These techniques include the analysis of OGD catalog user feedback, manual and automatic detection and correction of quality issues, manual and automatic validation of the newly created or updated catalog records, automatic metadata authorship, use of controlled vocabularies and use of a data cataloging methodology.

Future research should focus on the quality dimension of the OGD catalogs. The list of techniques for improvement of the OGD catalog quality proposed in this paper is not comprehensive. More attention should also be paid to the automation of the quality improvement steps because OGD catalogs may contain large amount of catalog records. Solely manual identification and correction of the quality issues might not be feasible in large OGD catalogs.

Acknowledgements. The research is supported by the EU ICT FP7 under No.257943, LOD2 project and the project of the Internal grant agency of the University of Economics, Prague, no. F4/3/2013.

References

1. About datacatalogs.org, `http://www.datacatalogs.org/about`
2. Bauer, F., Kaltenböck, M.: Linked Open Data: The Essentials. Edition mono/monochrom, Vienna (2011)
3. Batini, C., Cappiello, C., Francalanci, C., Maurino, A.: Methodologies for data quality assessment and improvement. ACM Comput. Surv. 41(3), 16:1–16:52 (2009)

4. Berlin: Interaktion. Offene Daten Berlin, `http://daten.berlin.de/interaktion`
5. Bolychevsky, I., Peltan, D.: LOD2 Deliverable 9.1.1. First release of the Publicdata.eu Website and Tools (2012), `http://static.lod2.eu/Deliverables/lod2-d9-1-1-publicadata-eu-launch.pdf`
6. Both, W., Schieferdecker, I.: Berliner Open Data-Strategie. Organisatorische, rechtliche und technische Aspekte offener Daten in Berlin. Fraunhofer Verlag, Berlin (2012)
7. Campbell, J., McDonald, C., Sethibe, T.: Public and Private Sector IT Governance: Identifying Contextual Differences. Australasian Journal of Information Systems 16(2), 5–18 (2010)
8. Cyganiak, R., Maali, F.: Use Cases and Requirements for the Data Catalog Vocabulary (2012), `http://dvcs.w3.org/hg/gld/raw-file/default/dcat-ucr/index.html`
9. Cyganiak, R., Maali, F., Peristeras, V.: Self-Service Linked Government Data with dcat and Gridworks. In: Proceedings of the 6th International Conference on Semantic Systems, pp. 37:1–37:3. ACM, New York (2010)
10. Chlapek, D., Kučera, J., Nečaský, M.: Koncepce katalogizace otevřených dat VS ČR (zkrácená verze) [Open data cataloguing strategy of the Czech public administration (abridged version)] (2012), `http://www.vlada.cz/assets/ppov/boj-s-korupci/otevrene-vladnuti/aktuality/Koncepce-katalogizace-otevrenych-dat-VS-CR-zkracena-verze.pdf`
11. Czech Statistical Office: Otevřená data pro volby (Elections Open Data) (2013), `http://www.volby.cz/opendata/opendata.htm`
12. Enel Spa: Enel Open Data, `http://data.enel.com/`
13. European Commission: Proposal for Directive of the European Parliament and of the Council Amending Directive 2003/98/EC on re-use of public sector information (2011), `http://ec.europa.eu/information_society/policy/psi/docs/pdfs/directive_proposal/2012/en.pdf`
14. European Commission: Joinup (2013), `https://joinup.ec.europa.eu/`
15. European Commission: Open Data Portal (2012), `http://open-data.europa.eu/open-data/`
16. European Commission: Directive 2003/98/EC of the European Parliament and the Council on the re-use of public sector information (2003), `http://eur-lex.europa.eu/LexUriServ/LexUriServ.do?uri=OJ:L:2003:345:0090:0096:EN:PDF`
17. European Commission: Directive 95/46/EC on the protection of individuals with regard to the processing of personal data and on the free movement of such data (1995), `http://eur-lex.europa.eu/LexUriServ/LexUriServ.do?uri=OJ:L:1995:281:0031:0050:EN:PDF`
18. Executive Office of the President: Open Government Directive (2009), `http://www.whitehouse.gov/open/documents/open-government-directive`
19. Friedman, T.: Magic Quadrant for Data Quality Tools (2012), `http://www.gartner.com/technology/reprints.do?id=1-1BOAK4L&ct=120809&st=sb`
20. Government of the Czech Republic: Action Plan of the Czech Republic "Open Government Partnership" (2012), `http://www.vlada.cz/assets/ppov/boj-s-korupci/otevrene-vladnuti/OGP_Action-plan_Czech-Republic_detailed.pdf`
21. HM Government: data.gov.uk - Opening Up Government, `http://data.gov.uk/`
22. House of Commons: Implementing the transparency agenda: Tenth Report of Session 2012–13 (2012), `http://www.publications.parliament.uk/pa/cm201213/cmselect/cmpubacc/102/102.pdf`

23. Kapidakis, S.: Comparing metadata quality in the Europeana context. In: Proceedings of the 5th International Conference on PErvasive Technologies Related to Assistive Environments, pp. 25:1-25:8. ACM, New York (2012)

24. Klessmann, J., Denker, P., Schieferdecker, I., Schulz, S.E.: Open Government Data Deutschland, Eine Studie zu Open Government in Deutschland im Auftrag des Bundesministerium des Innern (2012), `http://www.bmi.bund.de/SharedDocs/Downloads/DE/Themen/OED_Verwaltung/ModerneVerwaltung/opengovernment.pdf?__blob=publicationFile`

25. Kučera, J., Chlapek, D., Mynarz, J.: Czech CKAN Repository as Case Study in Public Sector Data Cataloging. Systémová Integrace 19(2), 95–107 (2012)

26. Ministry of the Interior of the Czech Republic. Informační systém o datových prvcích [Data Elements Information System], `https://www.sluzby-isvs.cz/ISDP/DefaultSSL.aspx`

27. Ministry of the Interior of the Czech Republic. Informační systém o informačních systémech veřejné správy [Public Sector Information Systems Register], `https://www.sluzby-isvs.cz/ISoISVS/Applets/DefaultSSL.aspx`

28. Mouzakitis, S., Tsavdaris, H., Psarras, J., Charalabidis, Y., Klessman, J., Flügge, M., Jeffery, K., Karayiannis, F., Yaeli, A.: Deliverable D7.7.1: Analysis Report of Public Sector Data and Knowledge Sources (2011), `http://www.engage-project.eu/engage/wp/wp-content/plugins/download-monitor/download.php?id=4`

29. National Audit Office: Implementing transparency (2012), `http://www.nao.org.uk//idoc.ashx?docId=3b4b9491-f7c8-4026-8ed4-1bbf02faa5e9&version=-1`

30. OECD: Public Sector Modernisation: Open Government (2005), `http://www.oecd.org/gov/34455306.pdf`

31. Open Government Partnership: Country Commitments (2012), `http://www.opengovpartnership.org/countries`

32. Open Knowledge Definition, `http://opendefinition.org/okd/`

33. Open Knowledge Foundation: CKAN Quality Assurance Extension (2013), `https://github.com/okfn/ckanext-qa`

34. Open Knowledge Foundation: Publish and manage data, `http://ckan.org/features/publish/`

35. Open Knowledge Foundation: The Open Data Handbook (2012), `http://opendatahandbook.org/pdf/OpenDataHandbook.pdf`

36. Queensland Government: Metadata management guideline (2010), `http://www.qgcio.qld.gov.au/SiteCollectionDocuments/Architecture%20and%20Standards/Information%20Standards/Current/Metadata%20Management%20Guideline.pdf`

37. Russell, G.R., Miles, M.P.: The definition and perception of quality in ISO-9000 firms. Review of Business 9(3), 13–16 (1998)

38. United States Government: Data.gov, `http://www.data.gov/`

39. U.S. Department of Energy: OpenEI, `http://en.openei.org/wiki/Main_Page`

40. Vickery, G.: Review of recent studies on PSI re-use and related market developments (2011), `http://ec.europa.eu/information_society/policy/psi/docs/pdfs/report/psi_final_version_formatted.docx`

41. Vláda České republiky: Usnesení Vlády České republiky ze dne 14. září 2011 č. 691 o přistoupení k mezinárodní iniciativě Open Government Partnership (2011), `http://kormoran.vlada.cz/usneseni/usneseni_webtest.nsf/0/4A3F809FCF5DB30AC125791200296E95/$FILE/691%20uv110914.0691.pdf`

Open Government Data – A Key Element in the Digital Society

Henning Sten Hansen, Line Hvingel, and Lise Schrøder

Aalborg University, Department of Development and Planning
A.C. Meyers Vænge 15
DK-2450 Copenhagen
hsh@land.aau.dk

Abstract. During the last decade several initiatives have worked towards open and freely available data. First, the success by the OpenStreetMap and partly the free use of Google Maps have been a revelation for many users, both in the public sector as well as in the private sector. Additionally, several legal frameworks like the EU directive on Re-use of Public Sector Information and the INSPIRE Directive on geographic information have in various ways encouraged the re-use of public sector information. As a consequence, a minor group of European countries have launched their own open government data projects, and the current research focuses on the role of open public sector information as a major step towards a digital society by analysing the background, extent and expected impact of the Danish open government data initiative.

Keywords: Spatial Data Infrastructure, Open Government Data, Public sector information.

1   Introduction

Data sharing is a fundamental component of the modern digital societies, and easier access to data and information has been a vision since the early days of the information society. However, very little progress has been achieved in this field until quite recently, and the success of the free OpenStreetMap is perhaps the best positive example on a worldwide solution on data sharing. Due to its extensive use, Google Maps also share this success although the use of data is imposed some restrictions. Generally there is a growing tendency to release at least to some degree various sorts of public data allowing citizens and businesses to freely re-use public data for their own purposes [1]. The real driver towards free sharing of data and information comes from the government sectors, including the European Union. Thus the launch of the so-called Digital Agenda of the European Union [2] has emphasised the need for maximising the economic and social benefits of Information and Communication Technology (ICT) towards a sustainable future.

A. Kő et al. (Eds.): EGOVIS/EDEM 2013, LNCS 8061, pp. 167–180, 2013.
© Springer-Verlag Berlin Heidelberg 2013

Large amounts of data and information are daily produced by the European public authorities being the largest single source of information in Europe with an estimated market value of 32 billion Euros.

Open government data has received increasing awareness during the last ten years in parallel with the preparation and implementation of the INSPIRE Directive [3]. Traditionally geographic information in Europe has been financed through the so-called cost recovery principle, where the revenue obtained by selling data is used for updating the data and maintaining the data quality. However this model has been under pressure from the EU by the PSI and INSPIRE Directives although the cost recovery is not directly in conflict with this legislation.

Several European countries have initiated open government data in various extents. Last autumn the Danish Government decided a new initiative on Basic Data, which is considered an essential basis for public authorities to perform tasks properly and efficiently across units and sectors, as outlined in the Danish e-Government Strategy 2011-2015. The vision is that Basic Data is to be the high-quality authoritative common foundation for public sector information – including the private sector. A general principle is that all basic data will be freely available for all public authorities, private businesses and the individual citizens.

The aim of the current research has been to analyse the background, extent and expected impact of the Danish decision on opening up government data for free re-use as a step towards the implementation of the digital society. After this introduction follows a chapter describing the background and theoretical foundation for the tendency towards open government data. The third chapter describes and analyses the national Danish implementation of open governmental data. Chapter four analyses the Danish approach to open data. The paper ends with a discussion and some concluding remarks including perspectives for subsequent research.

2   Background and Theory

The EU Digital Agenda is the first of seven so-called flagship initiatives included in the Europe 2020 Strategy presented in May 2010 [2]. The aim of the Digital Agenda is that Europe's citizens and businesses should get maximum benefit from the digital technologies. The Digital Agenda contains 101 actions organised into 7 pillars: 1) Digital Single Market, 2) Interoperability and Standards, 3) Thrust and security, 4) Fast and Ultra-fast Internet access, 5) Research and innovation, 6) Enhancing digital literacy, skills and inclusion, and 7) ICT-enabled benefits for the EU society. One of the actions (no. 3) within the Pillar 1: Digital Single Market are concerned with opening up public data resources for re-use. Already back in the 2003 the Directive on Re-use of Public Sector Information aimed at regulating and stimulating the reuse of public sector information (PSI). Although the PSI Directive [4] deals with all kinds of public sector information, a majority of this information has a geographical reference. Thus the focus for public sector is to manage and service people, businesses, real properties, roads and areas, which all are located somewhere on the surface of the earth.

2.1   Data Sharing in the Digital Society

The issue of data sharing goes back to the 1990es, where the book 'Sharing Geographic Information' [5] explored organisational issues in the context of sharing geographic information. Herein Campbell and Masser [6] concluded that within the UK local governments very little data sharing took place even between departments. Paper maps were still at that time a major source to information. However during the last 10 – 15 years the development towards a digital society has really put data sharing on the political agenda. However, the principle of data sharing is not enough to ensure an open, transparent and efficient public sector. Frequently bottlenecks connected with costs, legal restrictions, and proprietary data formats have hindered real re-use of data for the benefits of the society.

Globally the value of data sharing and free data has been demonstrated by the emergent free map services like Google Maps and not at least the OpenStreetMap, which have put severe pressure on the National Mapping Agencies. Surveys have demonstrated that not only the citizens and smaller private companies are using these map services, but also public organisations like agencies and municipalities. However, the most important reason for the recent focus on Open Government Data is the implementation of digital governance with extended use of self-service solutions. This requires access to data and information across the public sector – from municipalities over regional authorities to the national governments.

According to the recently started 'Open Government Data' initiative (http://www.opengovernmentdata.org) 'open data' means 'data free for anyone to use, re-use and re-distribute', and 'government data' refers to 'data and information produced or commissioned by government or government controlled entities'. This definition is applied in the current paper. The 'Open Government Data' initiative has produced a handbook aiming at supporting implementation of open government data around the world, and at the same time building a common framework for assessing existing open government initiatives. The Open Data Handbook [7] points to several areas, where open government data may create additional value including: a) Transparency and democratic control, b) Public participation, c) Self-empowerment, d) Improved or new private products and services, e) Innovation, f) Improved efficiency and effectiveness of government services, g) Impact measurement of policies, and h) New knowledge from combined data sources and patterns in large data volumes. These advantages can be organised into two main groups. One group (items a – c) can contribute to enhanced democracy and participation, while the other group (items d – g) primarily focuses on the economic benefits obtained through more efficient public sector and improved innovation and business possibilities in the private sector.

In order to discuss open government data some clear definitions must be stated, and several attempts have been made in this connection. Through a consensus process among 30 experts within this topic in December 2007 the 'Open Government Data' initiative has defined a set of principles, which must be met to be compliant with the open government data definition (table 1). In addition to the eight principles, a criteria

'Compliance must be reviewable' was defined by the 'Open Government Data' initiative. These principles have no authoritative role or legal bindings, but may serve as guidelines and inspiration for emergent open data initiatives, and will be applied in the analysis of the Danish implementation in chapter 3. Furthermore, the principles are all considered of equal importance, which are not true in practice. However, as shown in the section below the principles are to a large degree contained in the PSI and INSPIRE directives.

Regarding open government data it is clear, that open data is not the same as free data applying a strict definition of the word 'free'. All government data are produced by the public employed or bought from private companies and the associated costs are fully paid by the taxpayers. Thus, it may be argued that without a principle of free re-use, the taxpayers have to pay for the data twice.

2.2   European Legal Frameworks on Open Government Data

The PSI Directive [4] was implemented in July 2005 aiming at regulating and stimulating the reuse of public sector information. The initial intention of the European Commission was to make all public sector information in the Member States available for re-use. However, this caused some Member States and public institutions great concerns, as many of these institutions are expected to provide for, at least parts of, their own funding. Therefore, in the negotiation process between the European Parliament and the Council the general principle was toned down to a mere encouragement for the Member States to make their information available for re-use. Nevertheless, the PSI directive has gained a lot of impacts in the Member States as demonstrated in the next paragraph.

A key objective of INSPIRE was to make more and better spatial information available for Community policy-making and implementation in a wide range of sectors. Initially, it would focus on information needed to monitor and improve the state of the environment - including air, water, soil, and natural landscape - and later extended to other sectors such as agriculture and transport [8]. The INSPIRE Directive was adopted by the European Council and Parliament in spring 2007 and entered into force May 2007 [3]. The INSPIRE Directive is a framework, where the details are defined through a set of so-called implementing rules, where the Member States provide experts for drafting the rules, which are finally adopted by the INSPIRE Committee. Thus a high degree of Member States involvement is ensured. In a national Danish context, the so-called Geodata Law was a derived effect of the INSPIRE Directive. The INSPIRE Directive relies on a set of basic principles of which the one on data availability and accessibility 'Spatial data needed for good governance should be available on conditions that are not restricting its extensive use' is of major importance regarding open government data.

Altogether, there were several reasons and encouragements for opening up public sector information in a broader scale among the European countries. As an example, the next section will describe the Danish approach to Open Government Data.

Table 1. The principles of Open Government Data (http://opengovdata.org)

1. Data must be complete	All public data which are not subject to valid privacy or security limitations
2. Data must be primary	Published as collected at the source with finest level of granularity
3. Data must be timely	Made available as quickly as necessary to preserve the value of data
4. Data must be accessible	Available to widest range of users and purposes
5. Data must be machine processable	Reasonably structures to allow automatic processing
6. Access must be non-discriminatory	Available to anyone without registration requirement
7. Data formats must be non-proprietory	Available in formats over which no entity has exclusive control
8. Data must be license free	Not subject to any copyright, patent, trademark or trade secret regulation
Compliance must be reviewable	A contact person must be designated to respond to user requests

3   Implementation Strategy

Similar to the other Nordic countries, Denmark has a leading role in digitisation of the society. In the 2012 United Nations E-Government Surveys rankings, Denmark is ranked in the top as number four after the Republic of Korea, the Netherlands and the United Kingdom [9]. E-Government is generally being defined as the use of information and communication technologies (ICT) to improve the activities of public sector organisations and their agents and e-Government has been the key driver for all activities regarding information and communication technology in the public sector.

Since the mid-1990es various Danish governments have put e-Government on the political agenda with initiatives like "Information Society by the year 2000" [10] and not at least "Project Digital Government" [11], which sat up a so-called Digital Task Force aiming at enhancing e-Government solutions across the public sector.

To underline the importance of the Digital Task Force the Ministry of Finance chaired it. The Danish e-Government strategy for 2007-2010, entitled "Towards better digital services, increasing efficiency and stronger cooperation" (Danish Government, Local Government Denmark and Danish Regions, 2007) has three overarching strategic priority areas: a) better digital service, b) increased efficiency, and c) stronger collaboration. The national SDI is one of the prerequisites for fulfilling the strategy and handling the new dependencies. This policy was followed by an updated strategy concerning the period 2011-2015 [12].

3.1   The Stepwise Approach to Open Government Data

Generally access to and re-use of public sector information has been imposed with high costs and severe restrictions. However, several steps towards open government data have been launched during the last ten years. The *first* step towards Open Government Data in Denmark was the decision taken by the Ministry of Environment in the late nineties to make open access to all environmental information. This was a natural consequence of the Aarhus Convention from 1998 [13] emphasising the importance of public participation in all decisions related to the environment, which requires access to data and information. Thus open access to government data is addressed in Directive 90/313/EEC of 7 June 1990 [14] by stating the aims of 'ensuring freedom of access to, and dissemination of information on the environment held by public authorities and to set out the basic terms and conditions on which such information should be made available'.

The *second* step was the open access to the Address Register and Building and Dwelling Register in 2002. The decision gave open access to the data, and in principle the data was 'free', but only through a set of private distributors, who required rather high delivery costs. Thus the profit from selling and delivering the data was transferred from the public authorities to private companies. Nevertheless, the price for acquiring the Building and Dwelling Register including the Address Register was significantly cheaper than before, and the result was a substantial increase in the number of users.

Following the two INSPIRE principles of 'Data should be collected once and maintained where this can be done most effectively' and 'It should be possible for information collected at one level to be shared between all the different levels', an agreement between the Danish national Geodata Agency and Local Government Denmark was made in 2007 [15]. This so-called FOT-Denmark aims to establish a national base map for use at all administrative levels by combining the nationwide topographical database with a specified accuracy of 1 meter, and large-scale technical maps with an accuracy requirement of 10-20 cm used by the municipalities. Currently all municipalities have joined FOT-Denmark, and in 2012 the Geodata Agency acquired full rights to the FOT database.

The FOT-Denmark cooperation facilitated the *third* step by inventing a new funding model for geographic information. Traditionally, the Danish funding model for geographic data has been partly based on government funding and partly by cost recovery, but from 2009 a new funding model was launched for the central government sector. All ministries pay an annual fee to the National Mapping Agency, and in return all the central government agencies and institutions have access to the spatial data and services. Later in 2010, a similar agreement was obtained with the Local Government Denmark providing a free flow of geographic data among public authorities. However, the use of data was still imposed by several restrictions – e.g. publishing even derived data on the Internet.

The three steps mentioned above all focused on different sectors without being planned and implemented as part of an overall strategic vision. Nevertheless these steps represent important building stones in the Danish Infrastructure for geographic information as described and analysed by Hansen et al. [16]. From a governmental point of view a spatial data infrastructure is seen as an important dimension in several e-Government initiatives. Thus the Digital Task Force recognises the importance of geographic information by claiming that for many public authorities, the combination of geographic location and other registers or databases has proved a valuable tool in a number of administrative tasks. Recently, the Digital Task Force even stated that geographic information is a backbone in e-Government [17].

Although the initiatives taken during the first three steps, the visions of an advanced e-Society with extensive use of self-service solutions in the public sector are counteracted by several bottlenecks. Accordingly, the *fourth* step is a significant move towards extensive open government data. From 1 January 2013 several important registers and all terrestrial geographic data – i.e. topographic data, the Danish digital elevation model, and the cadastral map are freely available, and during the next months more data from the public registers will be made freely available in form of what is called basic Data [18].

3.2   The Basic Data Concept

By using a common geographic basis for administration, it is possible for example to link relevant data about the environment, traffic, health, property, companies and people. Basic data constitutes the core information needed by public authorities in their daily work, and contains information about *Persons*, *Businesses*, *Real properties*, *Addresses*, *Roads* and *Areas*. All these data has a spatial reference, and accordingly geography and maps are important elements in the Basic data concept (fig. 1). This figure illustrates clearly the interconnection between the different components of the Basic Data set. Each person, business unit, property, house and road has for decades been provided with unique identifiers, and a cross-reference register has ensured the interconnection between the different objects in the infrastructure. Besides, all persons and business units are assigned an address. Finally, the addresses, properties (parcels) and buildings are assigned a geographic reference, ensuring its connection with geography (maps). Thus the basic Data set constitutes an integrated system facilitating the core functions in public administrations.

At a later stage in the process it is expected to expand the Basic Data set to include personal data, income data, business financial statements, and road infrastructures. In order to maintain the authoritative status required for public administration, management and decision-making, the Basic Data needs to comply with the following

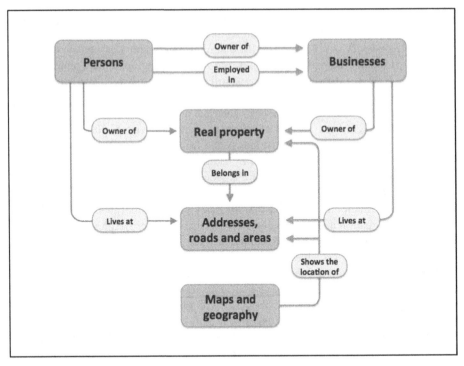

Fig. 1. The Basic Data concept in the Danish Open Government Data Strategy

principles: 1) Basic Data needs to be as correct, complete, and up-to-data as possible; 2) All public authorities must use the Basic Data in their daily work; 3) As far as possible Basic Data must be made freely available to businesses as well as the public (sensitive personal data excluded); 4) Basic Data must be distributed efficiently and accommodate the needs of the users.

In order to produce, maintain, and ensure data quality a specific business model has been developed. The Danish National Government and the organisation of local authorities – Local Government Denmark – have agreed to share the costs of Basic Data through a mutual agreement. Particularly in the first phase of the implementation additional costs for setting up facilities for data distribution, the costs may balance the benefits, but based on previous experiences from making address data freely available, the Danish Ministry of Finance has estimated that a revenue of more than 100 million Euro is expected when the Basic Data initiative is fully implemented by 2020. One third of this is expected from a more efficient public sector, and two-thirds from the private sector through enhanced innovation and competitiveness.

3.3   Cost-Benefit and Expected Impact

During the last twenty years major discussions have taken place regarding the benefits versus costs of various initiatives on the digitisation of the society based on establishing spatial data infrastructures and providing public data open and freely available. Few studies have tried to estimate the costs and benefits connected with such initiatives but rather few really cost-benefit analyses. However a survey carried out in the Netherlands estimate the economic value of the Dutch geoinformation sector to be 1.4 billion Euros – corresponding to 0.25% of the national Dutch GNP [19]. During the 1990es the national Danish Address Register went through a major harmonisation and quality upgrade, and from 2002 the Address Register including addresses coordinates was made open and free to use for everybody [20]. An analysis from 2010 concluded that the direct benefits from the open and free access to the Address Register in the five years period from 2005 – 2009 were more than 60 million € [21]. The analysis assumes that the economic value of the open and free addresses corresponds to the price paid by the users of addresses before the new open policy on address data, which is equivalent to 78 million €. These figures may even represent an underestimation due to the wider scope for use in the new agreement, where everyone may add value to the data and sell them for profit aims. On the other side you may claim that the general movements towards the digital society, inevitably would have led to lower prices on address data. In order to reduce the uncertainty in the analysis the value of address data is reduced with 25% - i.e. (75% x 78 million €) = 59 million €. Contrary, the authorities as well as the users have saved thousands of person hours earlier spend on negotiations, agreements, and data delivery, and in the calculations these savings are estimated to be 5 million €. This adds to 64 million € for the years 2005-2009 – and 13 million € yearly. However these figures do not include indirect and derived benefits obtained from: a) no need for alternative address data sets; b) higher security for police, ambulances, fire brigades etc. due to the same and accurate address data set.

Based on these figures, the Danish Ministry of Finance tried to estimate the costs and benefits from the new initiative on open public data at the broader scale. When the new Open Government Data policy is completely in operation in 2020, it is expected that the public sector yearly will save about 36 million € (table 2), and for the private sector the yearly benefits will be more than 65 million €. Thus the total yearly economic benefits for the Danish society will be about 100 million €. Although Basic data is freely available for everyone, the cost of producing the data is still there. As mentioned above the funding of the open government data project is based on shared costs between the different administrative layers in the Danish public sector. The expected benefits are more uncertain, but the calculations carried out by the Ministry of Finance are based on recent cost/benefit studies from Finland and Australia, and generally the estimates are conservative. Based on experiences from Australia, Houghton [22] concludes that 'the direct and measureable benefits of making PSI available freely and without restrictions on use typically outweigh the costs. As framework for estimating cost-benefits Houghton used the following formula: 'Benefit/Cost' = ('Agency & User Savings' + Increased Returns to Expenditure on PSI production') / 'Agency & Users Cost'. This formula was also applied in the cost-benefit analysis carried out by the Ministry of Finance. The Research Institute of Finnish Economy carried a major analysis on the impact of the pricing of public sector information on performance in the business sector, and based on data from 15 countries during the years 2000-2007 it was found that pricing of PSI really had an effect on company growth - particularly for small and medium sized enterprises [23]. Although the figures varies from country to country it was found that for example free access to geographic information contributes to a 15% higher growth rate (on average) compared with traditional pricing based on the cost recovery principle.

Table 2. Net profit for the public sector in millions € [18].

	2013	2014	2015	2016	2017	2018	2019	2020
The Ministries	-14	-11	-7	-3	1	1	4	6
The Municipalities	-3	3	11	19	22	23	23	24
The Region	0	1	3	4	6	6	6	6
Net effect	-17	-7	7	20	29	30	33	36

4   Analysis and Discussion

The principles outlined by the Open Government Data initiative (table 1) will be applied as a discussion frame for the Danish approach to open government data. Besides, the Danish approach will be assessed in relation to overall strategic aims. The nine principles identified by the Open Government Data initiative considers all principles of equal weight although some kind of weighting may have improved the appropriateness of using the principles as framework for the analysis. However, assigning weights to the principles is a major task beyond the focus of the current research, and accordingly the weights are considered equal in the discussion below:

1. Data must be complete: Although the Danish initiative is one of the most encompassing open government data projects as it covers all terrestrial geographic data, addresses, data on buildings, properties, and businesses as well as individuals unless the data is confidential personal information, a lot of data belonging to Statistics Denmark are still only available on commercial conditions. Clearly, it can be discussed if data from Statistics Denmark belongs to the group of public sector information.

2. Data must be primary: All data included in the new open government data policy are available as originally collected by the authority and with the finest granularity. Thus the data are not aggregated in any way.

3. Data must be timely: As soon as the new data distribution facility is in operation by summer 2013 the data for download or available as services will be the latest version used in the public administration.

4. Data must be accessible: The data will be available for public authorities, private companies and individuals for all purposes – including commercial aims. Thus no restrictions for legal use.

5. Data must be machine processable: The data are all well structured according to the current state-of-the-art methods, and all details about the underlying data models are freely accessible by download in order to serve the users

post-processing and applications. Metadata following the latest ISO standards are provided for all data within the Basic Data set.

6. <u>Access must be non-discriminatory</u>: The data can be downloaded by anyone without any registration, but currently the new data distribution portal is not in operation, and therefore it is unclear if some kind of registration will be required.

7. <u>Data formats must be non-proprietary</u>: The data is available in XML-formats, and other international standards including Web Feature Services, Web Map Services as well as industry standards like shape files from ESRI and Excel from Microsoft, and more.

8. <u>Data must be license free</u>: There are no regulations, patents or similar restrictions, but it is expected that the users mention the data source and attach the associated metadata. However, besides being free the final conditions are still not clear.

    <u>Compliance must be reviewable</u>: Contact persons are currently available for the individual parts of the Basic Data set, but it is still unknown if the new data distributor unit will serve as a common contact point, when the data distribution portal are in operation later this year.

Summarising the analysis above the Danish approach to open government data seems to be highly compliant with the 8 principles developed by 'Open Government Data' from 'Open Knowledge Foundation'. However, two dimensions have to be discussed. First, the new open data policy in Denmark is still under implementation, and although you can at the moment download all the data belonging to the Basic Data set without any restrictions the final conditions, except data being open, are still uncertain. Therefore, an exact conclusion on being compliant with the eight Open Government Data principles is associated with uncertainty. The second issue is related to the lack of priority within the nine principles. Looking at the nine principles from top to bottom gives in our opinion some kind of priority. Thus the first 4 items seems to be of more fundamental importance than the remaining 5. For example this does not mean that the use of non-proprietary data formats (7) and registration requirements (6) are not important, but they do not possess the same kind of fundamentality than for example data being primary (2) and accessible for all users and purposes (4). Considered in this light the Danish Open Government Data project seems to be highly in accordance with the core principles (1 – 4) from the Open Government Data initiative.

The Danish OGD project is a result of a top-down effort initiated by the Ministry of Finance based on purely financial considerations and cost-benefit calculations. During the previous ten years many partners involved in handling geographic information and associated public register have worked on setting up an Infrastructure for Spatial Information in Denmark as described by Hansen et al. [16] but without any power to launch a process towards open public information like the one described above. Only the top ministers including the minister of finance have the necessary power to do this.

A concern often put forward in the discussion of open government data is related to the costs of maintaining and updating the data. Who should pay, when the public data is open and according to the definition 'freely' available to anyone? The public registers are being produced and updated through the day-to-day work in the public agencies regarding the administration of persons, properties, buildings, businesses, etc., and accordingly there are no additional costs associated with their production and maintenance. However, some public organisation may loose income from selling register data to the private sector, and although the amount of money is rather low compared to the total public budgets, this income is of importance for some specific departments.

Concerning geographical data (digital maps) the so-called cost-recovery model has been the traditional economic foundation for production and maintenance. The geographic data have had a group of stabile customers like the Ministry of Defence and the Ministry of the Environment, and then ad hoc sales to other public organisations and in minor degree to the private sector. Hence, the new open government strategy will have a major impact on the economic model for the operation of the National Mapping Agency. As mentioned above the lack of income from selling geographical data will be compensated by direct economic support from the National Government, the Danish Regions, and Local Government Denmark – at least on the shorter term (2 – 3 years). The long-term funding of the digital maps remains to be decided. In addition the Ministry of Finance has decided a continuous 2% yearly cut of the public budgets due to increased effectiveness in the public sector. Finally, a continuing of the European economic and financial crisis will inevitably put the public budgets under renewed pressure, which indirectly may lead the lower data quality. Therefore, many fears that the geographical data will suffer from lack of update and quality control. However, one of the main arguments for making the decision on open government data was a more effective public sector and a more innovative and competitive private sector, and these aims will be strong drivers for providing up-to-date and high quality open public data.

The visions on getting public data re-used among citizens and in the private sector has recently been analysed by Bjoern-Moeldrup and Colding [24]. Until 1 January 2013 the Danish National Map Supply operated by the Geodata Agency had about 800 registered users, but this figure was enhanced to about 4000 registered users of the Map Supply by 1 April 2013. Within the same period the number of downloaded data sets has increased from less than 1000 thousend more than 15000. A majority of the new users (62%) are citizens, while 28% are private businesses, but the latter has made most of the downloads.

Thus an immediate effect of the Danish open government data initiative is promising, but the next interested aspect concerns the use of the data. Does the enhanced interest for public data among ordinary citizens mean increasing interest to being involved in participatory processes, and empowering new groups of people in the public participation? As shown by Hansen and Reinau [25], this is still a major challenge for the public authorities. Although many analyses have shown the great potentials for increased innovation and effectiveness [22, 23], and the demonstrated huge interest for the open government data is a fact [24], it still has to be proven that the potential will be realised in practice. Open government data is just one factor for innovation. Highly skilled specialists and researchers, entrepreneurship, and venture capital are perhaps more important.

5   Conclusion

During the last decade several initiatives have worked towards open data. Particularly, the success by the open and free OpenStreetMap and Google Maps with few use restrictions have challenged the traditional pricing model based on cost-recovery of the national mapping agencies. Additionally, several legal frameworks like the EU directive on Re-use of Public Sector Information and the INSPIRE Directive on geographic information have in various ways encouraged to opening up free re-use of public sector information. Also the Open Government Data initiative from Open Knowledge Foundation has been a driver towards open government data. As a consequence a minor group of European countries have launched their own open government data projects. The current research has focused on the role of open public sector information as a major step towards a digital society by analysing the background, extent and expected impact of the Danish open government data initiative. The Danish project is rather new being from 1 January 2013 and some details are still unclear. However, it can be concluded that by having the Ministry of Finance with high power and legitimacy as the main driver for the planning and implementation the decision-making process is easier than the previous efforts on establishing a Danish national infrastructure for geographic information. The Danish open government data decision is entirely based on a wish to increase the efficiency in the public sector and as a parallel effect stimulating innovation and growth in the private sector. The next steps in our research on open government data is a comparative analysis of the open government data implementations in 6 European countries in order to identify best practices.

References

1. Kulk, S., van Loenen, B.: Brave new open data world? International Journal of Spatial Data Infrastructure Research 7, 196–206 (2012)
2. European Commission: A Digital Agenda for Europe. Communication from the Commission to the European Parliament, the Council, the European Economic and Social Committee and the Committee of the Regions. COM (2010) 245 (2011)
3. European Commission: Directive 2007/2/EC of the European Parliament and of the Council of 14 March 2007 establishing an Infrastructure for Spatial Information in the European Community (INSPIRE). Official Journal of the European Union (2007)
4. European Commission: The reuse of public sector information, Directive 2003/98/EC of the European Parliament and of the Council. Official Journal of the European Union L345, 90–96 (2003)
5. Onsrud, H.J., Rushton: Sharing Geographic Information. Published 31 July 1995 by Center for Urban Policy Research (1995)

6. Harvey, F., Tulloch, D.: Local-government data sharing: Evaluating the foundations of spatial data infrastructures. International Journal of Geographical Information Science 20, 743–768
7. Open Knowledge Foundation: Open Data Handbook Documentation, Release 1.0.0 (November 14, 2012)
8. Vanderhaegen, M., Muro, E.: Contribution of a European spatial data infrastructure to the effectiveness of EIA and SEA studies. Environmental Impact Assessment Review 25, 123–142 (2005)
9. United Nations: E-Government Survey 2012: E–Government to the people. United Nations, New York (2012)
10. Ministry of Research: Information Society by the year 2000. Danish Government, Copenhagen (1994) (in Danish)
11. Ministry of Finance: Digitalisation and efficiency in National Government. Danish Government, Copenhagen (2002) (in Danish)
12. The Danish Government, Danish Regions & Local Government Denmark: The Digital Path to Future Welfare – eGovernment Strategy 2011-2015, August 2011 (2012)
13. UN ECE: Convention on Access to Information, Public Participation in Decision-making and Access to Justice in Environmental Matters. ECE Committee on Environmental Policy, Aarhus (1998)
14. European Commission: Council Directive 90/313/EEC of 7 June 1990 on the freedom of access to information on the environment, EuroLex (1990)
15. FOT-Denmark: Regulations for FOT – 8 October 2007. FOT Denmark, Copenhagen (2007) (in Danish)
16. Hansen, H.S., Schrøder, L., Hvingel, L., Christensen, J.S.: Towards Spatially Enabled e-Governance – A Case Study on SDI Implementation. International Journal of Spatial Data Infrastructure Research 6, 73–96 (2010)
17. Larsen, B.C.: Geodata – The Backbone of effective e-Government. The Digital Task Force. Ministry of Finance, Copenhagen (2006)
18. The Danish Government & Local Government Denmark: Good Basic Data for Everyone – A Driver for Growth and Effiency. The eGovernment Strategy 2011-2015 (2012)
19. Castelein, W.T., Bregt, A.K., Pluijmers, Y.: The economic value of the Dutch geo-information sector. International Journal of Spatial Data Infrastructure Research 5, 58–76 (2010)
20. Lind, M.: Addresses as an infrastructure component - Danish experiences and perspectives. In: Proceedings from ISO Workshop on Address Standards, Copenhagen, May 25, pp. 94–105 (2008)
21. Danish Business Authority: The Value of the Danish Address Data. Societal benefits of the free access of address data in 2002. The Danish Business Authority, July 2002 (2010) (in Danish)
22. Houghton, J.: Costs and Benefits of Data Provision. Report to the Australian National Data Service. Centre for Strategic Economic Studies, Victoria University, Melbourne (2011)
23. Koski, H.: Does Marginal Cost Pricing of Public Sector Information Spur Firm Growth. ETLA – The Research Institute of Finnish Economy, Report no. 1260, Helsinki (2011)
24. Bjoern-Moeldrup, M., Colding, T.S.: Data released – Free geographic data. Geoforum Perspektiv, No. 23, pp. 10–15 (2013) (in Danish)
25. Hansen, H.S., Reinau, K.H.: The citizens in E-participation. In: Wimmer, M.A., Scholl, H.J., Grönlund, Å., Andersen, K.V. (eds.) EGOV 2006. LNCS, vol. 4084, pp. 70–82. Springer, Heidelberg (2006)

Cloud Computing in E-Government across Europe
A Comparison

Bernd Zwattendorfer[1], Klaus Stranacher[1], Arne Tauber[1], and Peter Reichstädter[2]

[1] E-Government Innovation Center (EGIZ), Graz University of Technology, Graz, Austria
{bernd.zwattendorfer,klaus.stranacher,arne.tauber}@egiz.gv.at
[2] E-Government / ICT Strategy at Austrian Federal Chancellery, Vienna, Austria
peter.reichstaedter@bka.gv.at

Abstract. Cloud computing has many advantages which also governments and public authorities can benefit from. Therefore, a couple of European countries have already adopted cloud computing in the public sector or are planning to do so. In this paper, we evaluate eight European countries on their use of cloud computing in e-Government and compare them. As a result, the dominant cloud computing deployment model in those countries is a so-called G-Cloud (Governmental Cloud), a private or community cloud especially designed for national governmental use. In addition, no favored cloud service model has emerged, hence all standard cloud service models (Infrastructure, Platform, and Software as a Service) are adopted by most countries. Finally, half of the evaluated countries have anchored cloud computing in one of their national ICT strategies.

Keywords: Cloud Computing, e-Government, Europe, Public Sector, G-Cloud.

1 Introduction

Cloud computing is currently one of the dominating topics in the IT sector. In general, cloud computing enables the provisioning of IT services such as computing power or data storage just on demand. Additionally, only those resources which have been effectively consumed are charged by a cloud service provider. The NIST[1] defines cloud computing the following:

"Cloud computing is a model for enabling ubiquitous, convenient, on-demand network access to a shared pool of configurable computing resources (e.g., networks, servers, storage, applications, and services) that can be rapidly provisioned and released with minimal management effort or service provider interaction." [1]

In other words, IT resources such as computational power or data storage are shared across multiple customers and are easily accessible through a network by different devices (e.g. PC, mobile phone, etc.). Furthermore, the resources are provided dynamically, highly elastic, and customers can easily access them just on demand. Finally,

---

[1] National Institute of Standards and Technology

A. Kő et al. (Eds.): EGOVIS/EDEM 2013, LNCS 8061, pp. 181–195, 2013.
© Springer-Verlag Berlin Heidelberg 2013

consumed resources are measured by the provider and only effectively consumed resources are charged.

Cloud computing has many advantages such as cost savings, scalability, or high availability, which make cloud computing interesting for many sectors. In particular, due to limited budgets of many governments, cloud computing and its advantages are also interesting for the public sector. Moreover, Khan et al. [2] concluded that - by adopting cloud computing - governments and public authorities can rather focus on their core business, which is serving the citizenry, instead of thinking on IT resource allocation and IT maintenance tasks.

The importance of cloud computing and its benefits for the public sector has already been noticed by several European bodies. For instance, the European Network and Information Security Agency (ENISA) put cloud computing on their current and emerging research trends in 2010 [3]. Moreover, the European Commission explicitly refers to cloud computing in their Digital Agenda for 2020 [4]. In more detail, the European Commission aims on an EU-wide strategy on cloud computing for governments to strengthen the European internal market.

Not only European bodies, but also several European countries jumped on the cloud computing bandwagon or are planning to do so. Hence, they also want to take advantage of cloud computing benefits. In this paper, we compare the adoption of cloud computing within the public sector in eight European countries. For instance, we evaluate which cloud computing deployment models or service models are planned to be used or are already in use for e-Government applications. The evaluation of these countries is based on a thorough literature review and web research, thereby examining various existing articles and studies.

As a result, the dominant cloud computing deployment model in those countries is a so-called G-Cloud (Governmental Cloud), a private or community cloud especially designed for national governmental use. In addition, there is no favored cloud service model, hence all standard service models (Infrastructure, Platform, and Software as a Service) are adopted by most countries.

The remainder of the paper is structured as follows. In Section 2 different cloud computing models are briefly introduced. In Section 3 we discuss the importance of cloud computing in the e-Government sector. Furthermore, we oppose advantages with issues and challenges. In Section 4 we give details on cloud computing adoption in the public sector in eight selected European countries. The adoption of cloud computing in the public sector across those countries is compared in Section 5. Finally, we draw conclusions.

2   Cloud Computing Models

Cloud computing can be differentiated into different types of models. Mell and Grance [1] separate between model types which focus on technical and service aspects, and model types which consider organizational and deployment aspects. In the following sub-sections we briefly introduce different types of service and deployment models according to [1].

2.1   Cloud Computing Service Models

Cloud computing service models are differentiated based on the type of service provided by cloud providers. Usually, three different service models are distinguished.

- *Infrastructure as a Service (IaaS)*
  In this model cloud providers offer basic IT infrastructure such as computing power, virtual machines, or data storage as a service. Customers are usually allowed to install arbitrary operating systems or software of their choice, but do not get access to the underlying hardware.
- *Platform as a Service (PaaS)*
  Applying this model, cloud providers offer specific interfaces and platforms where customers can develop and deploy their own cloud applications to. Here, the cloud provider manages the underlying operating system too.
- *Software as a Service (SaaS)*
  In this case complete software solutions such as e-mail, calendar, or collaboration services are offered by the cloud service provider as a service. Customers can access the software via a simple web browser and do not need local installations on their PC.

2.2   Cloud Computing Deployment Models

Cloud computing can also be separated based on the chosen deployment approach. Usually, four types of deployment models are differentiated.

- *Private Cloud*
  A private cloud is only deployed and operated for a single organization.
- *Community Cloud*
  A community cloud is deployed and operated for a couple of organizations that share common interests.
- *Public Cloud*
  A public cloud is deployed and operated for the general public and can be used by everyone.
- *Hybrid Cloud*
  A combination or interconnection of different cloud models (e.g. between public, private, or community cloud) is called hybrid cloud.

3   Cloud Computing and E-Government

Cloud computing is penetrating many areas because of its advantages. High scalability, low maintenance efforts, enormous cost savings potential, and several other benefits make cloud computing also interesting in e-Government. Especially, the increasing tightness of governmental budgets can benefit from cloud computing adoption, as the amount of IT expenditures could be decreased [5]. Saving costs in the governmental sector is essential. For instance, the aim of decreasing costs for public services was also anchored in the Austrian governmental programme [6].

The cost savings potential of cloud computing in the governmental sector is enormous. Alford [7] estimates a saving potential between 50 to 67% by moving governmental applications into private or public clouds. Harms and Yamartino [8] conclude similarly in their economic analysis of cloud computing for the public sector. Particularly, they argue that public clouds have always higher cost benefits for public services compared to private clouds, irrespective of the required amount of IT resources or the cloud size.

3.1 Advantages

Besides cost benefits, cloud computing has several further advantages for public services. Bhisikar [9] lists a couple of advantages of cloud computing for the public sector. Based on these findings, we list the most important advantages of cloud computing in the governmental sector:

- Scalability
- Pay-as-you-go pricing model
- Easy implementation
- Low maintenance
- Availability

One main advantage of cloud computing for public services is scalability. Depending on the e-Government application, only resources, which are actually required, are consumed. This especially helps to absorb high load peeks of applications (e.g. e-Procurement, tendering, or election days), which may have higher access rates in a limited time period.

The flexible pricing model of clouds allows for just paying the very amount of IT resources, which effectively have been consumed. This pay-as-you-go pricing model enables public services to save a lot of IT costs.

Cloud applications are easy to implement. Public services do not need to buy hardware or software licenses but just can use the IT infrastructure (IaaS, PaaS, or SaaS) of the cloud service provider. Usually, cloud service providers offer some kind of APIs (application programming interfaces), where individual cloud applications can be developed to.

The use of cloud services also lowers maintenance tasks. Patch or update management can be fully handled by the cloud service provider, hence no manual maintenance tasks, e.g. for updating operating systems or installing security patches, are required.

Finally, the use of clouds can increase availability of applications. Applications can be deployed in different cloud data centers, distributed around the world. In case of a breakdown of one data center, the application may still continue running in another cloud data center of the cloud provider.

3.2   Issues and Challenges

Although cloud computing offers a lot of advantages to public services, several issues and challenges need to be targeted or to be met when applying cloud computing in the public sector. Hindering issues might be, for instance, security or privacy concerns when processing or transferring sensitive data into the cloud [10, 11]. We briefly list some requirements, which must be fulfilled when taking advantage of cloud computing in the public sector. Of course, whether those requirements can be simply fulfilled or not heavily depends on the cloud computing deployment or service model applied. According to Deussen et al. [12], Reichstädter [13], Wyld [5], and Repschlager et al. [14] the main issues and challenges for adopting cloud computing in the public sector are:

- Security
- Data protection and compliance
- Interoperability and data portability
- Identity and access management
- Auditing

Providing a high level of security for public sector cloud computing is essential. Security requirements must be fulfilled on several layers. This means, for instance, that network, application, or data security must be assured by the cloud.

Data protection defines one of the main issues when talking about cloud computing. In e-Government applications and services usually sensitive data are processed, hence meeting this requirement is indispensable. Particularly, some data protection regulations do not allow the storage of sensitive data in other countries, which is basically not accomplished by most cloud service provider as their data centers are usually spread around the world. Hence, being compliant to such regulations is essential.

Cloud computing has a fast growing and emerging market. Up to now, this mainly led to a heterogeneous landscape on service and interface offerings of cloud service providers. Due to that, the so-called "lock-in" effect can be often recognized. This means that although another cloud service provider offers better pricing conditions than the current one, switching to the other cloud service provider is still uneconomic because the opportunity costs for data and application transfer are too high. To bypass this issue, standardized services and interfaces might help to achieve interoperability between cloud service providers.

E-Government applications usually require more secure and reliable authentication and identification mechanisms. While most traditional e-Government services stick to stronger authentication and identification techniques, current cloud applications still lack in adoption of such techniques. However, e-Government services in the cloud require the same strength of authentication and identification as current e-Government applications do.

Auditing becomes essential e.g. in situations where compliance to specific regulations or policies must be verified. Cloud providers currently do not offer detailed auditing possibilities, hence further research in this field might be required.

Summarizing, e-Government applications and services in the cloud have to fulfill stronger and stricter requirements as needed e.g. for simple informational cloud services. A more comprehensive list on requirements of e-Government applications in the cloud can be found in [15].

3.3   E-Government Applications in the Cloud

Cloud computing has many facets and characteristics. Basically, cloud computing can be applied either in service or deployment models. While sensitive data is processed in most e-Government applications, the selection of the cloud model to be applied for e-Government applications in the cloud requires a thorough and systematic analysis. In fact, none of the existing cloud deployment and service models needs to be bared out for e-Government adoption from the beginning. However, some models might be easier applicable for e-Government than others. ENISA [16] or Zwattendorfer and Tauber [17] provide an overview of strengths and weaknesses of individual deployment models for e-Government adoption.

The decision on which cloud computing deployment model can be adopted for e-Government is difficult. According to [16] the private and community cloud model is recommended for the public sector as it allows more control with respect to security, privacy, or compliance with legal regulations. However, the public cloud model should not be neglected for e-Government adoption because of their low costs [17]. Non-sensitive data processing e-Government applications can be easily mitigated into a public cloud. Hybrid clouds are a mix of different clouds. Hybrid clouds could be also used for e-Government but usually require data separation as sensitive data should not be stored in public clouds.

Regarding the adoption of services models (IaaS, PaaS, or SaaS) for e-Government applications, generally all models are feasible. The IaaS model could be, for instance, used for archiving e-Government data or making backups. Additionally, it is conceivable to place open government data applications into an IaaS cloud. The PaaS model might be applicable for the development of customized public sector applications in the cloud. Such customized public sector services may include national or regional specific services, such as tax or electronic delivery services, or just simple services for filing applications to be processed in the public authorities' back-office. Finally, the SaaS model could be used for collaboration suites, workflow management systems for electronic documents, informational services for business or citizens, or any other "X as a Service"-based model such as "Identity as a Service" [18].

Summarizing, cloud computing offers a couple of benefits to public services and their e-Government solutions. According to [5] and [9], the main benefit is that governments can focus on their core business, which is serving the citizenry, instead of spending high efforts on server or IT management. Nevertheless, before moving public services to the cloud an extensive analysis is required whether the same level of security and data protection can be achieved as for traditional and existing e-Government services.

4   Cloud Computing in E-Government in Europe

The adoption of cloud computing in e-Government is not only a vision, it already became reality. Many countries or cities, especially across Europe, have already adopted cloud computing solutions in the public sector or are planning to do so [5]. In the next sub-sections we give some details on governmental cloud computing adoption within eight European countries, which currently also have a well-established and successful e-Government infrastructure in place.

4.1   Austria

Austria or Austrian cities have not adopted cloud computing in their public services yet. However, the Platform Digital Austria of the Federal Chancellery has published a position paper for the use of cloud computing in the public sector in 2012 [13]. This position paper especially covers legal, organizational, economic, and technical aspects, as well as opportunities and risks of cloud computing for public sector use. According to this paper, Austrian e-Government applications might be deployed in a private, community, or public cloud in the future. Moreover, they see all service levels applicable. IaaS could be used for archiving or backup purposes. By relying on PaaS, a particular platform supporting an easy applicable framework for developing e-Government cloud services is imaginable. On software level, future cloud services might include specific collaboration suites for public authorities or more security related services such as Identity as a Service [18].

4.2   Denmark

The Local Government Denmark started discussions on using cloud computing in the public sector already in early 2009 [19]. Moreover, according to KPMG [20] Denmark is one of the leading countries regarding the adoption of cloud computing in the public sector. For instance, in 2011 a Danish municipality planned to use Google Apps Services such as calendar or e-mail in their school systems [21]. In addition, a Danish procurement organization of a Danish municipality moved procurement services into the cloud in 2011 [22]. Although Denmark still struggles with security and privacy issues [20], the Danish Data Protection Agency e.g. judged the cloud service of Microsoft - Office 365[2] - to be compliant with the EU and Danish legislations [23]. In addition, cloud.dk offers public cloud services fully compliant with the Danish data legislation.

4.3   Finland

According to [24], Finland currently has no common strategy on cloud computing in the governmental sector. The government has only started an explanatory research for

---

[2] http://www.office365.com

centralizing ICT services where cloud computing could play a major role. Particularly, the aim of such centralized ICT infrastructure is bundling maintenance and support tasks as well as monitoring and helpdesk services. Referring to [24], no statistics exist which public authorities eventually use cloud computing services already. However, the Finish Government particularly emphasizes cloud computing in its report "Productive and Innovative Finland – Digital agenda for the years 2011-2020" [25].

4.4   France

France is currently one of those countries, which favor the development and installation of a nation-wide cloud for governments, a so-called G-Cloud (Governmental Cloud). France started its development of the G-Cloud named "Andromeda" in 2011. This G-Cloud, which is - in this particular case - a IaaS platform for governments, is currently set up and implemented by the two companies Orange[3] and Thales[4] [26]. The main aim for developing an own G-Cloud in France are data protection and legislative issues. A cloud especially developed for France can guarantee full compliance with national law in terms of data protection and security. Such compliance may not be achieved by e.g. adopting US-based services. Furthermore, Accenture is currently building up some kind of G-Cloud for the French Directorate of Legal and Administrative Information (DILA). This cloud shall offer French citizens fast and performing access to French public services [27].

4.5   Germany

Cloud computing is one of the main pillars of the ICT strategy of the German Federal Government [28]. This strategy has been published by the Federal Ministry of Economics and Technology in 2010 and aims on the digital future in Germany until 2015. Focusing on cloud computing, the objective is to facilitate and foster the development and installation of cloud computing services. In particular, both small- and medium-sized enterprises and the public sector should take advantage of cloud computing as fast as possible. The challenges (e.g. data security, quality assurance, easy integration, open standard, etc.), which need to be addressed for adopting cloud computing in Germany, are targeted in the so-called Cloud Computing Action Programme [29]. These challenges particularly arise when adapting existing IT concepts to the specific requirements of cloud computing.

4.6   Ireland

Ireland anchored cloud computing in their national governmental strategy. This strategy of the Irish government with the name "Technology Actions to Support the Smart Economy" was introduced by the Ministry of Energy and Communications and the Ministry of State in 2009 [30]. In more detail, Ireland sees cloud computing as one of

---

[3] http://www.orange.fr
[4] http://www.thalesgroup.com

the key drivers for economic growth in Ireland. They estimate high reductions in server and energy costs by expecting high value job generation at the same time [31]. Therefore, they released a separate "Cloud Computing Strategy" paper in 2012 [31]. They plan several governmental services based on cloud computing offered to their citizens, aiming on increased productivity by decreasing public expenditures at once [31]. Finally, the Irish government provided some kind of guidance for businesses when adopting cloud computing. This guidance entitled "SWiFT 10: Adopting the Cloud – Decision Support for Cloud Computing" consists of a set of standards which shall help businesses to lower obstacles when moving services into the cloud [31].

4.7   Spain

Pérez San-José et al. [34] did a thorough analysis on cloud computing in the Spanish public sector. This study concludes that there is still limited adoption of cloud computing in the public sector in Spain. Reasons are information integrity, privacy, and legal concerns. The central government is not the driving force behind cloud computing adoption but moreover local governments are. Local governments have a limited financial capacity in contrast to the central government and here cloud computing can tremendously help in saving costs. However, a lot of governments have adopted cloud computing already since more than three years. The favored deployment model in Spain is the private cloud (app. 58%), followed by the public cloud (app. 31%) and the hybrid cloud (app. 17%). The private cloud is favored because of higher control in terms of security and privacy. The community cloud model is generally seldom in Spain because it targets a fusion of specific sector applications (e.g. health), which seems to be undesired. [34]

4.8   United Kingdom

In 2011 the UK government published an ICT strategy, which also covers the topic on cloud computing [35]. This strategy particularly involves the implementation and installation of a G-Cloud in the UK. The main objectives of this G-Cloud are reducing ICT costs for governments, optimizing the use of data center infrastructure, and increasing public sector agility [35]. In fact, the installation of this G-Cloud is an iterative process. The first step, the realization of the so-called CloudStore[5], has been achieved in 2012. This CloudStore offers infrastructure, software, platform, and specialist services which can be bought online.

5   Comparison of Cloud Computing in the Public Sector across Europe

In this section we evaluate the adoption of governmental cloud computing within the eight European countries. We further also illustrate how governments benefit from

---

[5]   http://gcloud.civilservice.gov.uk/cloudstore/

cloud computing by placing sample cloud services as example. Furthermore, we discuss how challenges are being met or can be met in future.

5.1   Comparison across European Countries

In this sub-section, we compare whether cloud computing has been anchored in a national governmental strategy or not. Moreover, we elaborate whether cloud computing has been adopted more on national, regional, or municipality level. We further list, which cloud computing deployment models (public, private, community, or hybrid cloud) or service models (IaaS, PaaS, SaaS) are applied in the public sector. However, we do not distinguish whether those models are already in place or it is just planned by the individual country to adopt them. Finally, we list a sample on which government-related services were or are planned to be moved into the cloud.

Our comparison is based on a thorough literature review and web research, involving the countries Austria, Denmark, Finland, France, Germany, Ireland, Spain, and the UK. Table 1 shows the comparison of governmental cloud computing between these countries.

As can be seen, five of the eight investigated countries have anchored the adoption of cloud computing in the public sector in some kind of national strategy. For the remaining three countries, cloud computing is individually applied by local governments such as municipalities or cities.

Two of the evaluated countries have already adopted cloud computing and hence are in an executional stage. The other countries are still in the developing or planning phase. All countries, which have manifested cloud computing in some national strategy, are mostly still in the planning phase. However, the UK has already some governmental cloud services running. Nevertheless, the full implementation of their national cloud computing strategy will still take another few years.

Most countries plan the adoption of cloud computing in the public sector on national level. The reason for this is probably that security and privacy issues can be easier faced. In particular, Austria, France, Spain, and the UK are planning or are already developing a so-called G-Cloud (Governmental Cloud), a nation-wide private or community cloud. For Finland and Germany no further information was available to compare them against the other countries.

The most frequent planned and developed cloud computing deployment models amongst the evaluated countries are the private and the community cloud. This is because many of those countries tend to implement a national G-Cloud. The use of public clouds is also common across those countries. However, public clouds are and will be only applied if certain security and privacy requirements can be met or even be neglected.

When comparing cloud computing service models, 50% of the evaluated countries rely on the most common service models: Infrastructure as a Service (Iaas), Platform as a Service (PaaS), and Software as a Service (SaaS). France will set up a G-Cloud and focuses on IaaS. However, public authorities, which will take advantage of the offerings of this G-Cloud, will still be able to provide cloud computing services on

Table 1. - Comparison of cloud computing in e-Government across eight European countries

Country	Cloud Computing anchored in a National Strategy	Cloud Adoption	Cloud Adoption Level	Cloud Deployment Models	Cloud Service Models	Cloud e-Government Sample Services
Austria	Yes	Planned	National Regional City	Public Cloud Private Cloud Community Cloud	IaaS PaS SaaS	Backup/Archiving Cloud Framework for e-Government applications Collaboration Suites Identity as a Service
Denmark	No	Planned Executional	Municipality	Public Cloud Private Cloud Community Cloud	SaaS	E-Mail Procurement
Finland	No	Planned				
France	Yes	Development	National	Community Cloud	IaaS	
Germany	Yes	Planned				
Ireland	Yes	Planned	National	Public Cloud Private Cloud Community Cloud	IaaS PaaS SaaS	Open Data Public Information Repositories Collaboration Suites E-Mail
Spain	No	Planned Executional	National Regional City	Public Cloud Private Cloud Community Cloud Hybrid Cloud	IaaS PaaS SaaS	E-Government Services Open Government Citizen participation E-Mail Storage/Backup Office and Collaboration
UK	Yes	Development Executional	National	Private Cloud Community Cloud	IaaS PaaS SaaS	E-Mail Office Customer Relationship Management

other levels, i.e. PaaS or SaaS. For Denmark, information could only be found on the application of SaaS services.

Finally, in Table 1 we compared which services might be or are already moved to the cloud. The list is not exhaustive, so we named only the most important services. Applying IaaS, many countries think about cost-effective backup and archiving solutions. Additionally, IaaS can also play a major role for open data initiatives. For PaaS, the evaluated countries tend to offer some kind of cloud framework for e-Government solutions. This framework can be further taken as a basis for local governments or cities, where individual e-Government applications could be developed to. Finally, the most frequent SaaS services to be moved to the cloud are e-mail services. In addition, many countries think about the use of collaboration services or office suites in the cloud.

5.2   Benefits and Challenges

Cloud computing brings up many benefits for the public sector. However, several challenges must be coped with at the same time. In the following we briefly describe how individual countries can and could benefit from cloud computing and how challenges were or are going to be met by placing specific examples. We thereby refer to the benefits and challenges generally described in Section 3.

Benefits

Denmark, for instance, profited from cloud computing *scalability* during the "World Climate Conference" in 2009, where IT services where consumed from a community cloud. The reason for choosing a cloud approach was that high load peaks were expected before and during the conference [25].

The UK is going to set up a G-Cloud, which will also provide a marketplace for offering public sector applications to be shared and re-used. Those applications shall be offered based on a *pay-as-you-go pricing model* [31].

The government of Catalonia, a federal state in Spain, benefited from an *easy implementation* of cloud computing services by transferring their e-mail system (10.500 users) to the cloud in 2010. As they moved to Microsoft, their local Microsoft exchange system was easily upgraded by the system hosted in the Microsoft cloud.

The Calpe Municipal Council in Spain replaced the desktop PCs of its civil servants with virtual desktop terminals. The main objectives were cost savings and *low maintenance* [34].

All public authorities moving IT services into the cloud benefit from *high availability*. For instance, Amazon EC2[6] or Microsoft Azure[7] promise about 99.95% availability in their service level agreements (SLAs) supporting 24/7 uptime of governmental services.

Challenges

Security is still one of the biggest challenges in cloud computing, hence this challenge is not particularly relating to governmental cloud computing only. Currently, many countries rely on private and community clouds as they provide more control on the set up and infrastructure used for securing and protecting data [17]. An appropriate level of security is usually guaranteed by the cloud provider via SLAs or certification (e.g. ISO27001). Germany, for instance, published a whitepaper on security recommendations for cloud computing providers, which includes minimum information security requirements to be fulfilled for public sector cloud computing [37].

---

[6] http://aws.amazon.com/ec2/
[7] http://www.windowsazure.com/en-us/support/legal/sla/

To be compliant with *data protection* regulations, countries (e.g. France or the UK) favor the deployment of G-Clouds, which geographically store sensitive data only in the respective country [34]. Public cloud models are generally avoided by the individual countries due to the lack of data protection if sensitive data needs to be processed.

To avoid *interoperability* or *data portability* issues, many countries rely upon open source components and the implementation of open standards within their G-Cloud. For the UK Government CIO, this is also one main strand to build up the UK G-Cloud [31].

E-Government applications usually require more *secure and reliable authentication and identification mechanisms*. Cloud providers already start supporting such mechanism for their cloud services. For instance, the Austrian cloud provider Fabasoft[8] offers secure authentication supporting the national eID of Austria, Germany, and Switzerland. Such a support can act as key enabler for further migrations of e-Government services into the cloud.

Auditing is still an issue, which cannot be easily fulfilled by public cloud providers. However, relying on private or community clouds within the individual countries helps in overcoming this challenge.

Summarizing, according to [16] national governments of all EU countries should prepare national strategies for cloud computing in the public sector. Such strategies should particularly focus on security and resilience of cloud computing in their national economies over the next years. Moreover, they see a national strategy essential to avoid incompatible approaches and hence guarantee interoperable platforms and data formats.

6   Conclusions

High scalability and enormous cost savings potential are advantages of cloud computing also the public sector can benefit from. Many European countries have already adopted cloud computing in some public sector areas and others are still planning to do so. In this paper, we evaluated eight European countries on their cloud computing adoption in e-Government. Most of those evaluated countries are still in an early development phase for applying cloud computing services in the public sector. However, the use of cloud computing is anchored in some national strategy in half of the evaluated countries. The dominant cloud deployment model is the so-called G-Cloud, which constitutes a special private or community cloud for governmental services in the respective country. G-Clouds offer better compliance possibilities with national regulations and legislations than public clouds. However, a couple of countries still stick to public clouds for low risk and non-sensitive services. For public sector adoption, all cloud computing service models (IaaS, PaaS, and SaaS) are applicable. There also exist a couple of services which may be moved into the cloud by public authorities. Examples are backup/archiving services, open data applications, e-Government platforms, or collaboration and office suites for back-office procedures.

---

[8] http://www.fabasoft.com

While European countries already take advantage of cloud computing on national level, several initiatives also try to foster and facilitate cloud computing adoption on pan-European level. For instance, the EuroCloud[9] project constitutes an exchange platform for knowledge sharing and common interests on cloud computing across Europe. Currently, 27 countries participate in this project. Finally, the European Commission is currently setting up a co-funded €10 million project called "European Cloud Partnership"[10] within the 7th Framework Programme (FP7). The aim of this project is the development of a common framework for public sector cloud computing across Europe, especially focusing on electronic procurement requirements.

References

1. Mell, P., Grance, T.: The NIST definition of cloud computing. NIST (2010)
2. Khan, F., Zhang, B., Khan, S., Chen, S.: Technological leap frogging e-government through cloud computing. In: 4th IEEE International Conference on Broadband Network and Multimedia Technology, pp. 201–206 (2011)
3. ENISA. Priorities for Research on Current and Emerging Network Trends (2010)
4. European Commission. A Digital Agenda for Europe (2010)
5. Wyld, D.C.: Moving to the Cloud: An Introduction to Cloud Computing in Government (2009), http://www.businessofgovernment.org/sites/default/files/CloudComputingReport.pdf
6. Austrian Ministry of Finance. Verwaltungskosten senken für Bürger/innen und Unternehmen (2011)
7. Alford, T.: The Economics of cloud computing. Booz Allen Hamilton (2009)
8. Harms, R., Yamartino, M.: The Economics of the Cloud for the EU Public Sector (2010), http://www.microsoft.eu/portals/0/document/eu_public_sector_cloud_economics_a4.pdf
9. Bhisikar, A.: G-Cloud: New Paradigm Shift for Online Public Services. International Journal of Computer Applications 22(8), 24–29 (2011)
10. Zissis, D., Lekkas, D.: Addressing cloud computing security issues. Future Generation Computer Systems 28(3), 583–592 (2012)
11. Armbrust, M., Fox, A., Griffith, R., Joseph, A., Katz, R., Konwinski, A., Lee, G., Patterson, D., Rabkin, A., Stoica, I., Zaharia, M.: A view of cloud computing. Commun. ACM 53(4), 50–58 (2010)
12. Deussen, P., Strick, L., Peters, J.: Cloud-Computing für die öffentliche Verwaltung (2010), http://isprat.net/fileadmin/downloads/pdfs/cloud_studie.pdf
13. Reichstädter, P.: Cloud Computing - Positionspapier, pp. 1–42 (2011)
14. Repschlaeger, J., Wind, S., Zarnekow, R., Turowski, K.: A Reference Guide to Cloud Computing Dimensions: Infrastructure as a Service Classification Framework. In: 45th Hawaii International Conference on System Science, HICSS, pp. 2178–2188 (2012)
15. Zwattendorfer, B., Zefferer, T., Tauber, A.: Requirements for E-Government Applications in the Public Cloud (2013) (under review)
16. ENISA. Security & Resilience in Governmental Clouds (2011)

---

17. Zwattendorfer, B., Tauber, A.: The Public Cloud for E-Government. In: IADIS International Conference Collaborative Technologies (2012b)
18. Roessler, T.: E-Government und Cloud-Computing (2010),
    https://demo.egiz.gv.at/plain/content/download/678/3913/
    file/E-Government%20und%20Cloud-Computing.pdf
19. EUPractice.eu. (2009), http://www.epractice.eu/en/news/292790
20. KPMG. Exploring the Cloud: A Global Study of Governments' Adoption of Cloud (2012),
    http://images.forbes.com/forbesinsights/StudyPDFs/exploring-
    cloud.pdf
21. Datatilsynet. Processing of sensitive personal data in a cloud solution (2011),
    http://www.datatilsynet.dk/english/processing-of-sensitive-
    personal-data-in-a-cloud-solution/
22. OurBusinessNews.com.   (2011),   http://www.ourbusinessnews.com/tdc-
    gets-danish-cloud-computing-framework-deal/
23. E-Commerce Law Week. Issue 719 (2012),
    http://www.lexology.com/library/detail.aspx?g=2419f3a4-186e-
    4c45-9d16-dfbbb4d2cf94
24. Ylätupa, T.: Cloud Computing in the ICT of Finnish Public Administration (2011),
    https://publications.theseus.fi/bitstream/handle/10024/
    34651/Ylatupa_Tuomas.pdf?sequence=1
25. Frelle-Petersen, L., Valli, T., Sigurðardóttir, G., De Brisis, K., Enzell, M.: Nordic Public Sector Cloud Computing – a discussion paper (2012),
    http://www.norden.org/en/publications/publikationer/
    2011-566/at_download/publicationfile
26. Auffray, C.: Cloud Andromeda: Orange and Thales welcome and are ready to start. ZDNet (2012), http://www.zdnet.fr/actualites/cloud-andromede-orange-
    et-thales-se-felicitent-et-se-disent-prets-a-demarrer-
    39770969.htm
27. Zacks Equity Research. Accenture to Build French G-Cloud (2012),
    http://www.zacks.com/stock/news/67978/
    Accenture+to+Build+French+G-Cloud
28. Federal Ministry of Economics and Technology (BMWi). ICT Strategy of the German Federal Government: Digital Germany 2015 (2010a)
29. Federal Ministry of Economics and Technology (BMWi). Action Programme Cloud Computing (2010b)
30. Irish Government. Technology Actions to Support the Smart Economy (2009)
31. Robinson, N.: Computing in the public sector: rapid international stocktaking (2010)
32. Howlin, B.: Cloud Computing Strategy 2012 (2012), http://per.gov.ie/wp-
    content/uploads/Cloud-Computing-Strategy.pdf
33. Bruton, R.: New standards to provide guidance to business on adopting cloud computing, Department of Jobs, Enterprise, and Innovation (DJEI) (2012),
    http://www.djei.ie/press/2012/20120521.htm
34. Pérez San-José, P., de la Fuente Rodríguez, S., García Pérez, L., Gutiérrez Borge, C., Álvarez Alonso, E.: Study on cloud computing in the Spanish public sector, p. 178 (2012)
35. UK Cabinet Office. Government ICT Strategy (2011),
    http://www.cabinetoffice.gov.uk/content/
    government-ict-strategy
36. European Parliament (Directorate General for Internal Policies – Policy Departement A: Economic and scientific policy). Cloud Computing – Study (2012)
37. Federal Office for Information Security. Security Recommendations for Cloud Computing Providers. White Paper (2010)

Towards a Linked Geospatial Data Infrastructure

Sonya Abbas and Adegboyega Ojo

Digital Enterprise Research Institute, National University of Ireland,
Galway, Ireland
{sonya.abbas,adegboyega.ojo}@deri.org

Abstract. The pressure of opening access to public sector geospatial information traditionally managed within disparate spatial data infrastructures (SDI) is driven by a combination of factors. These factors include the adoption of open data programs and the need to integrate spatial data across sectors and levels of government for specific applications. Informed by the success of the Linked Open Data community, efforts to leverage Linked Data in enabling global access to spatial data currently managed within national and regional SDIs are emerging. However, these early efforts do not provide guidelines for implementing such Linked SDI nor articulate the socio-technical requirements for a successful Linked Geospatial Data strategy. By analyzing existing SDI architectures and emerging Linked SDI requirements, we develop Reference Architecture for building interoperable Linked SDIs.

Keywords: Linked Geospatial Data, Spatial Data Infrastructure (SDI), INSPIRE, e-Government Infostructure.

1 Introduction

Geospatial or geographic data describing information tied to some locations on Earth's surface [1], constitute an important and rapidly growing category of government data assets. This category of data are considered critical for planning, policy making and delivering innovative location based services in domains including disaster mitigation, public health, geology, civil protection and agriculture [2].

An important aspect of managing geospatial data is the provisioning of the so-called Spatial Data Infrastructure (SDI); an information infrastructure providing access and enabling interoperability among spatial information based on standards, policies, regulations and coordination mechanisms [3][4]. As at 2009, over 120 countries have developed one form of National SDI or another [4]. With increasing information integration efforts at regional and global levels and wide spread adoption of Open Government and data programs by governments in Europe and other parts of the world, there are compelling arguments for revisiting the notion of "Global SDI" (GSDI). GSDI encompasses the policies, technologies, standards and human resources necessary for the effective collection, management, access, delivery and utilization of geospatial data in a global community [5]. According to [6], a GSDI is expected to integrate information from regional SDIs to provide so-called global datasets with global spatial coverage.

A. Kő et al. (Eds.): EGOVIS/EDEM 2013, LNCS 8061, pp. 196–210, 2013.

While efforts by organizations like Open Geospatial Consortium (OGC) [7] and the United Nations Geospatial Information Working Group (UNGIWG) [8] in producing standards and reference models have significantly advanced the interoperability and exchange of geospatial information, the goal of realizing a global SDI is far from realized. Specifically, no single or distributed repository of geospatial data with global spatial coverage based on OGC standards and reference framework is available.

Although not strictly a GSDI, the INSPIRE (Infrastructure for Spatial Information in the European Community) SDI [9] which employs OGC standards like the Geography Markup Language (GML); presents an innovative approach to integrate National SDIs in a specific region based on a legally enforceable instrument. The SDI defines several spatial data themes and services; metadata standard, network services and technology specifications, agreement on sharing and access, coordination and monitoring mechanisms as well as processes and procedures. Unfortunately, the use of legally enforceable instrument as way to mandate the adoption of standards is not feasible at a global level.

Interestingly, the Linked Data community has arguably built a truly global space of data maintained by a dedicated community of researchers and practitioners based on standards and best practices provided by the World Wide Web Consortium (W3C) [10]. This success could be attributed to the simple representation format of the data - Resource Description Framework (RDF), its widespread adoption, and the strong global influence of the W3C consortium. Not surprisingly, the concept of Linked Geospatial (or Geospatial Linked) Data, i.e. geospatial data stored in RDF, created, managed and accessible based on the Linked Data principles and standards has appeared in the last few years [11][12]. Most of Linked geospatial studies have so far aimed at providing an alternative representation format and access method to geospatial data maintained within SDIs. For example, the Linked Geodata platform [13][11].

However, current studies on Linked geospatial data are fragmented and do not provide concrete guidelines for implementing a Linked SDI nor do they provide the policy, standards and community imperatives for a successful Linked geospatial data strategy. Our goal in this work is two folds: 1) to integrate and organize existing work on Linked geospatial data and Linked SDI into a reference model for government and 2) to highlight the policy, standards and organizational requirements for Linked SDI. For illustration, the paper also shows how Linked Data could be employed in the context of the INSPIRE SDI.

The rest of the paper is organized as follows: Section 2 presents the background on SDI and Linked Data. Our approach for developing the Linked SDI reference model is presented in Section 3. The synthesized SDI reference model is presented in Section 4 and refined for Linked Data enabled implementation in Section 5. Validation of the LSDI reference model is presented in Section 6 and discussed in Section 7. Finally, some concluding remarks are presented in Section 8.

2   Background

This section provides conceptual underpinnings and characteristics of SDIs and highlights how Linked Data concept provides a complementary semantic information integration approach for implementing SDIs and global SDIs.

2.1   Spatial Data Infrastructure

SDI is a multi-disciplinary concept that includes people, data, access networks, institutional policies, technical standards and human resources [14]. According [6], the notion of SDIs is continually evolving and also an inherently hierarchical, where one SDI is related to another belonging to different jurisdictional levels, typically global, regional, national, local and corporate levels.

As a platform, SDIs link data users to providers on the basis of the common goal of data sharing. Regardless of the jurisdiction of SDIs, they enhance the capability of governments to engage in systems-based, integrated and holistic decision making about the future of that jurisdiction [14]. They operate subject to policies that govern access, use, pricing of services, sustained financing, quality management and human resources development [15].

A number of features are commonly associated with SDIs [14]: 1) they enable communication and sharing of information, 2) they are networked infrastructures that allows all user benefits when a user joins the network, 3) they encompass both technical and social elements and therefore are socio-technical systems, 4) they support wide array of stakeholders in the communication and sharing of spatial data, 5) they operate within unstable environments and so need to adaptive, 6) they develop institutionalized properties in their ability to communicate, connect and share between stakeholders.

These functionalities are realized through a number of core components. Table 1 identifies the typical elements of SDIs as described in literature: [1], [3], [4], [6], [9], [16] and [17]. Consistent with the description of SDI above, elements of an SDI are essentially of the following types: Policy, Standards, Data, Network Access and People.

Efforts to integrate geospatial information across SDIs rely on the use of set of standards and institutional agreements such as those of OGC and UNGIWG. Given that effectiveness of standards is linked to the degree of its adoption, standards by global an influential entities such as W3C are relatively more likely to succeed. In addition, meaningful spatial information integration requires adopting of shared vocabularies by geospatial data providers or SDIs. The Linked Data approach presented in the next section is recognized as a global standard for publishing semantically-rich open (or enterprise) data.

Table 1. Elements of Spatial Data Infrastructures

No.	Source	SDI Elements
1	[9]	Data, Network, Policy, Standards, and People
2	[3]	Applications, Network, Policy, Data (foundation, framework, application-specific), Metadata and Partnership
3	[6]	Policy, Fundamental Datasets, Technical standards, Access Network and People
4	[4]	Legislative Framework, Content and Data Framework and Metadata and Standard, Quality Issues, Geo-portals and Distributed Information Systems, Architecture, Human Factors, Dissemination and Implementation
5	[1]	Communities, Roles (user, contributor, custodian, governing body, operational body, contact, educator, promoter, funder, member, communication channel, SDI catalog), Spatial asset (core asset, spatial asset metadata), Enterprise objects (person, team, organization, spatial dataset, spatial application, spatial service, geo-portal), Policies (governance, role assignment, infrastructure, standards, quality, promotion, education, funding, access, membership), Interactions and Objectives
6	[17]	Services (web service, SDI service, processing service – transformation service-, information management service-portrayal service, access service, catalog service, gazetteer service, knowledge model service-, application service) SDI client (application, geo-portal) Repository (metadata, knowledge model, dataset –spatial-)
7	[16]	Clients (user applications), Middleware (geo-processing, catalogue services, catalogues), Content repository (geospatial data, other data)

2.2   Linked Data and Spatial Data Infrastructure

Linked Data refers to a set of good practices for publishing and connecting structured data on the web [10]. Technically, Linked Data is a machine-readable data that is linked to external data sets on the rapidly expanding Web of Data Cloud. The goal of Linked Data according to Berners-Lee is to create a single global data space on the web. The notion of Linked Data is underpinned by four core principles [10]: 1) use of URIs (Uniform Resource Identifier) as names for things, 2) use of HTTP URIs so that people can look up those names, 3) URI should return useful information when looked up by utilizing standards such as RDF and SPARQL and 4) include links to URIs, so they can discover more things.

In recent years, studies on the adoption of Linked Data and Semantic Web in developing SDI have grown [18]. The W3C Incubator Group for example, provides many annotation methods and defines XLINK as a language for adding hyperlinks to XML and RDFa to enrich metadata for OGC standards like GML [19]. Works such as [19] and [20] have also shown how OGC services and semantic technologies can be integrated. Specifically, [20] highlights how Linked Data can be used within an SDI and compares RDF with GML. In [21], the treatment of Geo-Linked Data includes proxies which incorporate references to Geoweb and services in Semantic Web. In their work, URI describes a real world resource and the user can access either RDF or HTML through Geo Linked Data server or a GML representation in a Geoweb service.

Other works in this domain seek to refine Linked Data principles to meet geospatial community requirements. They address more specific issue related to Linked Data such as URI design, data models for representing and querying spatial data on the Semantic Web. For instance, the United Kingdom Government through its CTO council has developed best practices and guidelines for designing URIs for geospatial data [22]. In [23], proposal for refining existing W3C data models to meet the representational and querying needs of spatial data in the Semantic Web was presented using stRDF and stSPARQL standards. stRDF is an extension of RDF that allows for the representation of temporal geospatial data while stSPARQL adds filters to SPARQL queries to enable the discovery of topological relations between geometries.

Research on linking URIs is fundamental in enabling integration of data into the web of data cloud. Different approaches have been proposed for linking. Authors of [24] encode hierarchical topological relations between geographic entities over traditional spatial queries to link Great Britain datasets even in the absence of explicit geometric information. Other researches focus on the ontologies linking level to discover semantic relationships [25][26]. In [27], issues arising when interlinking the LoD cloud was addressed. They propose the use of upper level ontologies and schema level links to address these issues. They also commented on the misuse of the "owl:sameAs" in the LoD cloud. Authors of [24] support this argument by clarifying that "owl:sameAs" relation is over-used for linking entities which leads to mismatching problems. Instead they propose using alternative relationships such as "rdfs:seeAlso" and "coref:duplicate" to find related URIs no matter the nature of the relationship.

3   Approach

The objectives of our study includes: 1) providing a reference architecture for a Linked Data enabled Spatial Data Infrastructure, 2) showing how the reference architecture could be employed in analyzing the requirements a Linked Data strategy, using the INSPIRE initiative as example. Our SDI reference model aims to capture the major elements of existing SDIs as described in different scholarly works and international standards such as those related to The Open Geospatial Consortium [7]. The reference model will also consider future SDI needs.

The Linked SDI reference model is developed in two major steps in line with approach for developing reference architectures [28]: 1) Construction of a base reference architecture for traditional SDIs, 2) Refinement of the base reference architecture based on the Linked Data principles and existing work on Linked SDI to produce a Linked SDI reference architecture. These steps are explained below:

Step 1 - Constructing the SDI Base Reference Architecture (SDI-BRA):
Constructing the SDI-BRA consists of the following five activities: 1) identifying scholarly publications describing specific SDIs, 2) carrying out content analyses of the definition, form or nature and elements of SDIs described in these papers, 3) identifying the core dimensions of the SDI-BRA and core elements constituting each dimension, 4) integrating the dimensions and their elements to produce the SDI BRA, and 5) validating the SDI-BRA with respect to existing SDI architectures.

Step 2 - Refining SDI-BRA to Linked SDI Reference Architecture (LSDI-RA):
The refinement of the SDI-BRA is done through three major activities including 1) analyzing and consolidating information in literature on SDI and Linked Data, 2) articulating requirements for a Linked Data SDI from information obtained in activity #1 as the architectural vision, and 3) extending the SDI-BRA developed in Step #1 based on the architectural vision to obtain the reference architecture for Linked SDI.

Finally, we highlight the use of the Linked SDI-RA in identifying and prescribing critical actions for moving towards a Linked Data enabled INSPIRE SDI.

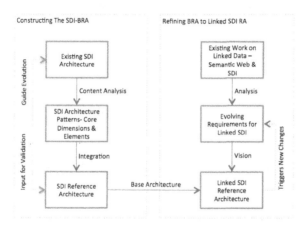

Fig. 1. Approach for Linked SDI Reference Architecture

4   Reference Model for Spatial Data Infrastructure

In this section, we develop the base reference model based on our review of SDI related work, partly presented in Section 2. SDIs have evolved from product and database-oriented infrastructures to a new generation of infostructures that are more process-oriented and emphasize partnerships and stakeholders involvement [9].

To obtain the overall structure or core dimensions of our SDI-BRA, we carry out content analysis on the various aspects of SDI described in Table 1. Our analysis showed that the five classic dimensions of SDI which include Data, Network, People, Standards and Policy; were structurally adequate to describe SDIs. These five dimensions are elaborated below.

Data Dimension describes the typical categories of datasets maintained by SDIs. At least five kinds of data are identified by SDIs including: 1) framework datasets that provide thematic information in a national context such as land cover and hydrography [3], 2) foundation datasets that covers geospatial aspect of SDI such as geodetic control, basic topography and geo names datasets [3], 3) application-specific datasets [3], 4) knowledge model that defines knowledge about the type, location, quality and ownership of datasets [5], and finally the 5) catalogue of meta data to facilitate the process of discovery of the available data through the SDI and the conditions of use [3].

Network Access Dimension consists of services and clients applications. At least three kinds of services are provided by SDIs including generic SDI services, processing and transformation services to information management services. SDI services cover geo-services, geographic information services and all web services in an SDI [17]. Information management services include portrayal services for visualization of spatial datasets, access services for downloading, and gazetter services to link toponyms and their spatial locations [17]. SDIs should also provide geo portals and applications as clients to allow geographic information access.

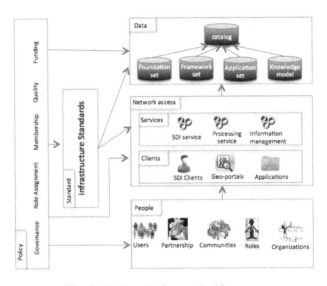

Fig. 2. SDI Base Reference Architecture

People Dimension includes all stakeholders, both users and producers of spatial information interacting with the SDI to drive the development and utilization of the SDI [6] such as organizations, roles, partnerships and communities.

Infrastructure Standards Dimension constitutes an important SDI component which provides technical guidance and enforceable rules to be followed by spatial data providers and communities in the development and use of SDIs [9]. The dimension enables interoperation across SDI hierarchies.

Policy Dimension specifies important decisions on core aspects of the SDI including governance, role assignment to memberships, quality and funding. Two categories of policies have been defined which are legislation/senior policy and regulation/local policy. Relationships between these two classes of policies are elaborated in [3].

We present in Fig.2 the five dimensions and their core dimensions in Fig.1. We present in Section 5 how this reference model could be refined to support Linked Data enabled SDI development.

5   Blueprint for Linked Geospatial Data Infrastructure

This section describes the core elements of a Linked SDI Reference Architecture (LSDI-RA). We understand a Linked Data enabled SDI or simply Linked SDI as an information infrastructure with traditional SDI capabilities and that is in addition capable leveraging Linked Data principles in the management and integration of its datasets by utilizing Semantic Web technologies. We consider an LSDI or indeed any SDI as a socio-technical system and thus organize the description of its elements into two categories: 1) the technical elements comprising the data and network access components described in Section 5.1 and 2) the socio-organizational components consisting of the enabling and constraining policy, standards as well as people and community responsible for creating, using and evolving the technical components of the SDI, described in Section 5.2. Fig.3. presents a summary of the Linked SDI Reference Architecture discussed in Sections 5.1 and 5.2.

5.1   Technical Components

We identify here the major elements of the Data and Networked Access dimensions of our LSDI reference model by refining the elements of the BRA in Section 4 with the emergent semantic requirements obtained from the existing work on Linked Data and SDIs.

Data – The data dimension of LSDI consists of the three categories of datasets, a knowledge model, and catalog as described in the SDI-BRA. The Foundation dataset in LSDI includes resources describing places or locations in RDF format [18] such as Geonames [10]. The representation and management of foundational data in Linked SDI is based on the Linked Data principles. For instance, places or locations described in the foundational datasets are expected to have URI with links pointing to other related places based on one or more geospatial relations   [29]. In addition, Linked SDIs are also expected to manage thematic Geospatial data (or Framework datasets), such as Earth Observation [18], Land Cover [7], Topography [19] and Administrative Hierarchy [30] datasets as Linked Data. Likewise, application-specific datasets such as DBpedia dataset [18], Linked Geodata [31] and Geoweb [9] are also maintained as Linked Data on the Linked SDI. Ontologies [19], [32], [9] and ontology mapping resources [5] underpinning RDF-based datasets are maintained as part of the knowledge model in Linked SDI. User-generated contents from the social processes enabling user contributions such as geo-tagging or resource tagging [30] are also managed by Linked SDIs. Finally the LSDI catalog contains metadata of datasets. In summary, the requirements for the Data component of a Linked SDI are abstracted in Table 2.

Table 2. Requirements for LSDI Data Component

Element	Requirement	Source
Foundation dataset	Support the management of reference or location information like geographical names as Linked Data	[18], [19]
Framework dataset	Enable the management of thematic geospatial data such as topography, administrative hierarchy, earth observation and cover; as Linked Data	[19], [30], [31], [31]
Application specific dataset	Should manage other application specific geospatial information (e.g. "Geoweb") as Linked Data	[18], [31], [26]
Knowledge model	Ontologies, vocabularies and other semantic assets for describing geospatial datasets should be managed as part of the knowledge model	[19][32][26], [11]
User generated Contents	Given the social contexts for SDIs, an LSDI must support semantic annotations of user-generated contents based on sematic assets that is part of the knowledge model	[30]
Catalog	Catalog must support semantic description and retrieval of geospatial data items based on or more of the semantic assets maintained in knowledge model	

Network Access - LSDI are expected to provide Linked SDI services and semantic client applications as part of the network access components. The Linked open services [32], Semantic Web services [32], resource-based services [32] and Geoweb services with RDF and OWL support [26] are examples of Linked SDI based services that could be provided. In addition, transformation services such as GML2RDF/XML transformations [18], query rewriting [30] and others are expected to enable transition from traditional SDI to Linked SDI. At information management level, Linked SDI should offer a variety of services ranges from map viewing [18] [26], publishing and sharing services [30], semantic ontology alignment [11] to SPARQL endpoints [30] and Geo Linked Data endpoint [26]. For Linked SDI clients, there is a need to provide portals and applications enabling access to stakeholders. For example, DBpedia mobile application provides Linked Data browser [18] whereas authors of [31] provide Linked geodata portals. Other available LSDI applications include location-centric DBpedia client [18], location-aware Semantic Web client [4], DBpedia mobile application [4][30], Linked Data-aware client [32], NOA fire monitoring and management applications [31] and Semantic Web applications [26].

Table 3. LSDI Network Access Component

Element	Requirement	Source
SDI services	Support RDF and OWL based Semantic Web services, resource based services and Geoweb services that interacts with the other components	[18], [9]
Processing Services	Transformation tools from traditional SDI languages to the new Linked SDI languages (e.g. GML2RDF/XML) should be covered by the processing services	[19], [30]
Information management Services	Support the management of Linked SDI by providing publishing and sharing services, web mapping services and geo Linked Data endpoint (SPARQL) that enable semantic geospatial data searching	[18],[30], [26]
SDI clients	Support semantic and Linked Data based query and retrieval of geospatial information	
Geo-portals	There is a need to provide geo-portals that enable use cases of stakeholders	[18], [31]
Applications	Should provide location-based applications that support Semantic Web and Linked Data	[9],[18], [30], [31], [32]

5.2 Policy and Organizational Requirements

People – LSDI realization requires the existence of people and stakeholders that can interact and develop the LSDI. Stakeholders consists expert, normal users, and government organizations [18]. As part of this dimension, we also indicate interests groups related to specific projects that have contributed to the development Linked SDI. These initiatives include DBpedia [30], EU Projects like SOA4All and SEALS [32], SemsorGrid4Env project, TELEIOS project, NOA [31], and Bio2RDF project [8]. Increasingly important stakeholder category are the communities that interact with, develop and shape the future of LSDI, e.g. the Linked Open Services LOS community [32], Semantic Web and Linked Data community [31], Geoweb community [9].

Table 4. LSDI People Component

Element	Requirement	Source
Users	LSDI should support different user categories including experts, public, private and non-governmental organizations or researchers	[21]
Communities	LSDI requires cooperation between Linked Data communities and Geoweb communities. The infrastructure must also enable these communities contribute contents (e.g. upload datasets) or to tag available existing datasets	[9], [31], [32]
Organizations	Supporting governmental organizations contributing to the development of geospatial contents managed on the LSDI	[8], [18], [30], [31], [32]

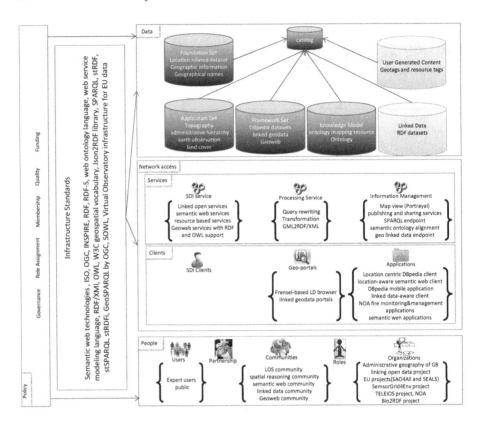

Fig.3. Linked SDI Reference Architecture

Standards – the LSDI infrastructure must support a host of Semantic Web and Linked Data related standards in addition to the traditional geospatial related technical standards. In particular, standards such as Resource Description Framework (RDF), Web Ontology Language (OWL), SPARQL and geospatial extensions of these standards such as GeoSPARQL by OGC, W3C geospatial web service modeling language, stRDF, stSPARQL, stRDFi,[31]. A list of standards related to Linked SDI implementation is provided in Table 5 below.

Table 5. LSDI Standards Component

Element	Requirement	Source
Infrastructure Standards	LSDI should support a number of Semantic Web and Linked Data related standards in addition to geospatial extensions of these standards. Examples of standards that such as that support geo-Linked Data implementation such as ISO, OGC, RDF, RDF-S, RDF/XMl, OWL, W3C geospatial vocabulary, SPARQL, stRDF, stSPARQL, stRDFi, GeoSPARQL, and SOWL	[19], [31], [32]

Policy – This dimension specifies additional policy issues arising from the adoption of semantic and Linked Data technologies SDI development. For instance, the vocabularies, ontologies and other semantic assets needs to be managed with additional roles defined to support additional activities [33]. At the same time, specific governance activities such as those related to URI management [22]. In addition, policies on adoption of best practices related to Semantic Web and by geo Linked Data, e.g. best practices for designing URIs for geospatial data or publishing Geoweb resources with RDF metadata [9], are designed in this dimension. Some policy requirements for LSDI are presented in Table 6.

Table 6. LSDI Policy Component

Element	Requirement	Source
Governance	Policies on the management of semantic assets related Linked geospatial datasets (e.g. URIs for geospatial data) must be available	[22], [33]
Membership	Policies on the roles of agencies in the development and management of these semantic assets must also be considered. For instance, how will the vocabulary for geospatial datasets be developed?	[33]

6   Using the Linked SDI Reference Architecture

This section briefly highlights the use of the Linked SDI Reference Architecture presented in Section 5 and shows how the reference architecture adequate captures elements the INSPIRE SDI as example. In Fig.4. we describe the intended use of our SDI-BRA to develop a SDI family architecture; such as the INSPIRE Family Architecture. Our SDI-BRA could also be directly employed in developing concrete SDIs such as the UK National INSPIRE-compliant SDI architecture. Our LSDI-RA could in general: 1) guide the development of new LSDI family architecture or instance architecture, 2) facilitate the development of LSDI across governance levels, from local to national and regional, 3) enable interoperability among LSDI instances, e.g. see Figure 5 showing how the INSPIRE SDI architecture can be mapped to our LSDI-RA.

Another use of our LSDI-RA in the case of the INSPIRE SDI is in the refinement of elements. For instance, the data components of the INSPIRE SDI (labeled as servers) could be refined into the Framework, Foundation and Application datasets. To transition from an INSPIRE-compliant SDI to a Linked SDI, a concrete approach is to implement the requirements described in Tables 2 to 6, guided by the LSDI-RA in Fig.3.

An important aspect of the LSDI-RA is the specified interactions among architectural components and the role of the Policy and Technical Standards elements in deciding how to implement the other three components.

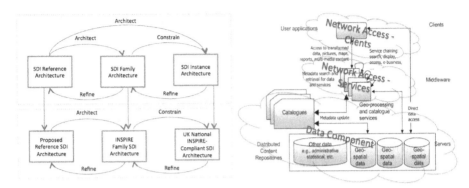

Fig. 3. Using the LSDI-RA   **Fig. 4.** Mapping INSPIRE to LSDI-RA

In summary, the value of the LSDI-RA like any RA includes [28]: 1) capturing the reusable concepts and implementations in past LSDIs for use in future SDI architecture initiatives, 2) controlling complexity of LSDI architectures through standardization on architecture patterns, 3) enabling common understanding of SDIs and emerging LSDIs based on common architecture patterns, and 4) reducing risk in future LSDI implementations.

7   Discussion

In the absence of comprehensive guidelines for developing Linked SDI, we have developed in this work a Linked SDI RA by consolidating existing work and analyzing emerging semantic and Linked Data geospatial requirements. While the state-of-the-art in Linked SDI is on transforming spatial data from GML and other native formats to RDF, developing ontologies to support such transformation and how to provisioning SPARQL endpoints for geospatial data [35], we provide an holistic perspective to the problem of transitioning from traditional SDI to Linked SDI.

However, gaining confidence in our LSDI-RA requires its demonstrated validity. Since the RA is based on existing SDI architectures and emerging Linked SDI requirements, we could argue for its contents validity by design – that it sufficiently captures key elements of existing and future (Linked) SDI architectures.

8   Conclusion

The contribution of this work lies in the elaboration of a Reference Architecture for Linked SDI based on existing SDIs and emerging Linked SDI needs. The developed Reference Architecture provides both a schema for contextualizing early efforts in LSDI and roadmap for future development of LSDI. We believe that the LSDI RA would be useful for governments and regional initiatives (e.g. INSPIRE) aiming to develop Global SDIs based on Linked Data and Semantic Web principle. Like all reference architectures, concrete use of the Reference Architecture will provide useful feedbacks for its refinement and evolution.

References

1. Béjar, R., Latre, M.Á., Nogueras-Iso, J., Muro-Medrano, P.R., Zarazaga-Soria, F.J.: An RM-ODP enterprise view for spatial data infrastructures. Computer Standards & Interfaces 34, 263–272 (2012)
2. Tóth, K., Portele, C., Illert, A., Lutz, M., De Lima, M.N.: A conceptual Model for developing Interoperability Specifications in Spatial Data Infrastructures (2012)
3. Groot, R.: Spatial data infrastructure (SDI) for sustainable land management. ITC Journal (1997)
4. Foley, R., Maynooth, N.U.I.: Integrated Spatial Data Infrastructure, pp. 507–511 (2009)
5. Rajabifard, A., Feeney, M.-E.F., Williamson, I.P.: Future directions for SDI development. International Journal of Applied Earth Observation and Geoinformation 4, 11–22 (2002)
6. Rajabifard, A., Williamson, I.P., Holland, P., Johnstone, G.: From Local to Global SDI initiatives: a pyramid building blocks. In: Proceedings of the 4th GSDI Conference, Cape Town, South Africa, p. 7 (2000)
7. The Open Geospatial Consortium: OGC Reference Model (2011)
8. UNGIWG: United Nations Spatial Data Infrastructure (2007)
9. Craglia, M.A.X., Annoni, A.: INSPIRE: An Innovative Approach to the Development 5 (2007)
10. Bizer, C., Heath, T., Berners-Lee, T.: Linked data-the story so far. International Journal on Semantic Web and Information Systems (IJSWIS) 5, 1–22 (2009)
11. Jain, P., Hitzler, P., Sheth, A.P., Verma, K., Yeh, P.Z.: Ontology alignment for linked open data. In: Patel-Schneider, P.F., Pan, Y., Hitzler, P., Mika, P., Zhang, L., Pan, J.Z., Horrocks, I., Glimm, B. (eds.) ISWC 2010, Part I. LNCS, vol. 6496, pp. 402–417. Springer, Heidelberg (2010)
12. Koubarakis, M., Karpathiotakis, M., Kyzirakos, K., Nikolaou, C., Sioutis, M.: Data Models and Query Languages for Linked Geospatial Data. In: Eiter, T., Krennwallner, T. (eds.) Reasoning Web 2012. LNCS, vol. 7487, pp. 290–328. Springer, Heidelberg (2012)
13. Schade, S., Granell, C., Díaz, L.: Augmenting SDI with linked data. In: Workshop On Linked Spatiotemporal Data, in conjunction with the 6th International Conference on Geographic Information Science (GIScience 2010), Zurich, September 14 (2010)
14. Crompvoets, J., Rajabifard, A., Van Loenen, B., Fernandez, T.D.: A multi-view framework to Assess SDIs. Space for Geo-Information (RGI), Wageningen University and Centre for SDIs and Land Administration, Department of Geomatics, The University of Melbourne (2008)
15. Grothe, M.: Implementing INSPIRE (principles) towards an Enterprise SDI for Rijkswaterstaat. Water Management
16. Paper, S.P., Smits, P.C., Murre, L., Gould, M., Sandgren, U., Murray, K., Pross, E., Wirthmann, A., Konecny, M.: Infrastructure for Spatial Information in Europe INSPIRE Architecture and Standards Position Paper. Presidency (2002)
17. Bejar, R., Latre, M.Á., Nogueras-iso, J., Muro-Medrano, P.R., Zarazaga-Soria, F.J.: An architectural style for spatial data infrastructures. Internal Journal of Geographical Information Science 23, 271–294 (2009)
18. Becker, C., Bizer, C.: Dbpedia mobile: A location-enabled linked data browser. In: Linked Data on the Web, LDOW 2008, pp. 6–7 (2008)
19. Goodwin, J., Dolbear, C., Hart, G.: Geographical Linked Data: The Administrative Geography of Great Britain on the Semantic Web. Transactions in GIS 12, 19–30 (2008)
20. Jain, P., Hitzler, P., Yeh, P., Verma, K., Sheth, A.: Linked data is merely more data. Linked Data Meets Artificial Intelligence, 82–86 (2010)

21. Schade, S., Cox, S.: Linked data in sdi or how gml is not about trees. In: Proceedings of the 13th AGILE International Conference on Geographic Information Science-Geospatial Thinking, pp. 1–10 (2010)
22. Davidson, P.: Designing URI Sets for the UK Public Sector (2010)
23. Koubarakis, M., Kyzirakos, K., Karpathiotakis, M., Nikolaou, C., Sioutis, M., Vassos, S., Michail, D., Herekakis, T., Kontoes, C., Papoutsis, I.: Challenges for Qualitative Spatial Reasoning in Linked Geospatial Data. In: Worskshop on Benchmark and Applications of Spatial Reasoning, IJCAI 2011, pp. 33–38 (2011)
24. Parundekar, R., Knoblock, C.A., Ambite, J.L.: Linking and building ontologies of linked data. In: Patel-Schneider, P.F., Pan, Y., Hitzler, P., Mika, P., Zhang, L., Pan, J.Z., Horrocks, I., Glimm, B. (eds.) ISWC 2010, Part I. LNCS, vol. 6496, pp. 598–614. Springer, Heidelberg (2010)
25. Cyganiak, R., Maali, F., Peristeras, V.: Self-service linked government data with dcat and gridworks. In: Proceedings of the 6th International Conference on Semantic Systems 1 (2010)
26. Lopez-Pellicer, F.J., Silva, M.J., Chaves, M., Javier Zarazaga-Soria, F., Muro-Medrano, P.R.: Geo linked data. In: Bringas, P.G., Hameurlain, A., Quirchmayr, G. (eds.) DEXA 2010, Part I. LNCS, vol. 6261, pp. 495–502. Springer, Heidelberg (2010)
27. Davidson, P., Sedgemoor, C.I.O.: Designing URI Sets for (2011)
28. Cloutier, R., Muller, G., Verma, D., Nilchiani, R., Hole, E., Bone, M.: The Concept of Reference Architectures, pp. 14–27 (2009)
29. Koubarakis, M., Karpathiotakis, M., Kyzirakos, K., Nikolaou, C., Sioutis, M.: Data Models and Query Languages for Linked Geospatial Data. In: Eiter, T., Krennwallner, T. (eds.) Reasoning Web 2012. LNCS, vol. 7487, pp. 290–328. Springer, Heidelberg (2012)
30. Becker, C., Bizer, C.: Exploring the Geospatial Semantic Web with DBpedia Mobile. Web Semantics: Science, Services and Agents on the World Wide Web 7, 278–286 (2009)
31. Koubarakis, M.: Challenges for Qualitative Spatial Reasoning in Linked Geospatial Data. In: Workshop on Benchmark and Applications of Spatial Reasoning (IJCAI 2011) (2011)
32. Norton, B., Krummenacher, R.: Geospatial linked open services. Proceedings of the Workshop Towards Digital Earth 640, 4–7 (2010)
33. Ojo, A., Janowski, T., Estevez, E.: Semantic Interoperability Architecture for Electronic Government. In: The Proceedings of the 10th International Digital Government Research Conference, pp. 63–72 (2009)
34. Tschirner, S., Scherp, A., Staab, S.: Semantic access to INSPIRE How to publish and query advanced GML data. Geography, 1–13

On the Duality of E-Participation –
Towards a Foundation for Citizen-Led Participation

Lukasz Porwol, Adegbojega Ojo, and John Breslin

Digital Enterprise Research Institute,
National University of Ireland,
Galway
{lukasz.porwol,adegboyega.ojo,john.breslin}@deri.org

Abstract. What remains unclear after a decade of e-Participation research and practice is the extent to which the social web and informal channels have empowered citizens in government-citizen interactions where government determines what, where and how to discuss. Lately, attention has shifted to how these informal channels could be better harnessed as part of a holistic e-Participation solution. However, this implicit notion of duality of e-Participation is yet to be explored or conceptualized. This paper provides a first step towards understanding the duality of Government-led and Citizen-led e-Participation based on structuration and dynamic capabilities theories. We employ structuration theory to understand how dynamics of power between government and citizen in deciding what is important for the society and the solutions to adopt could tilt towards the side of citizens through citizen-led deliberations. Through the dynamic capabilities theory, we determine additional capabilities required by governments to meaningfully exploit and sustain citizen-led e-participation as a part or a holistic e-participation framework. We show through a case study how our resulting analytical tool could be employed in identifying salient technical, organisational and political issues in an on-going Irish e-Participation initiative planning to adopt citizen-led deliberation.

Keywords: e-Participation, citizen-led e-Participation, e-Participation framework.

1   Introduction

e-Participation involves technology-mediated interaction between citizens and the politics sphere and citizens and administration [1]. Leveraging information and telecommunication technology (ICT) in political participation enables public participation and feedback simultaneously [2], opens up a new channel for political participation while strengthening existing citizen engagement areas [3]. These well-established notions of e-Participation as a consultative, democratic process with involvement of citizens in policy making does not capture or consider communication among citizens on informal channels such as social media.

A. Kő et al. (Eds.): EGOVIS/EDEM 2013, LNCS 8061, pp. 211–225, 2013.
© Springer-Verlag Berlin Heidelberg 2013

Macintosh et al. in [4] highlighted the need to design e-Participation research to consider deliberations on these increasingly important informal or so-called outsider communication channels as part of the political participation process. According to the authors, these channels present a new dimension of e-Participation, thus resulting in a form of duality of e-Participation. This dual nature of e-Participation involves on the one hand administration sponsored and driven by deliberation and on the other spontaneously conducted deliberations by citizens and special interest groups in their own way, using the many available Internet tools [4].

While some conceptualization of the duality of participation in the development context is offered in [5], studies conceptualizing e-Participation are few and those presenting (even tangentially) structuration analysis of e-Participation such as [6] are significantly fewer. Structuration analysis based on the Gidden's Structuration Theory [7] enables better understanding of how interactions among actors continuously shape, reproduce or modify institutionalized social structures. In the context of participation, it specifically enables investigating how values could be renegotiated, power re-distributed between administration and citizens [6] and what new rules are required to legitimize new forms of participation, e.g. use of new social media.

This paper provides a first step towards understanding the duality of Government-led and Citizen-led e-Participation. Our goal includes: 1) developing an analytical framework to understand the mutual reshaping of government- and citizen-led e-Participation; 2) determining necessary conditions under which the integration of citizen-led e-Participation and government-led e-Participation produces significantly improved e-Participation outcome; 3) determining the capabilities required by government and citizens to adopt citizen led participation.

To achieve these goals, we employ Structuration Theory (ST) to understand how dynamics of power between government and citizen in deciding what is important for the society and the solutions to adopt, could tilt towards the side of citizens through citizen-led deliberations. Through the Dynamic Capabilities Theory (DCT), we determine additional capabilities required by governments to meaningfully exploit and sustain citizen-led e-Participation as a part or a holistic e-Participation framework. We show through a case-study how our resulting analytical tool could be employed in identifying salient technical, organisational and political issues in an on-going Irish e-Participation initiative planning to adopt citizen-led deliberation.

2   Theoretical Framework

This section provides theoretical foundation of work - Structuration Theory (ST) and Dynamic Capabilities Theory (DCT). We provide a general overview of the theoretical framework and highlight the complementarity of the concepts.

2.1   Structuration Theory

Structuration Theory (ST) proposed by [7] deals with the creation and reproduction of social systems. The theory is used for the analysis of the relationships between agents and the structure. According to Giddens [7], Agency can be understood as the capability of individuals or groups to make free decisions or act, while Structure is defined as a patterned influence or limitation derived from rules and resources available to individual or group actions. In this context the theory describes the *duality of structure* in which structure is both a medium and an outcome of the social system reproduction process. Therefore, the rules together with resources are drawn from social actions are at the same time responsible for the social system reproduction and refinement of structures. Giddens further asserts that the constitution of agents and structures are not independent but act in synergy represented by duality. In principle the ST recognizes the knowledgeability of the agents who leverage the resources provided to change social practices imposed upon them by the structure. The knowledgeability is understood as the agents' awareness of their actions and reasons for the actions and is composed of three main so called memory traces: Domination (power) derived from authoritative resources – enable control of people and allocative resources – enable control of material objects, Signification (meaning) and Legitimation (norms) which can be referred to as the rules through which the recourses are obtained. The knowledgeability of agents is realized through *reflexivity*, which is described as constant monitoring of actions. The reflexive monitoring is a process dependent on factors such as time, space as well as the rationalization of the human agents.

Chitnis [5] employed ST to participatory communications to analyze the duality between agents and institutions, as well as to understand the role of power and empowerment in the social change. [5] argues that participatory communication constructs such as conscientization, empowerment and power could be framed directly with the constructs from the ST such as knowledgeable agents, dialectic of control and power and domination. According to [5] in participation, all actors gain from each other through sharing of political and economic power and subsequent structural changes leading to redistribute power.

The Structuration Theory provides a good framework for analyze the participation from the agency and structure perspective. However, the theory does not enable detailed or fine-grained analysis of the nature of capabilities requirements to support and sustain the social processes. ST also does not describe how the capabilities align to the organizational rules and routines. This gap could be addressed by employing the Dynamic Capabilities Theory [8] which enables more fine-grained analysis of capability and resources requirements for social and organizational changes.

2.2   Dynamic Capabilities Theory

The Dynamic Capabilities Theory (DCT) evolved from the Resourced Based View (RBV) [8]. The DCT extends the RBV with the acknowledgement of high dynamics of the market environments [9]. Unlike in 'static' RBV where basic capabilities allow organizations to draw from resources to produce results, the dynamic capabilities are intended to constantly integrate, re-create and reconfigure its resources as well as the basic capabilities [8]. The constant refinement enables the organization to adapt itself to fast changing environment [10]. The DCT identifies three general types of the dynamic capabilities with regards to change of the operational routines: 1) adaptive capability – organization's ability to capitalize on emerging opportunities through aligning resources and capabilities with environmental changes, 2) absorptive capability – ability to recognize and assimilate knowledge, 3) innovative capability – ability to develop new services and markets.

Additionally, [11] defines a set of principles for dynamic capabilities under conditions of high uncertainty and high market velocity: 1) the primacy of the goal of the actions over the methodology, 2) the need for creation of situation-specific knowledge (quick experimental actions and frequent iteration), 3) parallel consideration and partial implementation of multiple options, 4) unique skill set requirement (partnership and information sharing), 5) persistence in ensuring the capabilities.

3   Approach

A major goal of this work is to combine the ST and DCT described in Section 2, harnessing the complementarity of these theories to deconstruct the duality e-Participation. In particular, the integrated use of ST and DCT will help understand how citizen-led participation can complement the current government-led approach to e-Participation and also determine what kind of capabilities will be required to achieve significantly improved e-Participation outcome both from the perspectives of citizens and government. Specific goals of this paper include:

- Develop an analytical lens based on ST and DCT for exploring the duality of e-Participation.
- Identify salient capabilities that government and citizens needs to develop in order to undertake citizen-led participation of e-Participation.
- Demonstrate the use of our analytical model by using it to analyze the need of an e-participation initiative by a local authority in Ireland to planning to undertake integrate citizen-led e-participation with the ongoing government-led e-participation

Our analytical model was developed incrementally as follows:

S1. *ST based analysis of e-Participation* - we start by reviewing the structuration analysis of participation presented by Chitnis [5] to obtain core ST constructs relevant to the concept of participation. Following this, the obtained constructs were reinterpreted in the context of e-Participation. This is presented in Section 4.1.

S2. *Extending ST based analysis of e-Participation with Citizen-led participation* – We extend the model developed in Step 1 to include citizen-led participation. The resulting model explains the duality of e-participation; where both government- and citizen led e-Participation emerge as mutually supportive and shaping processes. This is presented Section 4.1.

S3. *Elaborating e-Participation structures and capability using DCT* – the final step involves the refinement of the resource and capability related constructs in the integrated model developed in step 2 with the dynamic capability theory. This enables the identification of specific types of capabilities required by government in particular to harness the dual nature of e-participation. The DCT-based analysis is presented Section 4.2 while the integration of ST and DCT for analyzing e-participation is presented in Section 4.3

To demonstrate the use of developed model, it is employed for analyzing the requirements for implementing citizen-led e-participation in the context of an ongoing government-led e-participation initiative.

4 Structuration and Dynamic Capability Model of e-Participation

This section develops our integrated ST and DCT based analysis of e-Participation. Section 4.1 presents structuration analysis of government-led e-Participation. Section 4.2 presents DCT-based analysis of the duality of e-Participation while Section 4.3 concluded with the integrated ST and DCT based analysis of the duality of e-Participation.

4.1 Structuration Analysis of e-Participation

Government-Led Participation
The government-led participation (GleP) is a common model exploited by the contemporary e-Participation solutions and driven by three main principles: inform, consult, empower [12–14]. GleP leverages an approach where the government 'educates' and mines citizens' opinion through dedicated e-Participation platforms. Although the approach acknowledges citizens' input (whenever government seeks citizens' opinion); substantial powers remain domicile with government as it owns the process. The supremacy of government's power in this context is implied by the insufficient resources appropriated to citizens. In Figure 1 we show a general overview of the GleP. The figure presents the pool of resources and rules (i.e. the structure) that are available to the government and citizens to run and transform e-Participation.

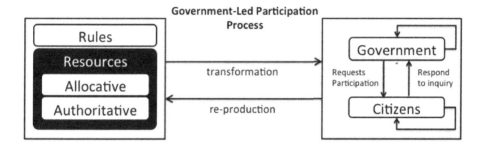

Fig. 1. GleP overview

Although citizens indeed are provided with allocative resources in a form of available e-Participation tools, their capability to draw from the authoritative resources is significantly limited. Therefore citizens are unable to implement their own ideas or resist the government's decisions. In addition, government decides what is important for policy making (signification). Furthermore, government alone shapes the system rules (full legitimation), which drive the system. Here, it is apparent, that the notion of *dialectic of control* is weak. A major implication of this scenario is that government may largely miss the knowledge of real needs of citizens, leading directly to the lack of engagement and ultimately lack of sustainability of e-Participation initiatives. Finally, GleP solutions designate the information and consultation as the two key, base levels for e-Participation [12]. Lastly, in the GLeP approach, there is an implicit assumption that citizens' knowledgeability is limited. Figure 1 presents a model for GLeP allowing for the reconfiguration of the power relationship between government and citizens as well as the empowerment of citizen and government agencies over time based on the interaction between government and its citizens. Next, we describe how CLeP can facilitate the re-distribution power between government and their citizenry over time.

Citizen-Led Participation
By CleP we understand a an approach where the citizens explicitly drive the e-participation agenda under the based on that government's recognition of citizens' knowledgeability. Macintosh et al. [4] identifies the lack of the exploration of the political discussions spontaneously conducted by citizens on ubiquitous social networking sites as one of the key gaps of e-Participation. In response, a salient principle of CleP is that the government continually attempt to reach out to citizens on media of their preference, such as the less formal social networking platforms rather than on dedicated e-Participation solutions. In particular, we operationalize CleP to proceed in three main steps: listen, shape and empower. The government continuously monitors (*listens*) citizens' deliberation on popular 'citizen owned' social media platforms (as shown on the Figure 2) for policy suggestions, and if necessarily *shapes* the discussion. Here, Government acts as an expert in the domain and enriches the discussion based on the domain expertise. As a result of this process, resources distribution and system rules are continuously updated and reproduced based on the citizens' contributions. In other words, in this model, citizens can effectively exercise the agency to change the structure, thus they are *empowered* in the decision making process.

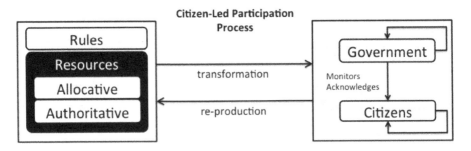

Fig. 2. CleP overview

Integrating Government and Citizen-Led e-Participation

Macintosh et al. [4] describes the duality of e-Participation as the integration of the disjoint ubiquitous, spontaneous citizen-driven participation and the government-led discussions. We attempt to operationalize this notion of e-Participation duality by offering an integrated approach to e-Participation, which combines both government-led as well as a complementary citizen-led e-Participation. In the integrated model the government can continue on traditional e-Participation routine while continuously monitoring the public opinion for guidelines and feedback on the new policies. The two pillars of GleP and CleP work in a synergy addressing the duality of e-Participation (Figure 3). The salient element of the synergistic model is that the government acknowledges citizens contributions and while acting as the domain expert, shapes the discussion in order to make it more legitimate. The citizens' discussions help decision-makers to better understand the issues and focus their agenda on the most important problems.

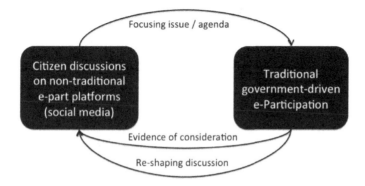

Fig. 3. Integrated approach to e-Participation

As shown on the Figure 4 there are two alternative modes of e-Participation available for the citizens' input. By default, government continuously explores CleP element and in case the government does not find enough input a new dedicated, more structured discussion can be opened through the GleP element. Unlike in the traditional GleP, the integrated approach allows both relevant allocative resources as well as the authoritative resources to be assigned to citizen through the recognition of citizens' knowledgeability. This approach therefore facilitates direct citizen input to the policy making process. Since citizens are given enough authoritative resources they are empowered to exercise the agency and resist not-satisfactory decisions (i.e. resist domination by government). The integrated approach also promotes greater government transparency and ensures freedom of information along with truly guaranteed democratic rights of citizens expressed in direct policy-making influence.

Our analysis of the integrated structuration model for e-participation leads to following propositions:

P1) The integration of citizen-led participation leads to better value outcomes for citizens when compared to traditional government-led participation.

P2) Deliberation that has potential impact on government programs carried out over citizens centric media leads to better sense of empowerment by citizens.
P3) CleP requires acquisition of special capabilities by governments.
P4) Adoption of CleP as legitimate bases for government actions, requires the legislative and regulatory updates.

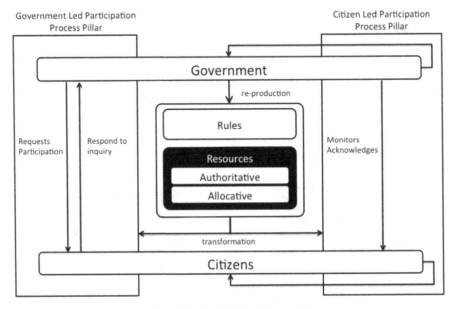

Fig. 4. Dual e-Participation model

4.2   Dynamic Capabilities Model for e-Participation

According to Wang et al. [8], dynamic capabilities are intended to constantly integrate, re-create and re-configure its resources as well as the capabilities. We demonstrate a specific adoption of DCT to e-Participation by considering continuous e-Participation re-production as an integral part of the e-Participation process. In order to effectively leverage e-Participation the government needs to harness the citizens' input and transform it into policies while continuously re-constructing the e-Participation process itself to ensure relevant stakeholders empowerment. The demonstrated approach demands high adaptivity to the dynamics of the social system environment. To conceptualize e-Participation capability requirements, we frame the dynamic capabilities constructs directly with the relevant e-Participation components and processes (Figure 5). The adaptive capability (AD) can be linked to the e-Participation resources rebalance and rules updates required for sustainable e-participation. In particular e-Participation requires AD capabilities like: *dynamic resources acquisition and distribution* (both allocative and authoritative resources) based on the current participation demand, e-Participation *rules re-production and reformation processes* based on participation process required improvements.

The absorptive capability (AC) can be seen as the knowledge exchange synergy between knowledgeable citizens and the government, learning from each other. In particular e-Participation requires AC like: *continuous monitoring process* intended to act as a seamless, rich source of information for the policy-makers agenda, *participation shaping process* necessary to ensure legitimate contributions, *citizen information services* guaranteeing freedom of public information and government transparency.

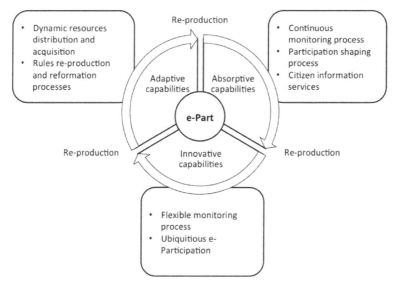

Fig. 5. Dynamic Capabilities Model for e-Participation

Innovative capability (IC) can be expressed in possible expansion of e-Participation reach and constant improvement of the e-Participation process. In particular e-Participation requires IC like: *flexible monitoring process* – citizen-opinion monitoring process independent from socio-technical platform, capable of expanding to the newly created participation places, *ubiquitous e-Participation* – e-Participation available to citizens via multiple channels of their choice (variety of hardware and software platforms).

e-Participation initiatives run in an environment of high dynamics and uncertainty. Therefore the building capabilities required by e-Participation should follow the principles such as creation of situation-specific knowledge (AC) that may involve invitation of domain experts from citizens as well as parallel consideration and partial implementation (AD and IC) of suggested ideas followed by routinized citizens feedback (AC). More importantly, the clearly defined, well-announced goals and persistence of the government in constant re-production of e-Participation capabilities is required in order to ensure sustainable citizen-decision-makers cooperation.

To summarize we have identified the following dynamic capabilities: 1) adaptive capabilities including dynamic resources distribution and acquisition, rules re-production and reformation process; 2) absorptive capabilities including continuous monitoring process, participation shaping process, citizen information services; and 3) innovative capabilities including flexible monitoring process, ubiquitous e-Participation.

The presented dynamic capabilities model structures the way the e-Participation is reshaped in the dual process (Figure 4). Next, we present and integrated model for e-Participation and then we apply this theoretical lens, to analyze an e-Participation case study in a city in Ireland.

4.3   Integrated Model for e-Participation

We have shown how the DCT can be applied in the e-Participation context. Now we shall attempt to structure the integrated e-Participation model. As shown on the Figure 6, the integrated model has been designed to exploit the facilitative aspects of the duality of e-Participation.

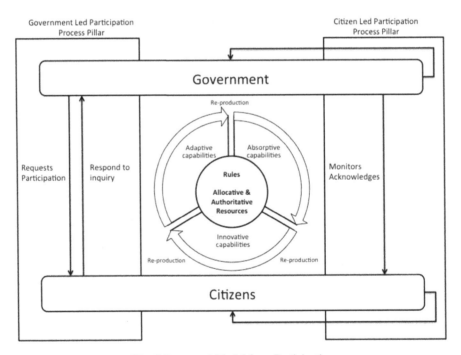

Fig. 6. Integrated Model for e-Participation

The two approaches to e-Participation: GleP and CleP are explored to support the dynamic allocative and authoritative resources and enable citizens to exercise their agency to re-produce the system regardless the level of engagement and the means of e-Participation. The legitimacy of citizens' contribution to policy making is strengthened directly by government's acknowledgement and indirectly by constantly updated system rules. The significance of citizens' input is supported by specially developed by the government, dynamic capabilities. These capabilities ensure continuous reflexive dialog and dialectic among citizens and between citizens and decision makers respectively characterizing the dual-nature e-Participation process.

This way the highly dominant role of the government is transformed into role of a facilitator, expert and executor for citizens' policy needs.

5   Case Study

We present an overview of our case study (Section 5.1), an analysis of the state of play of the initiative based on our theoretical lens (Section 5.2) and the application of the theoretical framework in determining future requirements for the e-participation initiative (Section 5.3).

5.1   Overview

The case study involves a transportation e-Participation initiative (Forum) established in 2011 as a volunteer initiative in Galway, Republic of Ireland, to identify a range of implementable, short-term traffic measures that will help alleviate some of the current city-transport difficulties. The core idea behind the solution has been to address the participation barriers, especially in context of social inclusion and impact on policy-making. The project involved most major local transportation stakeholder groups, ranging from government officials to ordinary citizens. The diverse group of stakeholders includes: the mayor, chamber of commerce, local development authorities, representatives of the enterprise sector, academia (especially civil engineering, social science and computer science), along with independent volunteers and finally the citizens.

5.2   State of Play

The Forum has been considered relatively successful, although our analytical lens points out a number of issues that may pose a serious threat to the sustainability of the e-Participation solution. The Forum, as indicated, has been initiated and managed by the mayor of the city; thus considered a GleP platform. The role of the e-Participation solution has been to increase local government awareness of the citizens needs regarding the transportation in the city as well as to ensure greater ownership of the key transportation decisions by citizens. Thus, based on GleP approach, the basic assumption of the project is to bring citizens over from many distributed spontaneous discussion places, and gather them on one platform to deliberate on the issues in a structured way. The solution offers multiple communication channels such as e-mail, digital forum, social media extensions (rich allocative resources), nevertheless the digital and paper surveys have been designated and recommended as the main contribution channel for citizens (what has been expressed in dissemination materials and reflected by the Forum design). The surveys have been designed with no input from citizens and have been shaped to answer very particular questions on transportation in the city. These facts imply that the citizens' contributions are very limited and actually 'censored' through narrow structure of contribution [15] with low level of significance assigned to citizens suggestions. Moreover one-way communication through mainstream media has been favored by the government, strengthening the image of the government's ownership of the initiative. What has been indicated on the platform, one of the key goals of the initiative has been to deliver a combined report, gathering together citizens' contributions that are handed over to the local transportation authority (LTA). Nevertheless, in the absence of any assurance that the ideas and solutions suggested would be implemented, citizens using the Forum are given very little authoritative resources, demonstrating the dominant position of the government. Moreover, LTA has been active on the Forum platform only on volunteer bases without taking full ownership of the solution which implies a lack of legitimacy assigned to citizen's contributions. Although citizens' contributions are very constraint due to fixed topics and questions, as the experience of this study shows, decision makers are surprised by many ideas proposed in the report. This supports the hypothesis that the government is not fully aware of the real needs of citizens. The experience showed also that the LTA finally did not acknowledge the suggestions presented in the report and followed their own agenda regarding the changes in the city (no signification power assigned to citizens' contributions). Without feedback from government to citizens on the extent of adoption of their contributions, citizen engagement on the platform systematically dropped. The LTA's inadvertent weak recognition of citizens' knowledgeability; its reliance only on their internal expertise, supports the observation of the existing gap between citizens' ideas and proposed improvements in the city. This has continued to cause growing public disappointment. Nevertheless, lack of significant authoritative resources or supporting system rules on citizen's side indicates that the citizen are not sufficiently empowered (i.e. no legitimation power). To conclude from the dynamic capabilities perspective the initiative misses absorptive capabilities by not taking into consideration the knowledgeability of citizens. The innovative capabilities have been rather missing apart from the multichannel communication, failing to provide citizens with seamless, ubiquitous e-Participation. The adaptive capabilities are not really present in the initiative as the initiative operators limited their actions only to minor fixes and improvements to the technological platform without any e-Participation re-production process in place.

5.3   Integrating CleP

The Forum initiative has been intended to address the common e-Participation issues. Nevertheless, with the consideration of the duality of e-Participation, the solution has been missing clear guidelines on structure of the process.

Therefore we would like to discuss the propositions regarding CleP integration posed in the section 4.1 that could help to alleviate the current issues of the e-Participation solution. Considering the proposition that CleP leads to better value outcomes than GleP alone (P1), we believe that CleP, promoting the open-structure of contributions, could help to avoid the mentioned aspects of 'censorship' that are present on the current platform, hence ensuring greater and richer source for deliberation. Moreover, citizens enabled to participate from their own social spaces would be given a better sense of empowerment. Therefore CleP would certainly help the Forum to bring more ownership of the e-Participation process to citizens and that should have direct implication in greater citizen engagement (P2). To ensure quality contributions in CleP the government is an active deliberation participant and shapes the discussion as a domain expert, thus again, regarding the better value outcome, the ideas and suggestions generated by CleP would have more legitimacy and better quality than in the current solution (P1). Nevertheless, as pointed out in the propositions before, these changes would require the government to generate new capabilities, especially the absorptive capabilities such as continuous monitoring and discussion shaping as well as innovative capabilities in a form of ubiquitous e-Participation and flexible input capability which are all rather very limited or non-existent in the current solution (P3). As the experience of the Forum shows, the weak legitimacy of the contributions in absence of authoritative resources has been the key obstacle for the initiative to fully succeed. This situation demands new rules and regulations to be set up, re-produced and routinized by the local government in order to provide enough legitimacy to citizen contributions, hence supporting the sense of empowerment of citizens (P4 and P2).

The future work will seek to confirm that the proposed CleP integration brings the expected benefits.

6   Discussion

Results from our theoretical work provide good evidence to support the claim of poor structuration of popular (GleP) e-Participation initiatives [13] leading these initiatives to ultimately fail. The application of the combined ST and DCT-based, theoretical framework exposes important e-Participation issues related to missing recognition of citizens' knowledgeability and imbalance of resources, while providing guidelines for future research in the field. It is apparent from this work that the common understanding of citizen-empowerment [15][16][17] is incomplete. In particular our findings expose the fact that e-Participation approach where citizens are given only limited, allocative resources in absence of signification and legitimation power is not sufficient and demands deep refinement. One could argue that given the less than a decade history of e-Participation research and practice, such level of development of the e-Participation domain is expected. Nevertheless in our opinion, developing a framework such as the integrated e-Participation model presented in this work and providing a robust conceptualization of the e-Participation process is a necessary condition for the sustainability of e-Participation initiatives.

The case study analysis presented in this paper confirms our previous observations. The framework proposed captures the key dimensions of participation, answering the question why the initiative seem to loose the citizen engagement although many 'traditional efforts' have been made (such us extensive media campaigns). The framework highlights the key improvements required and provides guidelines for the initiative designers that could help to ensure the e-Participation sustainability. One of the key improvements is to extend the existing GleP approach with the CleP and introduce the integrated e-Participation model presented. We believe that CleP is a visible option for the local government although due to limited resources on processing citizens' opinions the monitoring would have to be supported by relevant technologies.

Well-established social networking platforms are ubiquitous and witness far more engagement than any e-Participation solution. Moreover many people incorporated them into everyday activities as they are very easy to use [18] and indeed they became a spontaneous place for many political discussions. Therefore we believe the duality of e-Participation is a fact and there is a great challenge as well as an opportunity to leverage the potential of social media for participation purposes.

Apart from [5], we are not aware of any other significant attempts at applying Structuration Theory to social participation domain. Moreover we have not found any approach that would try to combine and apply in particular both ST and DCT to e-Participation. While there have been past efforts, aimed to scope e-Participation [16] and elicit its core dimensions [13], these studies present a very general view on e-Participation with lack of information on the theoretical basis for these work and providing low granularity level in regard to structuration of the participatory communication (or focus on technology), make them difficult to evaluate in terms of coverage and relevance.

Despite claims by [7][5][8] and the wide application of the ST and DCT in different social system related domains, we cannot claim "absolute completeness" of the presented approach with respect to e-Participation.

7   Conclusion

Motivated by the need to provide the necessary step towards structuration of e-Participation, we have presented an integrative theoretical lens for analyzing and improving existing e-Participation methodologies. Results from our work show immediate opportunities for consolidating the social-systems' related theories and the application to the democratic context for e-Participation.   While we have demonstrated the usefulness of the analytical lens, more detailed and formal models are yet to be developed. Next steps for the research include the implementation of CleP solution for the Forum e-Participation system and introduction of the integrated e-Participation approach followed by a detailed system analysis. Future steps should also bring series of applications of the theoretical lens as an analytical framework for analyzing and suggesting improvements for selected e-Participation initiatives.

Acknowledgement. The work presented in this paper has been funded in part by the European Union under Grant No 256261 (Puzzled by Policy – CIP-ICT-PSP-2009-3bis)

References

1. Sæbø, O., Rose, J., Skiftenesflak, L.: The shape of eParticipation: Characterizing an emerging research area. Government Information Quarterly 25, 400–428 (2008)
2. Chadwick, A.: Bringing E-Democracy Back In: Why it Matters for Future Research on E-Governance. Social Science Computer Review 21, 443–455 (2003)
3. Van Dijk, J.A.G.M.: Models of Democracy Ken Hacker & Jan van Dijk. Sage Publications Copyright (2000)
4. Macintosh, A., Coleman, S., Schneeberger, A.: eParticipation: The Research Gaps. In: Macintosh, A., Tambouris, E. (eds.) ePart 2009. LNCS, vol. 5694, pp. 1–11. Springer, Heidelberg (2009)
5. Chitnis, K.: The duality of development: recasting participatory communication for development using structuration theory 13, 228–249 (2005)
6. Paddon, R.W.: e-Participation in Canada: Probing Online Public Policy Development By (2009)
7. Giddens, A.: The Constitution of Society Elements of the Theory of Structuration (1984)
8. Wang, C.L.: Dynamic Capabilities: A Review and Research Agenda Dynamic Capabilities: A Review and Research Agenda 9, 31–51 (2007)
9. Teece, D.J., Pisano, G., Shuen, A., Shuen, A.M.Y.: Dynamic Capabilities and Strategic Management 18, 509–533 (1997)
10. Cepeda, G., Vera, D.: Dynamic capabilities and operational capabilities: A knowledge management perspective. Journal of Business Research 60, 426–437 (2007)
11. Connor, G.C.O.: Major Innovation as a Dynamic Capability: A Systems Approach, 313–330 (2008)
12. OECD: Engaging Citizens in Policy-making (2001)
13. Macintosh, A.: Characterizing e-participation in policy-making. In: Proceedings of the 37th Annual Hawaii International Conference on System Sciences, 10 p. (2004)
14. DESA: UN Global E-government Readiness Report 2005 From E-government to E-inclusion (2005)
15. Rose, J., Sæbø, Ø.: Designing Deliberation Systems. The Information Society 26, 228–240 (2010)
16. Tambouris, E., Liotas, N., Kaliviotis, D., Tarabanis, K.: A Framework for Scoping eParticipation. In: 8th Annual International Digital Govenment Research Conference, pp. 288–289 (2007)
17. Lee, D., Loutas, N., Sánchez-nielsen, E., Mogulkoc, E.: A Three-tiered Approach to eParticipation (2011)
18. Lane, M., Coleman, P.: Technology ease of use through social networking media. Technology, 1–12

Policy Making Improvement through Social Learning

Andrea Kő[1], András Gábor[2], and Zoltán Szabó[1]

[1] Corvinus University of Budapest
{ko,szabo}@informatika.uni-corvinus.hu
[2] Corvinno Technology Transfer Center Ltd.
agabor@corvinno.hu

Abstract. The world for which policies have to be developed is becoming increasingly complex, uncertain and unpredictable. Citizens are better informed, have rising expectations and are making growing demands for services tailored to their individual needs. The traditional policy-making process – where identification of problems and solutions given are defined by a small group of politicians and experts – is characterized by several inefficiencies: risk of false identification of problems, misled setting of goals, wasted resources, unsatisfactory evaluation and, above all, inefficiently addressed societal problems. The main goal of paper is to address the above mentioned challenges through the exploitation of social learning and supporting ICT techniques for a more efficient and open policy making process. These will enable better motivation to participate by taking each opinion into account for the final solution. The paper discusses our Centralab ICT solution as a supporting environment for policy modeling. The aim of our solution is not to change policy-making processes but rather to support them with innovative ICT tools to reach the overall goal when policy-making results in better quality of democracy and improved civic capacity.

Keywords: e-government, policy modeling, ICT enabled policy making, social learning.

1   Introduction

In the last two centuries the civilized world has fought to institutionalize civil, political, and social rights. In a time of great global transformation the new challenge is to spread and deepen democracy as a way of life. Now, in the early 21st century, participatory democracy [1] is not an alternative to liberal democracy [2] – it is a challenge to it, a deepening and broadening of 'actual existing' democracy.

Nowadays, transparency and participatory democracy become essential to facilitate good governance. By strengthening the relations with citizens and engage them in policy making will contribute to building public trust, raise the quality of policies and politics that will result in better quality of democracy and improved civic capacity.

The traditional policy-making process - where identification of problems and solutions given were defined by a small group - is characterized by several inefficiencies: risk of the false identification of problems is high, setting of goals are mislead,

A. Kő et al. (Eds.): EGOVIS/EDEM 2013, LNCS 8061, pp. 226–240, 2013.

resources allocated are wasted and overall the societal problem is not addressed. The role of politicians and selected experts is overrated and the decision making process is not transparent enough and accountability and responsibility have no limitation on attitudes, accountability matters only when elections take place. The stakeholders are only informed at the end of the process.

The weaknesses of the above mentioned practice and the evolution of the society and technology give space for new policy-making procedures where active participation of citizens is a core element. Strengthening the government – citizen relationship is fundamental in order to establish the most suitable policy-making process. Main benefits arising from a well-functioning relationship are:

- improved quality of policies – wider sources of information, perspectives and potential solutions are available
- challenges of the emerging information society - faster interactions and better knowledge sharing and creation are met
- public opinion is integrated in the policy-making process
- citizens' expectations that their voices are heard and views and opinions are considered can be fulfilled, and greater transparency and accountability can be achieved.

These relations cover a broad spectrum of interactions at each stage of policy-making cycle: from the design through implementation to evaluation. These relations can be also analysed from the 'level of interactions' perspective as well [3-6]:

- Information: a one-way relation in which government produces and delivers information for use by citizens.
- Consultation: a two-way relation in which citizens give feedback to government, on prior definition by the government of the issue on which citizen's sought are required.
- Participation: an active relation based on continuous and not limited interactions between citizens and government. This form of collaboration enables citizens to be engaged in policy making process from the proposition of policy options to shaping the policy dialogue.

ICT has an outstanding potential to support new policy-making practices. While there is legal background and established mechanisms supported by ICT tools as well for information (e.g. portals and websites) and consultation (e.g. opinion polls and surveys) there are only a few experiments and pilots with ICT tools to engage actively the citizens in policy making. The dynamism of the policy modeling landscape point of view is aroused from the two competing legs of ICT support. On one hand the ICT infrastructure is developing, growing as broadband access penetration, new and powerful mobile devices, etc. On the other hand the application development is trying to keep up with the new opportunities (e.g. social media hype, cloud services, etc.). For policy modeling this competition gives always renewed opportunity to introduce new and new services. Looking back only one-two decades, the renewal cycles repeats each other in fairly short cycle times.

From application point of view also characteristic levels of development can be distinguished [3]. ICT enabled policy making might start with the one-way information, which is extended with very limited opinion articulation opportunities (mostly in the form of comments). This solution is a combination of informing and "water cooler", giving a surface for presenting opinion of citizens (any many cases dominated by certain subcultures). Stepping ahead the social consultation already takes in to account what are the distribution of the opinions in the sense of agree/disagree. Advanced sentiment analysis may calculate the degree of agree/disagree or like/dislike. On a more advanced level, we might call social dialogue [7], not only the articulation of opinions is in the focus, but searching for consensus. In policy making normally policy makers look for the good (optimal) solution, where optimum means the best compromise among the particular interests. The particular interests should be well articulated, argued in order to reach sufficient solution. There are many precondition can be mentioned at this level, but definitely one of the most important whether the participants, stakeholders are being well-informed, and having the sufficient knowledge concerning the policy in matter. The main benefits can be achieved at this level is the increased awareness, high level of inclusion by participation on the top of these the higher level of motivation. As a perspective, the next level can be the social learning. Social learning is assumed when individuals assimilate new information and apply it to their subsequent actions [8]. And it is considered as a deliberate attempt to adjust the goals and techniques of policy in response to past experience and new information. Learning is indicated when policy changes as the result of such a process. Milbrath [9] used 'self-educating community' expression to describe situation where people learn from each other and from the environment, he was one of the first author who linked the term social learning to sustainable development.

The process and quality of policy-making affect the citizens at several points during the course of the execution. The inclusion of citizens is nowadays a focal point in policy-making, especially together with preliminary impact analysis. Current policy-making practice suffers from several problems which undermine the productive operation of the process. The concept of interactive policy-making is a significant step to broaden the inclusion of citizens, as well as to support preliminary impact analysis. The method can be promoted by several ICT tools and methodologies.

Social media and a variety of participatory tools have become popular (web/text/opinion mining, online social networking, blogs, wikis, and forums). Using these tools public administration decision-makers, governance bodies and civil society actors have the possibility of bringing about significant changes in the way future societies will function. The emerging technological environment has dramatic impact on communication, information processing and knowledge-sharing among public administration participants and also within civil society. Participatory democracy can be approached by developing IT based channels for a clear voicing of opinions, expression of citizens' needs and a extension of participation. In this new setting, decision makers have access to a large amount of data and information concerning people's situations, what they think and what they believe. In the paper we address those problems which are related to the enhancement of knowledgeable policy modeling, decision support and decision making through social learning.

In policy making context the complex, fragmented nature and the immense quantity of data can cause several problems. To align public policies with emerging societal needs, requirements and expectations, policy-makers need feedback on their initiatives. Civil society requires transparency of the policy-making process. Importance of ICT and especially social media as tools enabling transparent, open and accessible information services was discussed by [10] and Jaeger and Bertot [11-12]. Gelders and Rijnja [13] have looked at external, public communication-related issues of policy-preparation stages (policy intention), emphasizing the importance of proactive and interactive communication with the citizen while realizing that successful interaction between communication professionals and policy professionals is critical for any successes, too. Risk is an inherent part of the policy life-cycle, and frameworks have been developed to take on board the risk aspects of e-government initiatives [14].

Optimal utilization of ICT for policy modeling raises several questions [15].One of the main challenges here is how to cope with a large volume of data and the time constraint against data processing. Questions related to our research as well are: How can we manage interaction and coordination in relation to civil society agents that might exploit this data? How can we facilitate communication and knowledge sharing so that it is not overly time-consuming, whilst avoiding information overload? How can we dig out the collective intelligence of different stakeholders, orient this so as to augment our ability to identify trends, and then find solutions? How can we rest assured that this flow of information is reaching the right government agencies or decision-makers? For in this regard it is essential to know that the right information goes to the right (i.e. competent) body, institution or person.

Innovative ICT solutions especially social media and web 2.0/web 3.0 solutions provide a new way for capturing those issues, problems, which require immediate actions in terms of new policies, or management of existing one. One of the main goal of our research is to explore and monitor the mid-term impacts of policy decisions, in their maximum complexity. Maximum complexity means the articulation of all the relevant arguments, viewpoints and their interdependences regarding the policy in question. Impact amongst others, can be captured through the "voice of citizens" by an online environment and serves as an additional input for fine-tuning decisions through the modeling. Feedback collected can be pre-processed with the data and text mining tools, in order to filter and aggregate stakeholders' opinion for the modeling and to modify model variables if it is needed. Finally, by using advanced visual analytics methods, our approach enables continual monitoring of a policy impact, providing a useful mechanism for managing the risk in policy implementation, especially in dynamically changing environments. Fast changes in the environment, as well as the instability and interconnectivity makes policy making challenging nowadays. ICT tools can promote the policy modeling process, giving supportive methods to design, implement and evaluate policies. The process of interactive policy-making can be supported by several ICT tools and methodologies. Promotion can be used at the design, implementation and evaluation process steps as well [16-17]. This paper will be structured as follows:

First, policy modeling and policy making -related problems and challenges are discussed from social learning aspect, then, theoretical background are detailed.

The following part presents our ICT solution for policy making improvement through social learning. Finally, conclusion part summarizes strengths and weaknesses of our approach with further improvement directions.

2   The State of the Art in Policy Modeling and Governance

Several approaches are discussed in the literature for policy-making [18-20]. The most frequently cited theories are the following:

1. The open-systems framework of Richard Hofferbert [21];
2. An approach involving rational actors within institutions, as developed by Elinor Ostrom and her colleagues - the IRA approach [22];
3. The "advocacy coalition" framework, as recently developed by Sabatier [23].

The general lifecycle of policy making consists of the following steps: articulating opinions, comments in connection with the draft policy, followed by the processing of comments. Based on the processing the policy maker get a feedback, whereas the periodicity of feedback lasts from one-time to continuous feedback, summary, evaluation. Considering the feedback, policy will be fine-tuned. The iterative solution may result the optimal policy solution, where one of the optimality criteria is the continuous monitoring of the policy effects, embedded into the process. Finally, not only the policy in question will be monitored, but also the policy making process. This latter self reflected feature of the solution will lead to step forward to the direction of social learning.Policy modeling implies the application of methods and tools from a broad range of disciplines and integrates various lines of research and the state–of- the-art.

Policy modeling is the method through which a precise model may be used to help understand and evaluate available policy options. These models can be of various natures, including: statistical, econometric, systems dynamics, micro-simulation and agent-based simulations. Each technique has different advantages and disadvantages, making different compromises in order to help bridge the gap between the complexity of the environmental/sociological/economic/political situations that exist and the decisions and understanding of the policy advisor that has to face these. Such modeling is mainly a technical affair and has been largely in the hands of specific experts, working with inputs and evaluations coming from policy makers. The main policy modeling approaches are the following [15]:

• Behavioral modeling
• System dynamics
• Multi-level and micro-simulation models
• Queuing models or discrete event models
• Cellular automata
• Agent-based social simulation
• Theory of complexity

Some governments do not yet have any policy making or modeling tools, but many models are starting to be used across governmental and non-governmental organisations, to support policy making also in developing countries. Modeling is used extensively in health, education, criminal justice environment, urban planning, transport etc. The traditional constitutional framework of policy-making suggests that politicians make policy and public servants implement it. In practice, this offers a limited understanding of policy-making, which fails to recognize the many competing factors which shape the way policy is formulated, implemented and evaluated.

In the last fifteen years the policy making process is in a permanent process of being (more and more) technologically-enhanced. Despite many successes, especially in the domain of e-government, policy-making process is still suffering from many early-detected problems: inefficiency, non-transparency, not-citizen-driven, etc. The main cause of the problem has been related to the unavailability of official data, low engagement of citizens and very rigid (inflexible) policy making processes. However, nowadays we are experiencing dramatic transformation in several domains that can influence the policy making process:

- Data has become Big (Data), i.e. big (and integrated) enough to provide the proper context for analysing a problem and /or a situation of interest.
- Information has become Open (Data), enabling creating awareness about any change in a wider context.
- Knowledge has been evolved in the wisdom of the crowd, by allowing that everyone can contribute to the resolution of a problem.
- Participation has started to be gamified, by fostering true engagement in any kind of (personal or collective) activities.
- From intuition-driven into data-driven policy making.

Policy making process is usually not driven by data, but mainly by so called "political intuition" and experiences (in the context of political goals). This has resulted in the policy not addressing the real needs of all citizens' groups. Big and Open- Data analytics will make them visible.

- From rigidly-defined into open, anticipatory and agile policy making process

Policy making processes are implemented as slow, well-structured workflows, without many possibilities to influence them in a bottom-up fashion. Crowdsourcing and gamification will enable that everyone will be better motivated to participate and each opinion will be taken into account for the final solution. It will result in a more flexible process that is sensing early indicators for changes and continuously improving the quality of the resulting regulations.

Several researches in the 1990s focused on the architectural issues of policy systems, and researches cited the importance of enforcement [25-26]. Marriott [25] abstracted the policy life-cycle as editing, distributing and deleting policies. Avitable [27] expanded this lifecycle approach, and differentiated a development phase (refinement, deploy, distribution, test), and an operational phase (activation/deactivation, enforcement, removal). These approaches have the common characteristic of focusing on technological issues. Zhang et al [24] developed the policy lifecycle model for system management, concentrating on internal organisational policies, and policy enforcement, identifying elements of the lifecycle as management objectives, policy definitions, policy deployment and policy enforcement.

The research took also into account different approaches meant to evaluate policy impact. There are many typologies currently used, and they mainly vary according to the specific policy to be evaluated, as well as according to the moment in which they are carried out: ex ante, monitoring and ex post. Ex ante analysis is a "what if" analysis, meant to capture differences between the proposed reform(s) and the status quo. Monitoring analysis is a "what's happening" process, meant to collect feedback while a new measure is deployed. Finally, ex post analysis, seeks for results achieved, given the initially fixed objectives. Some of the most common evaluation methods include cost-benefit analysis (CBA), an ex ante evaluation scheme which uses as measuring unit a monetary reference of the aggregate change in individual well being resulting from a policy decision, or also behaviour models, techniques designed to shed light on the potential distributional impacts of policies, that do not currently exist, but that might exist in the future. Furthermore another important classification distinguishes between macro- and micro-simulation models. Certain types of modeling problems are best dealt with using micro-simulation whereas for others an aggregate approach is more appropriate; micro-simulation models are computer models that operate at the level of the individual behavioural entity (person/family/firm), while aggregated approaches refer to explanatory variables already representing collective/National realities. Ex ante evaluation of policy impacts, the one using in most cases various typologies of simulation models, is usually carried out by experts, and still not so widely used among National governments, except for some Anglo-Saxon countries. Policy monitoring, as well as ex post evaluation, are sometimes carried out by governmental structures, but more commonly by university departments.

Another key issue in policy making processes is risk assessment. NAO [28] suggests six key questions which public administrations might ask them to assess whether they have a sound approach to managing risk. This is particularly important where initiatives require coordination between a number of parts of the same organisations or with other organisations. A possible solution for preventing risks to undermine public policies deployed are Early Warning Systems [15], which showed their potential benefit also in policy modeling. Early Warning Systems bases on one or more models of how the phenomenon monitored behaves. The model is being used to show what is likely to happen next. These models can range from simple to very complex systems. Early Warning Systems can base on quantitative and qualitative approaches using for instance either a more formal forecasting oriented approach through e.g. simulations or a more informal foresight approach using e.g. scenarios.

The involvement of citizens/stakeholders is vital in the policy making process. This involvement is starting to take place through innovative approaches, based on direct participation of stakeholders, often convoyed through IT means. Edelenbos [29] defines interactive decision making as a way of conducting policies whereby a government involves its citizens, social organizations, enterprises, and other stakeholders in the early stages of the policy-making process. The difference with more traditional public policy procedures is that parties are truly involved in the development of policy proposals, whereas in classic opportunities of public comment, citizen and interest group involvement only occurred once the policy proposal had been developed. Obviously active involvement of stakeholders brings along also a series of problems,

because in most cases it is quite different from traditional decision-making procedures, so separate organisational provisions have to be developed in order to conform
to these innovative decision-making procedures. Evaluating the connection of this
new policy practice with existing decision making and the elaboration of guidance
supporting this new practice is definitively important.

3   Policy Modeling Solution through Social Learning – Centralab Policy Modeling Framework

This section gives an overview about our policy modeling solution, which was developed in Centralab project (http://www.centralivinglab.eu) (Figure 1). CentraLab solution is based on "Living Lab" approach and incorporates the two novelties discussed
in previous section, namely data-driven and agile policy making. Data – driven feature means that policy making process is supported by data collected from various
other sources; while agility means the real-time support of policy maker through visualization and interpretation of data. In this ICT driven model, technology brings infrastructures into real-life contexts to enable a "co-design" process with end users. This
method supports faster time to market and more customised solution for R&D results,
as   demonstrated   by   the   212   Living   Labs   in   the   ENoLL   network
(www.openlivinglabs.eu). The specific objective of CentraLab is to apply the Living
Lab approach transversally across a broad range of policy fields relevant to Central
European regional development, constructing a multi-level governance network for a
trans-national Central European Living Lab. It thus contributes to "enhancing the

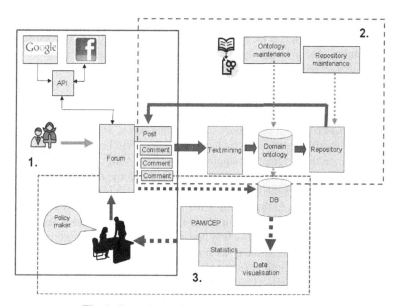

Fig. 1. General overview of Centralab solution

framework conditions for innovation", particularly in the organisational and policy dimensions of a new methodological research infrastructure. Centralab aimed to develop a new policy modeling framework that increases the knowledge economy component of regional development initiatives in a range of fields, amongst other in eco-tourism, energy, micro-SME networks, environment & education, waste management and rural development.

Centralab solution map the general lifecycle of policy making process, it has three main blocks: portal, ontology learning block and interpretation block. Portal is used to support posting, issuing draft policies, comments and opinion articulation about policies and discussion with stakeholders. Ontology learning block helps to analyse and understand discussion and provide the context for the discussion. Interpretation block provide feedback and interpretation for policy makers. Next section will give a brief overview of the main building blocks of Centralab solution.

1. Portal is the online interface where interactions and discussions among the policy maker and the stakeholders (users interested in the specific topic, local inhabitants, domain experts etc.) can take place (area 1 in Figure 1). Discussions at the portal are initiated by the policy maker by describing a new or modified policy, asking for opinions, raising a specific topic etc and stakeholders can react to the proposal or to each others' opinions. Forum will be available also from popular social media solutions, e.g. from Facebook through API to broaden the community to be involved in the discussion, especially involvement of younger generation to the discussion. Besides textual inputs, the forum allows users to share and upload web links and media content. This component supports social learning through the contribution in common understanding of a problem, reach mutual agreement and take collective actions.

2. Ontology learning block (area 2 in Figure 1). In this part the analyses of the post and comments of the forum will take place, with innovative data-, web-, and text-mining solutions in order to identify emerging issues, "hot topics". Open source web and text mining solutions are applied (Weka). Web- and text-mining are enhanced with semantic technologies in the form of ontology learning. Ontology learning component is responsible for the semi-automatic building the ontology by learning from pre-processed information sources (the web- and text-mining output). The other role of ontology is to structure knowledge repository elements, which include policy related objects, sources from regulatory environment, laws, and economic reports. Studio, Corvinno's ontology-based knowledge repository will be used for this purpose. In those cases, when the automatic mapping is not successful, there is a need for human maintenance. The identified "hot issues" are mapped to the domain ontology in order to identify that content of the knowledge repository which is relevant to the topic. The purpose of the feedback to the discussion is to enrich the discussion, to draw the attention to the related but to the moment not mentioned dimensions, aspects, details, data, additional concept, etc. This way the discussion will be "automatically" moderated, trying to highlight as many as possible details, aspects of the problem. If no repository item found, a limited (in number) search is done on the web, illustrating the first few most relevant hits. This component enhances social learning through co-creation of knowledge, understanding of interdependence and complexity of the investigated problem.

3. Interpretation block. This part of the system is responsible for visualization and interpretation of the discussion and provides feedback to the policy maker (area 3 in Figure 1). Database is applied as an additional tier, to link the ontology learning process environment and the evaluation, visualization, and interpretation part, to the knowledge repository. Logging the discussion the system is able to evaluate the affectivity of the discussion in statistical terms. The statistical evaluation will give a reliable picture of number of participants, the distribution in time, the dynamic view of discussion, e.g. what are the hot topics, and how they change their relative importance in time or in connection with other subtopics. Visual analytics provides a comprehensive view of the ongoing discussion. In form of dashboards not only the policy maker but also the participants get summary feedback, since the dashboard is published on the portal, as well. The interpretation component is based on the complex event processing (CEP) principle. The policy KPIs are monitored and evaluated, the rule-based notification system notifies in a readable and understandable form the policy makers when and where to change, modify the policy, where to focus or pay more attention. Social learning in this component leads to acquisition of factual knowledge of policy maker, change of their attitudes, increase trust.

4 Realization

This section provides a technical background, description about the main components of the backend, which are a) social media portal b) ontology learning c) interpretation.

4.1 Social Media Portal – Forum

The base of the front-end is a Content Management System (CMS) called WordPress (thereinafter WP) which is able to help the web developers to create dynamic web sites and blog systems. WP is free, open source under GPL license and easy to use. It is written in PHP language, and maintained by a large community. WP's functionality is easy to extend with plug-ins which is also free and easy to deploy. There is lot of pre-coded plug-ins in ZIP format, which are also written in PHP, but own extensions can be also developed. WP websites can be designed with pre-designed templates based on CSS stylesheets, also many community maintained templates is available on the internet. The CMS provides the authentication, the authorization (AAA) on a secure HTTPS connection. Content and daily tasks are managed on a pre-defined administration panel which is provided by the WP engine. The popular social media services (like Facebook or Twitter) can be integrated with the WP, thus the CMS functionality can be extended by these third-party contents. The WP system runs under an Apache 2 web server which supports the appearance of the PHP based web sites. The web server is on Trustix 3.0 (Tikka Masala) Linux server provided by VMWare virtualization environment. In the background of WP there is a MySQL database for storing data on the logical level. Web Developers can access to the MySQL database through a so-called Phpmyadmin web based panel.

4.2   Ontology Learning Component

Ontology learning will include text mining application. In Hungarian case the linguistic algorithm will be written in JAVA and will run on an Apache Tomcat server (open source software implementation of the Java Servlet and JavaServer Pages technologies (tomcat.apache.org)). Because the services of the program can be accessed via web services, an Apache Axis 2 web service, SOAP and WSDL engine has to be run on the server providing the standardized XML-based definition of the functions and allowing the front-end application to use them. The following main text mining functions will be applied: stop-words filtering, stemming, n-gram generation. For stemming purposes the open source JMorph morphological analyser will be used. The morphological process produces a list of words given in dictionary format to be analysed with statistical methods. It is based on the frequencies of the words, which will be calculated during the process. Most relevant terms will be defined and sent to the Studio knowledge repository for further processing. After that Studio gives back the list of the related knowledge elements for the most frequent terms in a structured JSON format which is transferred to the front-end. If there is no relevant related knowledge element for the given term in the knowledge base, the text mining component makes an internet search using the Google's AJAX web service API and gives back the most relevant hits to the front-end in a JSON format.

4.3   Ontology Update

Domain ontology maintenance will be semi-automatic; ontology learning, folksonomies and social bookmarking will provide some automatic support for the update, which will be finalised by a human expert. Folksonomies and social bookmarking, which are decisive in social media, will have key roles in our approach as well. Folksonomy combines the words "folk" and "taxonomy". It has been used to characterize the product which emerges from this tagging in a social environment. Social bookmarking sites such as Flickr, del.icio.us, and CiteULike have adopted folksonomic systems where users tag entities with keywords. In our solution tags, their initial structure and frequencies of occurrences will be extended from the users' conversation by text mining solutions. Next step will be to derive ontologies from these folksonomies. Saab discussed the ontology of tags in his work [30], and Alves and Santanchè [31] describe folksonomized ontology building (attaching folksonomy's tags (which come from ontology learning) to ontologies. We use their works as a starting point to develop our solution for the maintenance.

4.4   Studio – Knowledge Repository

Studio (http://abruzzo.corvinno.hu/studio-demo/index.html) is an ontology based online learning platform providing an elaborate but easy-to-use tool to represent a knowledge domain, discover the user`s knowledge gaps and access instant learning material. In its original form it consists of the Domain Ontology and the Repository that are the two major pillars of the whole solution and the Adaptive Testing Engine as well. The domain ontology provides the underlying structure of the content. The central element of content development and management is the Repository. Its content can be an image, an article, short texts like a useful paragraph or a famous quote or even audio and video materials. The role of the Content Repository is to store and manage these content elements while maintaining a rich set of metadata describing the contained elements. Each content element can be described with Dublin Core metadata and other useful descriptors, like tags or categories. Adaptive Testing Engine is responsible for determining the knowledge level of the test taker as precisely as possible with as low number of questions as possible. Studio is widely used in higher education in Corvinus University of Budapest (in BSc business informatics and business intelligence teaching, in MSc IT audit teaching) and in CISA exam preparation courses held by Corvinno and Hungarian ISACA. In our project Studio is customised and its ontology-driven content management functionality is applied.

4.5   Feedback to the Forum

The results of the text-mining process arrive to the front-end in JSON format via web service call. The WP functions process JSON string and store the data in the MySQL database. The related contents list will be displayed on the front-end to the user.

Fig. 2. Centralab screenshot

The user in order to view the details of the related content, must click on the specific item of the list of knowledge objects, and the content related to the selected object will be shown in a pop-up window with a JQUERY function. During this event WP calls another web service which collects the selected knowledge item from the Studio repository.

5   Conclusion

Opinions about social learning role in participatory decision-making processes are various. Muro and her colleagues [32] conclude that the utility of the social learning model for participatory processes still needs to be proven. They draw the attention that there is only limited evidence about the role of social learning in participatory processes and that the social learning model has a number of conceptual weaknesses. Centralab solution links between policy making process, method, and context (through ontology learning) and helps to reach shared views and a common understanding of the situation, which are an essential prerequisite for consensus and collective action. Considering the general overview of the model (figure 1) the technological impact categories can be linked to the model's different blocks or cycles and described as follows:

1. Centralab solution has a feedback strategy to policy maker about specific discussions: system fed back relevant knowledge material efficiently to a specific discussion and policy maker. Efficiency in this aspect means

— relevance and timeliness, i.e. how well the knowledge material that is fed back covers the actual topic of discussion and how well it follows the changes and fluctuations of the discussion during time;
— usability, i.e. if the participants of the discussion can truly absorb and use the new information that they get through the knowledge feedback for argumentation.

2. Semiautomatic ontology building: our research combined text mining and semantic technologies in ontology building. One of our solution main components is the repository feedback cycle. However, the effectiveness of this feedback in the project's model depends largely on the ontology based structure that is built up using the results of the text mining. Existing text mining solutions usually yield statistical results, in many cases combined with semantic analysis (e.g. emotional charge of found words). The innovation of our approach lies in the fact that, instead of only relying on the numerous expressions, it develops a semiautomatic method that uses the text mining results to build up an ontological structure of nodes and relations in order to better serve the knowledge feedback strategy.

As a summary of the above, we can say that our solution brings an important technological innovation in the way online discussions can be efficiently transformed into co-creative solution finding involving all the interested and affected stakeholders. Centralab solution provides an appropriate environment for social learning, amongst other it contributes in common understanding of a problem, support reaching mutual agreement and taking collective actions. It leads the acquisition of factual knowledge of policy makers, change of the citizens and policy makers' attitudes and increase trust between them. Future research will include the development of Centralab English version; fine-tuning of ontology learning process and its customization for additional domains (like tourism). English version of Centralab solution requires English text mining environment and its integration with the other Centralab components. In this step we plan to apply text mining components of Weka library and customize them. Another plan is to organize a real life test of Centralab solution; just now we are discussing with possible communities about the pilots.

References

1. Baiocchi, G.: Militants and Citizens: The Politics of Participatory Democracy in Porto Alegre. Stanford University Press (2005)
2. Wolterstorff, N.: Understanding Liberal Democracy: Essays in Political Philosophy Edited by Terence Cuneo. Oxford University Press (2012)
3. OECD: Promise and Problems of E-Democracy. Challenges of Online Citizen Engagement. OECD Publications Service (2003), http://www.oecd.org/governance/public-innovation/35176328.pdf
4. Gramberger, P.S.D.M.: Citizens as partners, OECD Handbook on Information, Consultation and Public Participation in Policy-Making, Published by : OECD Publishing (2001), http://www.ezd.si/fileadmin/doc/4_AKTIVNO_DRZAVLJANSTVO/Viri/Citizens_as_partners_hanbook_oecd.pdf
5. Aparajita, A., McConnachie, C., Sharma, D., Mehta, D., Carelli, F., Dhru, K.: A Comparative Survey of Procedures for Public Participation in the Legislative Process – Research Report, University of Oxford (2011), http://denning.law.ox.ac.uk/news/events_files/A_Comparative_Survey_of_Public_Participation_in_the_Legislative_Process.pdf
6. OECD: Evaluating Public Participation in Policy Making, OECD Publishing (2005), https://bvc.cgu.gov.br/bitstream/123456789/3674/1/evaluating_public_participation_policy_making.pdf
7. Cerda, B.C., Valenzuela, H.C.: Can Social Dialogue Be a Social Coordination Mechanism? Social Dialogue Policies in Chile between 1990 and 2010. Politics & Policy 40, 904–929 (2012), doi:10.1111/j.1747-1346.2012.00380.x
8. Bandura, A.: Social Learning Theory. General Learning Press, New York (1977)
9. Milbrath, L.W.: Envisioning a sustainable society. Learning our way out. State University of New York Press, New York (1989)
10. Bertot, J.C., Jaeger, P.T., Grimes, J.M.: Using ICTs to create a culture of transparency? - E-government and social media as openness and anti-corruption tools for societies. Government Information Quarterly 27, 264–271 (2010)
11. Jaeger, P.T., Bertot, J.C.: Designing, implementing, and evaluating user-centered and citizen-centered e-government. International Journal of Electronic Government Research 6(2), 1–17 (2010)
12. Jaeger, P.T., Bertot, J.C.: Transparency and technological change - Ensuring equal and sustained public access to government information. Government Information Quarterly 27, 371–376 (2010)
13. Gelders, D., Rijnja, G.: Dutch government communication professionals X-rayed - their role and attitude in public communication about policy intentions. Estudos em Comunicação (1), 26–42 (2007)
14. Bannister, F., Connolly, R.: A Risk Framework for Electronic Voting. International Journal of Technology and Policy Management 7(2), 190–208 (2007)
15. Lampathaki, F., Koussouris, S., Passas, S., Osimo, D., Mouzakitis, S., Tsavdaris, H., Charalabidis, Y., Askounis, D., De Luca, A., Bicking, M., Wimmer, M.: CROSSROAD: State of the Art Analysis. Brüsszel, European Commission (2010)
16. Macintosh, A.R.: Argument visualization to support democratic decision-making. In: Proceedings of the eChallenges e.2004 Conference, Vienna, Austria (2004)
17. Demirhan, K., Öktem, M.K.: Electronic Participation in the Policy Making Process: A Case Study. International Journal of e-Business and e-Government Studies 3(1) (2011), http://www.sobiad.org/eJOURNALS/journal_IJEBEG/arhieves/2011_1/05kamil_demirhan.pdf

18. Birkland, T.A.: An Introduction to the Policy Process: Theories, Concepts, and Models of Public, 2nd edn. M.E. Sharpe (2005)
19. Hill, M.: The Policy Process in the Modern State. Prentice-Hall, London (1997)
20. Parsons, W.: Public Policy. Edward Elgar, Cheltenham (1995)
21. Hofferbert, R.: The Study of Public Policy. Bobbs-Merrill, Indianapolis (1974)
22. Kiser, L., Ostrom, E.: The Three Worlds of Action. In: Ostrom, E. (ed.) Strategies of Political Inquiry, pp. 179–222. Sage, Beverly Hills (1982)
23. Sabatier, P.: An advocacy coalition framework of policy change and the role of policy-oriented learning therein. Policy Sciences 21, 129–168 (1988)
24. Zhang, Y., Liu, X., Wang, W.: Policy Life-cycle Model for Systems Management. IT Professional 7(2), 50–54 (2005)
25. Marriott, D.A.: Policy Service for Distributed Systems, PhD thesis. Imperial College of Science, Technology & Medicine, London (1997)
26. Koch, T.: Automated Management of Distributed Systems, Berichte aus der Informatik. Shaker Verlag (1997)
27. Avitable, M.: An Examination of Requirements for Metapolicies in Policy-Based Management, Thesis. Munich Technical University (1998)
28. NAO (National Audit Office): Supporting innovation - Managing risk in government departments. HC 864 Session 1999-2000. The Stationery Office, London (2000)
29. Edelenbos, J.: Managing stakeholder involvement in decision-making - a comparative analysis of six interactive processes in the Netherlands. Journal of Public Administration Research and Theory 16(3), 417–446 (2005)
30. Saab, D.J.: The Ontology of Tags. In: Proceedings of the iConference 2010, February 3-6, University of Illinois, Urbana-Champaign (2010)
31. Alves, H., Santanchè, A.: Folksonomized Ontologies – from social to formal. In: Proceedings of XVII Brazilian Symposium on Multimedia and the Web, pp. 58–65 (2011)
32. Muro, M., Jeffrey, P.: A critical review of the theory and application of social learning in participatory natural resource management processes. Journal of Environmental Planning and Management 51(3), 325–344 (2008)

Allowing Non-identifying Information Disclosure in Citizen Opinion Evaluation

Francesco Buccafurri, Lidia Fotia, and Gianluca Lax

DIIES, University Mediterranea of Reggio Calabria
Via Graziella, Località Feo di Vito
89122 Reggio Calabria, Italy
{bucca,lidia.fotia,lax}@unirc.it

Abstract. The continuous participation of citizens in the decisional processes of the community through the submission of their opinions is a key factor of e-democracy. To do this, it appears very promising the use of *lightweight* e-voting systems relying on existing social networks, as a good way to solve the trade-off among security, usability and scalability requirements. Among the other security features, anonymity of citizens (i.e., secreteness) should be guaranteed, at least to be sure that the action of people is actually free from conditioning. However, the decisional process would be better driven if the opinions of citizens were mapped to social, economic, working, personal, non-identifying attributes. In this paper, by extending a previous solution working on existing social networks, we overcome the above limit by re-interpreting the classical concept of secreteness in such a way that a preference expressed by a citizen can be related to a number of (certified) attributes chosen by the citizen herself, yet keeping her anonymity.

1 Introduction

The model of e-democracy is one of the most challenging innovations towards which any community which is a candidate to become a *smart city* should tend. Indeed, the continuous participation of citizens to the decisional processes of the community is actually one of the most important aspects to deal with, whenever the smart-city model is implemented. Recall that the concept of smart city has to be intended in an extended way, thus not necessarily limiting the scope of e-services and the dynamics of the involved processes just to a city, but to an entire community which could be sometime really a city, sometimes a region, sometimes an entire country. It is well known that e-democracy declines in many different forms, all sharing the presence of ICT-based processes allowing citizens to become actors of the government of the community [47,45]. Among these, all the processes aimed at collecting opinions, preferences, evaluations of citizens [11], assume a very important role in the e-democracy model, since represent the concrete way to adapt government decisions to the real expectations of citizens [40,50,48].

Consider for example the preliminary evaluation of a law or a reform, a political parties poll, a satisfaction survey, a primary election, just to mention a

A. Kő et al. (Eds.): EGOVIS/EDEM 2013, LNCS 8061, pp. 241–254, 2013.

few. In these cases, secretness (i.e., anonymity of citizens) should be guaranteed, at least to be sure that the action of people is actually free from conditioning. Moreover, all the remaining basic properties of e-voting systems [13,46], namely uniqueness, verifiability, uncloneability, robustness and scalability, are essential requirements. In [10], it is shown that a suitable use of cryptographic protocols and social networks can be a good way to implement this *light* form of public elections, supporting all the above features. But among such features, secreteness inhibits the possibility to relate the preferences expressed by citizens even to non-identifying attributes [12]. By contrast, this would be a feature very desirable in the considered setting, differently from the one of elections. Indeed, the decisional process would be better driven if the opinions of citizens were mapped to social, economic, working, personal, non-identifying attributes. In this paper, we overcome the above limit by re-interpreting the classical concept of secreteness in such a way that a preference expressed by a citizen can be related to a number of (certified) attributes chosen by the same citizen, yet keeping her anonymity. Besides the possibility to analyze citizens' preferences and to extract useful knowledge from them, it will be possible to enable filtering mechanisms aimed at collecting only preferences of a certain segment of the population, like all people with a certain age range, a certain job, a given region and so on. Observe that the above requirements evokes what is provided by selective disclosure and bit commitment approaches [8,44,37,52], but a direct application of such approaches to our case is not resolutive since the secret used by a citizen to enable the disclosure of the chosen attribute would allow third parties to trace the citizen herself, thus breaking anonymity. The problem is thus non trivial.

We propose a solution that extends the model presented in [10]. It is based on pre-existent social networks, allowing citizens to vote through their own profile and does not require complex overhead besides an electronic card to identify a citizen or any identity management system able to identify people (plausibly, we can consider this is for free in an e-government context), and the owing a profile by each voter in one of the existing social networks.

The paper is organized as follows. In the next section, we recall some background notions. An overview of our proposal is given in Section 3, where the differences of this proposal with the model presented in [10] are discussed. The protocol allowing the selective disclosure of some attribute in an e-voting session is defined in Section 4. In Section 5, we analyze the security of this protocol. Section 6 is devoted to the related literature. Finally, in Section 7, we draw our conclusions and sketch possible future work.

2 Background

In this section, we present the background necessary to the reader to understand the technical aspects of the paper. Such notions are *discrete logarithm problem*, *digital signature* and *partially blind signature*.

The difficulty of solving the discrete logarithm is exploited to guarantee the security of numerous cryptosystems [3]. The discrete logarithm problem can be formalized as follows. Let G be a multiplicative group and let $\langle g \rangle$ be the cyclic subgroup generated by $g \in G$. Given $g \in G$ and $a \in \langle g \rangle$, the problem consists in finding an integer x such that $g^x = a$. Such an integer x is the discrete logarithm of a to the base g (i.e., $x = log_g a$). Note that $log_g a$ is only determined modulo the order of g.

The digital signature mechanism relies on public key infrastructure. Each user owns two keys, a private key and a public one. The private key is kept secret and the public one is made public. Guessing a private key is computationally unfeasible for enough large keys. The first step of the signature generation process is the computation of a cryptographic hash function [28,26] of the document to be signed. The result, called digest, can substitute the original document in the signature generation process since the probability of having two distinct documents producing the same digest is negligible. Moreover, the problem of finding a document with digest equal to that of another given document is unfeasible, so that an attacker cannot corrupt a signed document without the signature detects it. The digital signature is produced by encrypting the digest with the private key using an asymmetric cryptographic cipher, typically RSA. The verification of the signature is done by checking that the decryption of the signature done with the public key of the subscriber coincides with the (re-computed) digested of the document.

Partially blind signatures [1] are a particular type of signature allowing the signer to explicitly include in unblinded form some pre-agreed information in the blind signature, like an expiry date, and are mainly used in the context of electronic cash (e-cash).

3   An Overview of the Proposal

In this section, we briefly describe the scenario we have designed in our proposal. The e-voting protocol will be described in the next section. The scenario is close to the one presented in [10]. We assume that citizens may use a smart card embedding a certificate granted by any Certification Authority including only a unique numeric ID and a list of pairs $\langle x, y \rangle$ where x is the attribute name and y is the obscured attribute value. This certificate, not existing in [10], includes information about the citizen in an obscured form, in such a way that the user may decide which information can be disclosed. Attributes encode standard information about users like personal data, but also more general information like job, qualification, marital status, etc. As usual, the certificate is a semi-structured document where the attributes are optionally included. For each attribute, its value is obscured by applying a one-way function using a key. A different key for each attribute is used. The keys are shared between the user and the Certification Authority. Thus, for a given attribute value A and a given key k, we obscure the attribute value by computing $g(A, k)$, where g is a one-way function. This means that it is unfeasible to compute A from the knowledge of just $g(A, k)$. For function g, we adopt the modular power function. The infeasibility of the computation of the discrete logarithm ensures us that the function is one way.

As in [10], the solution is based on the usage of existing social networks. Citizens vote by using their social network profile. The e-voting infrastructure is implemented by exploiting, for the selected social networks several profiles whose URL is of the form: http://www.socialnetwork.org/poll_Y, where Y is a cardinal number. These profiles are managed by possibly different government entities. Each entity replicates its profile over the most common social networks. The only requirement we have for these *super* profiles is the service continuity. These profiles are called *credential providers* and play the role of granting credentials to voters they can spend in order to submit their vote to a Trusted Third Party (TTP), responsible of generating the ballots for each e-voting. The domain of credential providers is built by collecting a large variety of subjects, like public sector offices, postal offices, universities, schools, military subjects and so on.

Recall that, differently from the model presented in [10] where both credentials and votes submitted by citizens do not include any additional information, our goal here is to associate votes with some attribute values chosen by the voter. It is worth noting that the trivial extension of the protocol of [10] consisting in including in the credentials granted by the credential providers also the attributes the voter wants to disclose does not work. Indeed, in this case the credential providers would able to incrementally relate information about the voter, as they know her identity. This way, the protocol would violate the confidentiality of the attribute certificate. By contrast, we want to relate votes to voters' attributes without discovering to anyone whom these attribute refer to.

To do this, we include in the credentials a further obscuration of the attribute values of the certificate by means of a different key per attribute. Each credential provider shares these keys with the user, but, obviously, it does not know the attribute values because operates only on already obscured values taken from the attribute certificate.

The credentials obtained by the voter contain a double obscuration of all the attributes of the voter, each with two keys, namely k and r (different for each attribute), in such a way that the knowledge of the product $k \cdot r$ allows us to obtain the final obscuration starting from the plain value of the attributes. Indeed, for the chosen function g, it holds that $g(g(A, k), r) = g(A, k \cdot r)$.

This way, whenever the voter submits her vote to TTP, she decides which attributes to disclose, simply by including into the vote record the attribute value, say A, and the product of keys $k \cdot r$. Then, TTP for each chosen attribute A, just has to compute the value $g(A, k \cdot r)$ and to verify whether this value is included in the related credential.

The scenario is summarized in Fig. 1. To avoid that the protocol is breakable by just one misbehaving credential provider, we use the common approach of replicating the responsibilities over a number of different independent parties [25,52,30,35]. In fact, the voter selects a suitable number $\bar{t}$ of credential providers on the basis of the value of her ID and asks them for the credentials necessary for the e-voting session. In Fig. 1, we describe the different steps related to an e-voting session. First, the user receives the obscured certificate from a

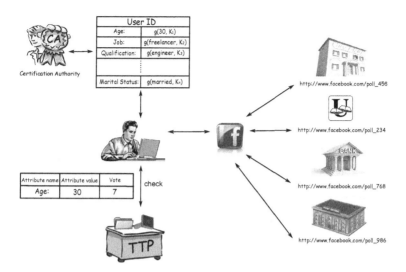

Fig. 1. The e-voting scenario

certification authority. Then, on the basis of her ID, the voter (we assume she has joined Facebook) computes four values (i.e., $Y_1 = 456$, $Y_2 = 234$, $Y_3 = 768$, and $Y_4 = 986$) identifying the respective credential users (in this example, $\bar{t} = 4$). The Trusted Third Party collects votes, verifies that they are admissible, and generates the ballots for each e-voting. The protocol ensures that the credential providers, even though may identify voters cannot link them to their vote, while TTP cannot identify voters but can only be aware about the attributes voluntarily disclosed by the voter.

As already done [10], the only assumption is that no more than t credential providers collude, where t is a parameter of the system. The number $\bar{t}$ of contacted credential providers per voter is directly related to t. The detail of the protocol is shown in the next section.

4   The E-Voting Protocol

In this section, we describe how the e-voting protocol works. Consider an e-voting session identified by ID_{vs}. For the sake of presentation, we assume that a preference is expressed by reporting the number i identifying the choice of the voter. For example, if the voting session regards the choice of one among 8 candidates in a primary election, then the choice of the voter could be represented by a number from 1 to 8. However, extending our technique to the cases in which preferences are given in a difference way (for example, in the case of a primary election, by indicating the name of the candidate) is possible with no impact on the model.

The e-voting process involves the following four basic entities:

1. The *Voter V*. We describe how the protocol run for the voting done by one user. Clearly, the overall e-voting session involves many user, each running these steps.
2. A *Certification Authority* CA granting attribute certificates to voters.
3. A set $\langle CP_1, \ldots, CP_c \rangle$ of c special users, named *credential providers*, issuing the credential exploited by the voter to prove her authorization to vote.
4. A *Trusted Third Party*, say TTP, responsible of generating the *certified ballots* for each e-voting.

Our technique is parametric with respect to a value t. It is chosen in such a way that the likelihood that t randomly selected users misbehave is negligible. This is a common assumption in this context [52,30,35,25].

Now, we describe how the e-voting process proceeds. It consists of the following steps:

1. *Certificate Issue.* In this first step, CA generates the attribute certificate for the voter V which contains ID_V (i.e., a value that uniquely identifies each voter) and a list of n associated attributes. All the attributes but ID_V are obscured, in such a way that a third party cannot know the values of such attributes by accessing the certificate. In particular, for each attribute, its value is obscured by applying a one-way function using a key. A different key for each attribute is used. The keys are shared between the voter and CA. In detail, for a given attribute value A and a given key k, we obscure the attribute value by computing $g(A, k)$, where g is a one-way function. This means that it is unfeasible to compute A from the knowledge of just $g(A, k)$. For function g, we adopt the modular power function $A^k \bmod m$, where m is a prime number greater than any possible A. In practise, m can be set by assuming a realistic upper bound for the values of attributes. If the above assumption is not applicable, we can use for each attribute a different module, which depends on the actual value of the attribute. In this case, the value of the module has to be saved in the certificate.

   Thus, CA selects a random vector of keys $(k_1, \ldots, k_n)$. Each attribute included in the certificate is a pair $(AN, g(AV, k_i))$, where AN is the attribute name and AV is the attribute value. Therefore, in the certificate, instead of the plain value AV, only the obscured value $g(AV, k_i) = AV_i^{k_i} \bmod m$ is inserted. At the end of this operation, CA signs the certificate and sends it to V together with the vectors $(k_1, \ldots, k_n)$ and $(AV_1, \ldots, AV_n)$. We denote by C the so obtained certificate.

2. *CPs Identification.* In the first step, V has to select $\bar{t} = 2 \cdot t + 1$ of the c credential providers that will generate the credentials. The p-th credential provider chosen by V, say CP_p^V, with $1 \le i \le \bar{t}$, is CP_j, with $j =$ SHA-$1(ID_V \| i) \bmod c$. Specifically, the first credential provider is obtained by applying the hash function SHA-1 to the concatenation between the voter identifier ID_V and the number 1 (i.e., $i = 1$), and then by mapping the result to one of the c credential providers through the mod operation. Note that the value j computed by SHA-1 corresponds to the number Y completing the

URL identifying the credential provider (recall the discussion done concerning the scenario described in Fig. 1).

3. *Credential Issue.* In this step, the voter starts a connection with each CP_p^V (among the $\bar{t}$ ones). CP_p^V verifies that it has been correctly contacted by recomputing the function SHA-1 as done by V at the previous step. If this is the case, then CP_p^V generates the credential C_p^V allowing V to participate to the e-voting session. Otherwise, the connection is terminated. Before the generation of the credential, V sends the certificate C issued in Step 1 to CP_p^V, together with a random vector $\langle r_1, \ldots, r_n \rangle$, where, we recall, n is the number of the attributes in C. Then, CP_p^V generates a n-tuple of pairs $AT = \langle (AN_1, g(AV_1, k_1 \cdot r_1)), \ldots, (AN_n, g(AV_n, k_n \cdot r_n)) \rangle$. Observe that the second element of the i-th pair is the further obscuration of the i-th attribute value by means of the random value r_i, i.e., $g(g(AV_i, k_i), r_i) = AV_i^{k_i \cdot r_i}$. We denote the attribute name AN_i by $AT(i).name$ and the attribute value AV_i by $AT(i).value$.

   At this point CP_p^V is ready to construct the credential C_p^V. It consists in the signature of the pair $\langle ID_{vs}, AT \rangle$, where ID_{vs} is the identifier of the voting session.

4. *Voting.* After the voter has collected the credential from each of the $\bar{t}$ credential providers, these credentials are presented to TTP in order to obtain the possibility to vote.

   In particular, TTP performs the following tests on the received credentials:

   (a) It checks authenticity and integrity of each credential and that the voting reference (i.e., ID_{vs}) in each credential coincide.

   (b) It verifies that in the past, no user has presented credentials issued from the same credential providers as the current voter for the same voting session (otherwise, it means that the voter is trying to repeat her participation to the same voting).

   If both the tests succeed, then the voter is authorized to vote possibly disclosing some attributes.

   Suppose now that V decides to disclose h attributes, with $h \le n$. In this case, she must send to TTP the h-tuple of pairs $T = \langle (B_1, e_1), \ldots, (B_h, e_h) \rangle$, where B_i is the value of a chosen attribute, say it the attribute A_x, and e_i is the i-th product $k_x \cdot r_x$, for $1 \le i \le h$. To verify that the voter choice is valid, it is necessary that TTP checks the consistence of T with AT. In particular, given the function $f : \{1, \cdots, h\} \to \{1, \cdots, n\}$, such that:

$$f(i) = \begin{cases} j & \text{if } \exists \, j \in [1, n] \mid AT(j).value = B_i^{e_i}, \\ undefined & \text{otherwise.} \end{cases}$$

TTP has to verify that f is total, i.e., is defined over all the domain $\{1, \cdots, h\}$. If this check fails, the vote is invalidated. Otherwise, TTP generates the ballot. The ballot consists in the partially blind signature of the quadruple $\langle ID_{vs}, \tilde{r}, \tilde{pr}, (AT(f(1)).name, B_{f(1)}), \cdots, (AT(f(h)).name, B_{f(h)}) \rangle$, where $\tilde{r}$ is a fresh 128-bit random sequence and $\tilde{pr}$ represents the preference specified by the voter.

The values ID_{vs} and $(AT(f(1)).name, B_{f(1)}), \cdots, (AT(f(h)).name, B_{f(h)})$ are unblindly signed, whereas $\tilde{r}$ and $\tilde{pr}$ are blindly signed. Finally, TTP stores the received credentials in order to detect a possible re-submission of the same credentials.

5. *Ballot Publication.* After the voter obtains the signed ballot, she unblinds it in order to obtain a new ballot still correctly signed by TTP but not linkable anymore to the voter. As usual, timing attacks are prevented by introducing an unpredictable delay before sending the new ballot back to TTP. The final ballot is thus $\langle ID_{vs}, r, pr, (AT(f(1)).name, B_{f(1)}), \cdots, (AT(f(h)).name, B_{f(h)}) \rangle$.

Observe that, due to the presence of the tuples $(AT(f(1)).name, B_{f(1)}), \cdots, (AT(f(h)).name, B_{f(h)})$, the list of attribute names and values that V has chosen to disclose is shown in the ballot.

At the end of the e-voting session, TTP verifies the signature of all received ballots and publishes valid ones. The presence of non identifying information about the voter enables the possibility to analyze citizens' preferences in order to extract useful knowledge from them.

5   Security Analysis

This section is devoted to the analysis of the robustness of our protocol against a large number of realist attack model. We extend the security analysis done in [10] taking into account the improvements introduced by our proposal. Also in this case, the basic assumption is that at most t users misbehave during the whole evaluation process.

We start by analyzing the possibility for a credential provider to be aware of information about the voter. Any selected credential provider, say CP, cannot guess the value of the attributes in the certificate. Indeed, let us assume that CP wants to know whether the real value of the obscured attribute $A' = A^k \bmod m$ is equal to F. Then, it has to find a value k' such that $F^{k'} \bmod m = A'$ which corresponds to find the discrete logarithm of A', which is unfeasible. With stronger reason, any other entity which is aware of the attribute certificate or credentials of the voter can guess the value of the non-disclosed attributes.

There is no link between the certificate and the credentials issued to the same voter. Indeed, the voter ID is not included in the credential and any attribute $g(AV_i, k_i)$ in the certificate is transformed to $g(AV_i, k_i \cdot r_i)$. Thanks to the further obscuration performed by r_i, there is no way, without the knowledge of this random value, to link the credential to the attribute certificate (and then to the voter). Clearly, ID_{vs} is the identifier of the voting session and is not included in the certificate. The only information known by TTP is the e-voting session and the disclosed attributes and cannot link the voter and the preference rate of her ballot thanks to the use of the partially blind signature (at Step 4). Observe that the collusion between TTP and a credential provider allows them to link the voter identifier to the disclosed attributes also in different voting sessions. However, they cannot know also the preference score which is indistinguishable among all the votes of the e-voting session (the partially blind signature of TTP on the ballot hides the preference score).

Our protocol allows each user to express only one preference. In case the voter tries to use the same credentials for a second time, the double vote is detected by TTP in Step 4.(b). Again, if the attacker requires to the certification authority a new certificate, the user ID is the same, thus resulting in the failure of the attack. Moreover, observe that in principle it could occur that two different voters V_1 and V_2 in the same voting session are considered the same by TTP in the case that the two voters share the set of credential providers due to the collision of the hash function SHA-1. This would result in improperly rejecting the latest vote erroneously detected as duplicated vote. However, this event can be considered impossible since its probability is negligible in a realistic scenario. For example, since the number of possible different sequences of credential providers is $c\,!/(c - \bar{t})!$ (we recall c is the number of credential providers and $\bar{t} = 2 \cdot t + 1$), for the realistic values $\bar{t} = 21$, $c = 200$, and even hypothesizing an unrealistically high number of users 10^{12} voters, we obtain that the probability of collisions is less than 10^{-20}.

The vote verifiability continues to be guaranteed. Each user can find its vote identified by r on the published ballot list and verify its correctness. The probability that two voters generate the same 128-bit sequence r is $p(u; D) \approx 1 - e^{-u^2/(2 \cdot D)}$ (birthday attack) where u is the number of users expressing her preference for a candidate and D is the domain of r. Assuming again a number of users u equals to 10^{12} (in the worst case), such a probability is negligible (in numbers, this probability is less than 10^{-15}).

Also uncloneability holds. This property ensures that generating a bogus ballot starting from a legal one must be detected. We observe that a valid ballot has been signed by TTP and thus it cannot be modified. Obviously, it cannot be duplicate thanks to the presence of the bit-sequence r identifying the ballot, according to the previous probability consideration.

Concerning the possibility that two obscured values $g(AV_1, k_1 \cdot r_1)$ and $g(AV_2, k_2 \cdot r_2)$ in AT collide (recall TTP verifies that the function f is total at Step 4), the probability of this event is negligible thanks to the randomness of r_1 and r_2 assuming that the number of bits of such random values is sufficiently large. According to this observation, even though from a formal point of view the definition of the function f does not allow us to guarantee that f is deterministic, from a practical point of view f returns always a unique value when it is defined.

It is worth noting that the application of the hash function SHA-1 at Step 2 returns a pseudo-random value depending on the voter (through her identifier) which allows us to assume that the credential providers selected by the voter can be considered randomly chosen. Thanks to this assumption, we can reach another important result. The unfair behaviour of at most t credential providers (according to our initial assumption in Section 4 about the possible misbehaving of users) is detected. Indeed, among the $\bar{t} = 2 \cdot t + 1$ credentials provided by the voter, at least $t + 1$ of them must be correct. As a consequence, fake credentials are detected since they are in the minority.

6   Related Work

E-government is a topic widely investigated in the last years by researchers [51,24,27]. In this section, we briefly survey the literature related to the topics of e-voting, which our proposal is clearly related to, and focus on selective disclosure, which represents a key issue in our approach.

Let us start with e-voting. Guaranteeing anonymity of the voter is an important requirement. For this purpose, Chaum [17] introduced the notion of *mix-net*, which exploits a sequence of servers. Each server receives a batch of input messages and produces as output the batch in permuted (mixed) order. An observer should not be able to tell how the inputs correspond to the outputs. Mix-nets are used to ensure voter privacy by providing the ballots of the voters as input to them. In Chaum's original proposal, before a message is sent through the mix-net, it is encrypted with the public keys of the mixes it will traverse in reverse order. Each mix then decrypts a message before sending it on to the next mix. A modified version of the protocol was published later by Chaum [20]. Here, a new kind of receipt improves security by letting voters verify correctness of the election outcome, even though all election computers and records were to be compromised. The system preserves ballot secrecy, while improving access for voters, robustness, and adjudication, all at lower cost.

Sako et al. [49] propose another approach to e-voting based on *re-encryption mix-nets* [43] and on *proofs*, used by voters to prove the correctness of the votes they sent. Zwierko et al. [52] propose an agent-based scheme for secure electronic voting. The protocol, presented in [32], is designed for large scale elections.

Chaum pioneered privacy-enhancing cryptographic protocols that minimize the amount of personal data disclosed. Chaum et al. defined the principles of anonymous credentials [18,19,22], group signatures [23], and electronic cash [18]. In all these papers, some party issues a digital signatures where the signed message includes information about the user (i.e., attributes). Subsequently, more efficient implementation of these concepts were proposed concerning group signatures [2,6,39], e-cash [7,14,31], and anonymous credentials [8,15,16]. Moreover, a number of new concepts were introduced, like traceable signatures [38], anonymous auctions [42], and electronic voting based on blind-signatures [32]. Many of these schemes use as building blocks signed attributes and protocols that selectively reveal these attributes or prove properties about them. Their implementations typically encode attributes as a discrete logarithm or, more generally, as an element (exponent) of a representation of a group element, resulting in protocols where the number of transmitted group elements and the performed commutations are linear in the number of encoded attributes.

An interesting approach for maximizing privacy protection is to selectively disclose attributes within a credential, so that only the needed subset of properties is made available to the recipient of the credential. A system to partially disclose credentials relies on the use of the bit commitment technique, which enables users to commit a value without revealing it. Bit commitment has been used for zero-knowledge protocols [33], [9], identification schemes [29], and multi-party protocols [34,21], and it can implement Blum's coin flipping over the phone

[5]. The idea of selectively disclosing credential attributes is not new [8,44]. [37] focuses on selective disclosure of credentials during negotiations and provides a prototype implementation. The focus of Bertino et al. [4] is to deeply analyze the impact of protected attribute credentials on trust negotiations, and to devise new strategies allowing interoperability between users adopting various credential formats. Further, instead of using the bit-commitment technique, the authors adopt a multi-bit hash commitment technique for attribute encoding, as the length of attributes will likely be longer than one bit.

Naor [41] shows how a pseudorandom generator can provide a bit-commitment protocol and also analyzes the number of bits communicated when parties commit to many bits simultaneously. Let $m(n)$ be some function such that $m(n) > n$. $G : \{0,1\}^n \to \{0,1\}^{m(n)}$ is a pseudorandom generator. $G_l(s)$ is used to denote the first l bits of the pseudorandom sequence on seed $s \in \{0,1\}^n$. $B_i(s)$ is used to denote the i-th bit of the pseudorandom sequence on seed s. The user selects seed $s \in \{0,1\}^n$ and sends $G_m(s)$ and $B_{m+l}(s) \oplus b$. In the reveal stage, the user sends s and the verifier checks that $G_m(s)$ is equal to the previously received value and computes $b = B_{m+l}(s) \oplus (B_{m+l}(s) \oplus b)$.

The system of Holt et al. [36] uses bit commitments to create selective disclosure credentials with a limited amount of data the holder must reveal. A selective disclosure credential has several attributes. When the user shows the credential to a verifier, she can choose to reveal only some of them. Credential sets accomplish this with the help of bit commitment that allows the user to commit to a value without revealing it. The user's commitment is the output of a one-way function $oneway()$ operating on the concatenation of her secret value s and a random string r. The user first sends it to the verifier. If she chooses not to reveal the value, the verifier can't determine what the value was. To reveal her secret, she sends s and r to the verifier who computes the one-way function and checks that the result equals the value sent previously by the user.

We observe that the approaches based on selective disclosure and bit commitment do not solve the problem investigated in our paper. Indeed, the secret used by a citizen to enable the disclosure of the chosen attribute would allow third parties to trace the citizen preferences in the different voting session, thus breaking unlinkability.

7   Conclusion

In this paper, we have proposed a lightweight e-voting system relying on the use of social networks and allowing the voter to graduate the privacy level of the vote. In particular, the citizen may decide, whenever she submits a vote, to reveal some non-identifying personal certified attribute to link to the vote. The e-voting system is oriented to all those processes aimed at collecting opinions, preferences, evaluations of citizens, which assume a very important role in the e-democracy model, since represent the concrete way to adapt government decisions to the real expectations of citizens.

The result we have obtained is a fair compromise between the secreteness of the vote and the necessity of government parties to conduct analyses on the collected opinions, in order to relate them to various types of information describing the inquired population. The solution shows also good features of feasibility since it does not require complex ad-hoc infrastructures by exploiting pervasive and user-accepted media (i.e., social networks). The security analysis also shows that all the basic properties of an e-voting system are satisfied and that a correct utilization of our extended notion of secreteness does not invalidate the anonymity of the voters. As a future work we plan to investigate the implementation issues with the goal of implementing a system prototype useful to perform real-life experiences also in limited (specific) domains.

Acknowledgment. This work has been partially supported by the TENACE PRIN Project (n. 20103P34XC) funded by the Italian Ministry of Education, University and Research.

References

1. Abe, M., Fujisaki, E.: How to date blind signatures. In: Kim, K.-c., Matsumoto, T. (eds.) ASIACRYPT 1996. LNCS, vol. 1163, pp. 244–251. Springer, Heidelberg (1996)
2. Ateniese, G., Camenisch, J., Joye, M., Tsudik, G.: A practical and provably secure coalition-resistant group signature scheme. In: Bellare, M. (ed.) CRYPTO 2000. LNCS, vol. 1880, pp. 255–270. Springer, Heidelberg (2000)
3. Bach, E.: Discrete logarithms and factoring. Computer Science Division, University of California (1984)
4. Bertino, E., Ferrari, E., Squicciarini, A.C.: Privacy-preserving trust negotiations. In: Martin, D., Serjantov, A. (eds.) PET 2004. LNCS, vol. 3424, pp. 283–301. Springer, Heidelberg (2005)
5. Blum, M.: Coin flipping by telephone a protocol for solving impossible problems. ACM SIGACT News 15(1), 23–27 (1983)
6. Boneh, D., Boyen, X., Shacham, H.: Short group signatures. In: Franklin, M. (ed.) CRYPTO 2004. LNCS, vol. 3152, pp. 41–55. Springer, Heidelberg (2004)
7. Brands, S.A.: An efficient off-line electronic cash system based on the representation problem (1993)
8. Brands, S.A.: Rethinking public key infrastructures and digital certificates: building in privacy. MIT Press (2000)
9. Brassard, G., Chaum, D., Crépeau, C.: Minimum disclosure proofs of knowledge. Journal of Computer and System Sciences 37(2), 156–189 (1988)
10. Buccafurri, F., Fotia, L., Lax, G.: Allowing continuous evaluation of citizen opinions through social networks. In: Kő, A., Leitner, C., Leitold, H., Prosser, A. (eds.) EDEM 2012 and EGOVIS 2012. LNCS, vol. 7452, pp. 242–253. Springer, Heidelberg (2012)
11. Buccafurri, F., Fotia, L., Lax, G.: Privacy-preserving resource evaluation in social networks. In: Proceedings of the 2012 Tenth Annual International Conference on Privacy, Security and Trust, PST 2012, pp. 51–58. IEEE Computer Society (2012)
12. Buccafurri, F., Lax, G., Nocera, A., Ursino, D.: Discovering links among social networks. In: Flach, P.A., De Bie, T., Cristianini, N. (eds.) ECML PKDD 2012, Part II. LNCS, vol. 7524, pp. 467–482. Springer, Heidelberg (2012)
13. Burmester, M., Magkos, E.: Towards secure and practical e-elections in the new era. Secure Electronic Voting, 63–76 (2003)

14. Camenisch, J., Hohenberger, S., Lysyanskaya, A.: Compact E-cash. In: Cramer, R. (ed.) EUROCRYPT 2005. LNCS, vol. 3494, pp. 302–321. Springer, Heidelberg (2005)
15. Camenisch, J., Lysyanskaya, A.: An efficient system for non-transferable anonymous credentials with optional anonymity revocation. In: Pfitzmann, B. (ed.) EUROCRYPT 2001. LNCS, vol. 2045, pp. 93–118. Springer, Heidelberg (2001)
16. Camenisch, J., Lysyanskaya, A.: Signature schemes and anonymous credentials from bilinear maps. In: Franklin, M. (ed.) CRYPTO 2004. LNCS, vol. 3152, pp. 56–72. Springer, Heidelberg (2004)
17. Chaum, D.: Untraceable electronic mail, return addresses, and digital pseudonyms. Communications of the ACM 24(2), 84–90 (1981)
18. Chaum, D.: Blind signatures for untraceable payments. In: McCurley, K.S., Ziegler, C.D. (eds.) Advances in Cryptology 1981 - 1997. LNCS, vol. 1440, pp. 199–203. Springer, Heidelberg (1999)
19. Chaum, D.: Security without identification: Transaction systems to make big brother obsolete. Communications of the ACM 28(10), 1030–1044 (1985)
20. Chaum, D.: Elections with unconditionally-secret ballots and disruption equivalent to breaking RSA. In: Günther, C.G. (ed.) EUROCRYPT 1988. LNCS, vol. 330, pp. 177–182. Springer, Heidelberg (1988)
21. Chaum, D., Damgård, I.B., van de Graaf, J.: Multiparty computations ensuring privacy of each party's input and correctness of the result. In: Pomerance, C. (ed.) CRYPTO 1987. LNCS, vol. 293, pp. 87–119. Springer, Heidelberg (1988)
22. Chaum, D., Evertse, J.-H.: A secure and privacy-protecting protocol for transmitting personal information between organizations. In: Odlyzko, A.M. (ed.) CRYPTO 1986. LNCS, vol. 263, pp. 118–167. Springer, Heidelberg (1987)
23. Chaum, D., van Heyst, E.: Group signatures. In: Davies, D.W. (ed.) EUROCRYPT 1991. LNCS, vol. 547, pp. 257–265. Springer, Heidelberg (1991)
24. Cordella, A.: E-government: towards the e-bureaucratic form? Journal of Information Technology 22(3), 265–274 (2007)
25. Cramer, R., Gennaro, R., Schoenmakers, B.: A secure and optimally efficient multi-authority election scheme. European Transactions on Telecommunications 8(5), 481–490 (1997)
26. Dobbertin, H., Bosselaers, A., Preneel, B.: RIPEMD-160: A strengthened version of RIPEMD. In: Gollmann, D. (ed.) FSE 1996. LNCS, vol. 1039, pp. 71–82. Springer, Heidelberg (1996)
27. Dunleavy, P., Margetts, H., Bastow, S., Tinkler, J.: Digital era governance: IT corporations, the state, and e-government. OUP Catalogue (2006)
28. Eastlake, D., Jones, P.: US secure hash algorithm 1 (SHA1). Technical report, RFC 3174 (September 2001)
29. Fiat, A., Shamir, A.: How to prove yourself: practical solutions to identification and signature problems. In: Odlyzko, A.M. (ed.) CRYPTO 1986. LNCS, vol. 263, pp. 186–194. Springer, Heidelberg (1987)
30. Fouque, P.-A., Poupard, G., Stern, J.: Sharing decryption in the context of voting or lotteries. In: Frankel, Y. (ed.) FC 2000. LNCS, vol. 1962, pp. 90–104. Springer, Heidelberg (2001)
31. Frankel, Y., Tsiounis, Y., Yung, M.: Fair off-line e-cash made easy. In: Ohta, K., Pei, D. (eds.) ASIACRYPT 1998. LNCS, vol. 1514, pp. 257–270. Springer, Heidelberg (1998)
32. Fujioka, A., Okamoto, T., Ohta, K.: A practical secret voting scheme for large scale elections. In: Zheng, Y., Seberry, J. (eds.) AUSCRYPT 1992. LNCS, vol. 718, pp. 244–251. Springer, Heidelberg (1993)

33. Goldreich, O., Micali, S., Wigderson, A.: Proofs that yield nothing but their validity or all languages in NP have zero-knowledge proof systems. Journal of the ACM (JACM) 38(3), 690–728 (1991)
34. Goldwasser, S., Micali, S., Wigderson, A.: How to play any mental game, or a completeness theorem for protocols with an honest majority. In: Proc. of the Nienteenth Annual ACM STOC, vol. 87, pp. 218–229 (1987)
35. Hirt, M., Sako, K.: Efficient receipt-free voting based on homomorphic encryption. In: Preneel, B. (ed.) EUROCRYPT 2000. LNCS, vol. 1807, pp. 539–556. Springer, Heidelberg (2000)
36. Holt, J.E., Seamons, K.E.: Selective disclosure credential sets (2002), Accessible as http://citeseer.nj.nec.com/541329.html
37. Jarvis, R.: Selective disclosure of credential content during trust negotiation. Master of Science Thesis, Brigham Young University, Provo, Utah (2003)
38. Kiayias, A., Tsiounis, Y., Yung, M.: Traceable signatures. In: Cachin, C., Camenisch, J.L. (eds.) EUROCRYPT 2004. LNCS, vol. 3027, pp. 571–589. Springer, Heidelberg (2004)
39. Kiayias, A., Yung, M.: Secure scalable group signature with dynamic joins and separable authorities. International Journal of Security and Networks 1(1), 24–45 (2006)
40. Medaglia, R.: eParticipation research: Moving characterization forward (2006–2011). Government Information Quarterly (2012)
41. Naor, M.: Bit commitment using pseudorandomness. Journal of Cryptology 4(2), 151–158 (1991)
42. Naor, M., Pinkas, B., Sumner, R.: Privacy preserving auctions and mechanism design. In: Proceedings of the 1st ACM Conference on Electronic Commerce, pp. 129–139. ACM (1999)
43. Park, C., Itoh, K., Kurosawa, K.: Efficient anonymous channel and all/nothing election scheme. In: Helleseth, T. (ed.) EUROCRYPT 1993. LNCS, vol. 765, pp. 248–259. Springer, Heidelberg (1994)
44. Persiano, P., Visconti, I.: User privacy issues regarding certificates and the TLS protocol: the design and implementation of the SPSL protocol. In: Proceedings of the 7th ACM Conference on Computer and Communications Security, pp. 53–62. ACM (2000)
45. Persson, A., Goldkuhl, G.: Government value paradigms-bureaucracy, new public management, and e-government. Communications of the Association for Information Systems 27(1), 4 (2010)
46. Pieprzyk, J., Hardjono, T., Seberry, J.: Fundamentals of computer security. Springer (2003)
47. Rose, J., Sæbø, Ø.: Establishing political deliberation systems: Key problems (2008)
48. Sæbø, Ø., Rose, J., Skiftenes Flak, L.: The shape of eParticipation: Characterizing an emerging research area. Government Information Quarterly 25(3), 400–428 (2008)
49. Sako, K., Kilian, J.: Receipt-free mix-type voting scheme. In: Guillou, L.C., Quisquater, J.-J. (eds.) EUROCRYPT 1995. LNCS, vol. 921, pp. 393–403. Springer, Heidelberg (1995)
50. Susha, I., Grönlund, Å.: eParticipation research: Systematizing the field. Government Information Quarterly (2012)
51. Viscusi, G., Mecella, M.: Information systems for eGovernment: A quality-of-service perspective. Springer (2011)
52. Zwierko, A., Kotulski, Z.: A light-weight e-voting system with distributed trust. Electronic Notes in Theoretical Computer Science 168, 109–126 (2007)

Author Index